Carnage, Cops and Deadlines

To: Mike Breton:
with warm regards always

Roscoe C Blunt, Jr.

Carnage, Cops and Deadlines

Roscoe C. "Rockie" Blunt, Jr.

Ambassador Books, Inc.
Worcester • Massachusetts

The Publisher wishes to thank the *Worcester Telegram & Gazette* for permission to use the cover photo of the 1968 I-290 bridge collapse. Rockie Blunt is seen taking notes at right in the photo.

Library of Congress Cataloging-in-Publication Data

Blunt, Roscoe C. (Roscoe Crosby), 1925-
  Carnage, cops, and deadlines / Roscoe C. "Rockie" Blunt, Jr.
    p. cm.
  ISBN 1-929039-23-9 (pbk.)
  1. Blunt, Roscoe C. (Roscoe Crosby), 1925- 2. Journalists--United States--Biography.
3. Crime and the press--Massachusetts--Worcester. I. Title.

  PN4874.B58A3 2004
  070.92--dc22

2004022617

Published in the United States by Ambassador Books, Inc.
91 Prescott Street, Worcester, Massachusetts 01605
(800) 577-0909

Printed in the United States.
For current information about all titles from Ambassador Books, Inc.,
visit our website at: www.ambassadorbooks.com.

contents

Acknowledgements 7

Introduction 9

The Exile Years 15

Working Conditions 26

Fire 33

Feature Stories 78

High Jinks: Humor to Break the Tension 92

The Oldest Profession 104

Drugs 114

Car Theft 130

The Silent Victims 141

Rivalries: Municipal, County, State,

and Federal Egos 157

Homicide 164

The Chiefs 198

The Evolution of Law Enforcement:

Constitutional and Civil Rights 216

Vehicular Fatalities 226

Gun Play 242

A Look Inside Headquarters 260

The Curtain Falls 268

acknowledgements

TO MY BEAUTIFUL WIFE, "BEASIE" FOR HER MANY HOURS OF MIDDLE-of-the-night sleep she lost while heating coffee every time the Fire Alarm sounded; for her patience during many hundreds of hours spent alone as I chased feature stories; for her never ending support through the countless trials and tribulations of my extremely demanding career, and for her unwavering strength and love, but most of all for her selflessness. I pray she finds happiness.

And with deepest gratitude to the Rev. Mike Nyman for spoon feeding a computer illiterate author through the myriad complexities of the electronic world of today without which this book never would have seen the light of day.

And to Steve Kellicker, who has become like an adopted son whose continuing loyalty and compassionate friendship has ennobled my life. I am deeply grateful for the countless hours spent enabling me to achieve many of my goals in life, militarily and journalistically. Steve: A rarity, a true friend.

introduction

ONE OF THE THINGS THAT HAS MYSTIFIED ME THROUGHOUT SEVEN plus decades on this earth is whether the course of our lives is preordained by fate or some other exterior force, or by a greater master plan governing our individual destinies. Along the path of life, are the many bends, curves, and grooves we encounter mere happenstance or are our destinations, aspirations, achievements, and failures strictly of our own doing? I wonder.

As a fuzzy-cheeked teenager, still pondering the intricacies of using a razor, I was thrown into the most cataclysmic event ever devised by man: war. In a matter of weeks, perhaps even days in many cases, the carnage, horrific slaughter of millions, total devastation of entire countries, and utter madness, turned a generation of boys into men. After surviving combat and being discharged, my life dream—becoming a writer—destined me to endure for another thirty years, and into old age an almost unending stream of cruelty, violent death, filth, deprivation, and hatred as a newspaper investigative police and fire reporter. Could fate have predetermined that I was best qualified for such an assignment because of previous combat experience? To understand more clearly the question of fate versus self-determination, perhaps it is better to go to the beginning of this odyssey.

Never before nor since had I felt as alone and vulnerable as on Christmas night 1944, when I was huddled in a forward outpost, the first alarm line of defense against a possible attempt by a German patrol to infiltrate our thinly held "Ghost Front." The foxhole, my home for four hours this night, consisted of a narrow, shallow passage scooped out of a snow drift with a battle-scarred steel helmet in the Ardennes Forest. It was just deep enough to deceive me into feeling protected. During World War I, my isolated position would have been described as "No Man's Land," a place half way between our forward defensive line and the unseen enemy.

As soon as the exploratory German artillery shelling and mortar barrage had stopped, and our ears were finally able to function again, the company commander barked, "Blunt, get out there and listen. They may be coming." This meant bellying out for a couple of hundred feet through the snow, trying to dig in, and listening for the stealthy approach of the enemy. The Germans generally did not attack at night, but in infantry combat one learns to expect surprises. I had found an open, exposed area—not a good idea generally—because I did not want to risk being showered with shrapnel in the event of a possible artillery or mortar shell tree burst. Squad radios were frozen and for the most part inoperable, so any warning of an attack or enemy infiltration would have to be by rifle fire or by scrambling back to what little safety our forward line offered.

The previous artillery barrage had been an attempt by the Germans to goad us into a retaliatory response, thereby exposing our position. That night we did not bite. There was an almost deathly silence all along the line. But, we still had no idea where or how strong the German forces were. It was a muddled situation that plagued the inadequately equipped, rag-tag, command-splintered American troops throughout December 1944, when Adolf Hitler ordered a massive, daring, and incredibly violent surprise counter offensive in an attempt to drive the Allies back to the English Channel. I could only guess that the invisible enemy facing us also had no precise knowledge of where we were. For nine days, both forces had jockeyed back and forth waging a cat-and-mouse guerrilla operation through the dense pine-studded forests, often emerging suddenly out of the early morning fog, so typical of Belgium in the winter, like gray ghosts with machine pistols and tank cannon blazing. In my lonely foxhole, all I knew for sure was that he, the German, wanted to destroy me and as many others behind me as he could find. I also knew that his forces seemed to be much stronger than ours.

The blizzard-like conditions and battering high winds that had, day and night for more than a week, physically tortured our poorly-clothed troops had finally abated, but the temperature had plummeted to well below zero. By curling into a fetal position I tried to conserve as much body heat as my equipment allowed. But, I felt no body heat, only painful, chapped hands and face, and numbness. The never-ending shivering intensified into all-out shaking. I tried to control it by wrapping myself in a tight bear hug, but the violent trembling was not to be stopped. Through the frost coating my face, I gazed almost hopelessly at a four-inch plastic and wire Christmas tree perched in the snow at the lip of my foxhole, only inches from my eyes. The tree, intended to be a morale booster, a "touch of home" had been packed in a food package sent by my parents. But, instead of raising my spirits, the small tree brought on a deeper, more morose melancholia at the paradox between Christmas and the massive killing everywhere around me. This night there would be no temporary Christmas truce as in World War I when the senseless slaughter of trench warfare had been put on hold for a few hours, while enemies sang "Silent Night" together in languages strange to each other. That was a different generation, a different morality, where chivalry still existed, even if ever so slightly. But, this was 1944 and nothing would stop the relentless massacre in the Ardennes Forest that resulted, in slightly less than six weeks, in the death of 19,000 Americans and at least as many Germans casualties.

The eerie stillness of the night was broken by a chorus of sounds which fed my fear and uncontrolled imagination. Ice or snow breaking off from evergreen boughs became German footsteps. The rustling of snow-laden branches around me became whispering enemy voices. The scrunching sounds of the snow, as I moved about in my makeshift hole, were unnaturally amplified. As my pain-wracked extremities ceased to function, I began to lose the battle against the elements. To shut out the world, I closed my eyes and gradually allowed thoughts of home to camouflage the pain, but the troubled reflections were jumbled and unfocused. I tried to fight off the thought that what I hoped for would probably never come to be. Like millions of others of my generation, my dreams and aspirations had hit a snag, a detour, caused by Uncle Sam, who was assisted by a former World War I German corporal, bent on ruling the world. I had not asked for much in my young life, only to be a drummer and a writer. Now, such childhood dreams were in jeopardy, and if I was ever to achieve them, the first thing I had to do was survive this night.

I struggled to remember the warm Spring evening of March 11, 1943, in a Victorian mansion on the Clark University campus, in Worcester, Massachusetts, when scholarly Professor Leroy Ames of the English Department had figuratively opened a door for me, turned on a light, and then pointed out the uncharted path he strongly urged me to follow in my life. Every word of his warm, fatherly voice had become indelibly etched in my memory. "I see a talent in you I seldom see in a freshman English student, Mr. Blunt. If you don't become a writer or a journalist you will be making one of the major mistakes in your young life," he had told me. At that moment in my teenage life, a dream had been born. And twenty-one months later in Belgium's "Battle of the Bulge," as I reached the lowest ebb in my life, struggling to survive another day, another night, even another hour, that dream offered me the strength and determination to survive and to some day write. But, that day seemed so remote, so far away. My numbed brain rationalized that the hopelessness of my daily existence would almost certainly preclude the realization of my dream. Many combat infantrymen whose world was mostly limited to their crudely dug foxholes, surrounded by the insane and horrifying carnage of war that fate was forcing them to endure, frequently did not see themselves as having much of a future. Their existence often included a form of fatalistic mental destiny. I prayed that I would have the strength to be different.

Since landing in Normandy only seven short weeks earlier, count-less scraps of paper and fountain pens or pencils from demolished villages had become my journalistic tools. Scribbling every emotion, every thought, every observation, every opinion had become my daily ritual during the infrequent momentary lulls in the fighting. I felt that even my minuscule contribution to history demanded to be preserved and some day told. Every scrap of paper was dutifully thrown into my barracks bag, eventually (three years after the war ended) to be corre-lated and typed into manuscript form by my future lovely bride, Beatrice.

After my survival and eventual discharge, I, as so may other return-ing veterans, became a victim of the uncertainty of the late forties, the post-war era. Repeatedly, for eleven years, I knocked on the door of the *Worcester Telegram & Gazette*, premier newspaper of Central Massachusetts, and each time I was unceremoniously bounced by a crusty, old, cantankerous managing editor. But perseverance, it is said, is the truest attribute of a newspaperman. I was not to be denied. Guided by advice from a family friend, a fifty-year veteran of the so-called "journalistic wars," I managed to sneak in a back door as a file clerk in the newspaper library, the so-called "morgue." The die had been cast.

Less than a year later, I finagled a transfer to the news staff where my initiation consisted in being shunted five times to night shift duty in various county bureaus. Each assignment was usually of less than two-weeks duration and all with absolutely no instruction or guidance as to what was expected of me. Eventually, I was able to figure out where the on and off switch was on the teletype machines and my journalistic career was off and running. Difficult beginning? Surely. But, it was the opening act of a thirty-two-year career which culminated, at the time of my retirement, in my description as the "dean of police reporters in Massachusetts, perhaps of all New England." by the Massachusetts State Police.

The early years as a journalist were, to be sure, slow, faltering, awkward, discouraging, and often quite nerve-wracking. But, they were nowhere as taxing as the "Battle of the Bulge." Here the only enemy was the competition morning newspaper and no one there was shooting at me!

the exile years

Displaying a smile, the Managing Editor announced: "Starting tomorrow, you are our new police reporter; You're a good leg man, you have lots of energy and you write well about people. You will be a good one." Those few terse words charted the direction of my whole future, and tailored my personality, ambitions, and goals.

For almost a year, at the highly respected *Worcester Evening Gazette*, I had bounced around as a general assignment reporter but had failed to distinguish myself in any particular area. On the city staff, the most exciting story I had covered, was a tear-jerker about a small, brown and white mongrel dog "Tippy" that refused to leave the scene of a car accident in a suburban town where her master had been killed.

General assignment reporters are like baseball utility infielders, OK at a few things but highly skilled at none. The role did not fit my mental makeup. Since childhood, I had to excel at everything I tackled. I constantly strived for perfection, and I was always trying to prove myself, mostly to myself. I knew that police reporting would be a lot more challenging than writing obits. I had previously endured a short stint on the religion beat trying to placate the constant publicity demands of ministers, priests, and rabbis. It was a difficult task at best, especially when one is not gifted with even a modicum of diplomacy, tact, or interest in religion. My complaints to management fell on deaf ears with the reply, "Good. If you aren't religious, you won't show any favoritism."

After finally receiving a reprieve from the world of religion, I inherited the federal beat. I was working my way up the ladder. The new beat consisted of hanging around post offices, military recruiting stations, FBI and Treasury Department offices, and federal district courts hoping that some generous soul, feeling sorry for a bored reporter, would throw out a tidbit of news. But that seldom happened. For the most part, the beat meant drinking coffee out of plastic cups and mouthing platitudes with a host of unresponsive people who, out of fear of their chains of command, dared not offer me anything substantive. After a few months of this, I was convinced that editors used the federal beat to get certain reporters out of sight so that they would not interfere with the publishing of the paper. A few weeks on this beat began to dry up my ambition and journalistic desire. Fortunately, I did not stay on the federal beat.

The health, education, and welfare beat—the next rung up the newspaper ladder—was no better. Here I tried to translate, into English, press releases from medical institutions, politically connected educators, and state bureaucracies. The most difficult part of this assignment was attempting to decipher the gibberish of the local School Department and of various educators, the so-called "egghead legalese" of the medical world, and the self-serving pap of state bureaucrats and paper shufflers. Then came the formidable task of trying to translate all this alleged "news" into language that readers age fourteen and older could understand.

We were constantly reminded that the few cents, which those readers planked down for the paper, contributed to our meager weekly salaries of fifty-five dollars. I was eager to rid myself of this assignment, for it seemed as if those spewing out the endless streams of press releases either had a back to pat, an ax to grind, or some smoke to blow at the public. I resented being manipulated as a back-slapper, an ax-sharpener, or a human smoke screen.

After the unexpected announcement of my transfer to the police beat, I returned to my desk in the newsroom with some degree of trepidation and started cleaning it out. As I dumped the contents of three drawers into my briefcase, I sensed that I was being ostracized for being a free thinker, a maverick who, on occasion, had been reluctant to conform to the company line. It was an opinion that remained with me throughout my reporting career. I did not, for a minute, buy the con job that, on the staff, I was the best-suited reporter for the police beat. It was a time-worn adage in the newsroom that the police beat was reserved for those so incompetent they could not line up three people in a photo and get the cut-line names in the correct order. But I did not foresee that the new assignment offered total freedom of thought and action, and an opportunity to improvise each story.

I also could not foresee that the abysmal working conditions under which I would be forced to live, and the daily adversity I was soon to confront would forge in me a resolve and determination never heretofore experienced. Nor did I know that the police beat would lift me eventually to the stature of one of the dominant reporters on the staff. The invigorating action, the occasional danger, the uninhibited freedom continually flavored by physical and emotional hardship coupled with longevity were all factors in elevating me, over the decades, to statewide prominence. I also could not foretell that this uninhibited, seat-of-the-pants style of reporting would, before I retired, shoehorn me into more journalism awards than anyone in the 123-year history of the paper.

But, as I vacated my newsroom desk for the last time, I put on a brave front, not for a minute giving the editors or staff any inkling of my innermost thoughts. I accepted the new post "promotion" with a forced smile and never once looked back. I severed myself from the newsroom staff and management for the next three decades.

As I headed toward the company parking lot, I fended off the jibes of the other news hounds. Their relief and sarcasm were obvious— they had escaped being exiled to Police Headquarters to replace the reporter whom editors deemed no longer productive.

I entered the unlighted, dungeon-like corridors leading to the dilapidated basement pressroom at Police Headquarters with foreboding. It was not that I was wary of cops; I was not. But, I knew full well that they were clannish, often difficult to work with, generally confrontational, unforgiving and tending toward greediness. Many cops, I also knew, worked on one-way streets: taking whatever they could, seldom giving anything in return.

All of this was compounded by the primitive, filthy working conditions in the cellar pressroom to which T&G police reporters had been relegated since 1918. It was with ominous trepidation that I entered a strange, new world, one in which I would have to acclimate myself if I was to survive. I knew that I would have to adapt quickly, and become a street fighter, or at least develop that persona. Cops do not like a reporter in a position to tell the public what they are up to. And if I did not counter the cops' daily barrage of cruel and demeaning insults with more caustic insults, they would never ease up on the verbal punishment and eventually they would beat me down. Standing up to them toe-to-toe brought their eventual, begrudging respect — not popularity certainly, but limited acceptance.

I had already spent more than two years on the county staff working with more than a dozen police departments of varying sizes — from rural towns where chiefs could not take phone inquiries until they had finished chasing down cows escaped from pastures, to cities with large forces where many officers were diligently lining their pockets "working their side of the street," or conniving to beat the pension system with faked injuries as soon as they could after being sworn in. I had held my own with many of them in pistol-shooting competitions; had drunk their rancid coffee; refereed their often violent feuds with their chiefs; and had even stashed my young sons to sleep in their dingy, unlighted back room cells when I occasionally baby sat on company time. I knew cops. They held no mystery for me, but still I realized I had my work cut out for me if I was to succeed this time around.

My first formidable obstacle would be to live down the fact that several years earlier I had been banished from headquarters for the cardinal sin of criticizing the department in print. This came about after the paper received a post card from a suburban town librarian claiming that the only safe place to park illegally and not get ticketed was around headquarters. "If it's true, there's a story there," the crusty old managing editor had roared. "Get going." It was futile to try to reason with him once an order had been given.

I followed orders. If I was anything, I was thorough, concise, and literal to a fault. I reported the story in my usual exhaustive fashion. I tallied every parked car within a two-block circumference of the station, counted every tagged car, and took the plate numbers of those without "paper hung on them." I even took a picture of a police officer's car illegally parked beside the station with a ticket neatly tucked under the windshield wiper blade. The only catch was that the picture clearly showed the ticket dated in May; the picture was taken and the story written in October. It was an old police ploy to assure the casual public that justice was being meted out even-handedly. The ruse would have been almost laughable, had it not been so blatantly corrupt.

My street by street survey proved that every car not ticketed belonged to a cop. I wrote the story just that way. It was by-lined and made Page One, despite my pleading that the by-line be dropped. I knew full well what the reaction and consequences would be, back at headquarters, but I just did not realize how swift the retribution would come and how many years it would linger, all because the managing editor would not "cover my ass." My reputation as an investigative reporter had been established but my future as a budding police reporter had been stunted, blindsided, and cold-cocked, depending on the angle from which you looked at it.

Daily journals were removed from front counters and hidden in inner offices. Division doors were locked. The coffee room was off limits to reporters. Former uniformed lunch partners ignored me. I was forced to park my car in commercial lots, safe from every ticket, book-carrying flatfoot just drooling at the chance to tag it. Gone too was "Big Dan," a moose-sized, all brawn, no-brains son of an Irish-come-over, noted in the department for how much his arm pits sweat. He rapped each noon with his billy club on my cellar pressroom window to join him for watered down soup at Louie's next to the fire station. This was the same Louie's where, as we ate, drunks passed out face down on the cigarette-scorched counters and slid off the stools with a thud onto the sawdust-strewn floor. The diner was the pits but "Big Dan" never paid for anything there so the price was right for him. Louie was street smart and knew that to demand payment was to risk vandalism or burglary if the congenial cop, while on protective patrol, started looking the other way. But, to "Big Dan," Louie's was the best lunch in town.

My shunning even included "Crazy Frank," a former mental patient and alcoholic derelict. When he saw me coming, he would yank the steel-splintered freight-passenger elevator (World War I vintage) from the station house cellar to the third floor. Threatening cops had coerced this simple man into leaving me to walk three flights of stairs every time I went news hunting to the Planning, Training, Juvenile, or Criminal Identification divisions.

I had one friend in the department, a polio-disabled war veteran dispatcher whom, when he was a boy, my parents had driven to swimming holes from the city's Swedish neighborhood. "Well, what the hell did you expect after a bullshit story like that," he offered for sympathy.

A head-to-head confrontation with the chief to bring the whole vindictive, narrow-minded, childish affair to a head did nothing to clear the air. "Where do you and your damned paper expect me to put those cops' cars? Hang them from sky hooks?" The steely-eyed chief glowered at me menacingly. With that vitriolic dismissal, the ostracism continued.

On occasion, if I thought it was worth the effort, I tried to reason with my antagonists. I drew comparisons to show them the similarities of our respective jobs: police search for fact, reporters for truth; police are not generally popular in the community, neither are reporters; and both police and the media spend much of their time interviewing people who are often reluctant to be interviewed.

A few cops, when shown the common bonds we shared, eased up slightly and some even became cautiously friendly. But, during the three decades I lived in their sordid, violence-wracked world, they never once allowed me to forget I was a civilian and not even an honorary member of the exalted brotherhood family. When the "blue line" went up, I remained an outsider to the end. There was always the unspoken, confrontational feeling that continued to exist on both sides. In a few instances, it erupted into screaming threats and counter-threats of reprisal. Several times there were physical assaults. Usually the standoffs between media and police were dissolved as cooler heads prevailed. But, the co-existence was always at arms length.

Once, when someone at the newspaper, asked what police were really like I defined this defensive police posture as, "Four hundred and fifty people trying to protect themselves from society." It was more truth than prose. Police lived by the survivalist philosophy of a "strong-offense-is-the-best-defense." As an illustration, one of the chiefs with whom I was expected to co-exist, was constantly being badgered by a well-known, influence-peddling city councilor. The chief pulled a "rap sheet" from the bottom drawer of his desk and scaled it at me. "One of these days he'll shoot off his mouth once too often. One of these days," the chief growled, almost in anticipation. The file showed where the local politician had been previously charged with publishing a pornographic newspaper in the greater Boston area.

I endured the shunning for months before the newspaper, perhaps mercifully, yanked me back to the newsroom where I began a string of feature stories. I had stonewalled it, but for the most part, my effectiveness in the police world led to my demise as a police reporter, all because of one parking story. The "Temple of Truth" had handed the victory to the police department.

Back in the News Room, most of the hot shot reporters entrenched there treated me as an outcast, a failure as a police reporter, rather than recognizing that I had been sucker-punched by the managing editor's stubbornness over a single story that probably was lining a parakeet cage the next day.

But, strange events sometimes happen in the news business. While serving my penance, I had an idea for a feature—I would accompany a city health inspector as he scoured the city for health and safety violations. Anything to escape the confines of the City Room and get back out on the street where I longed to be.

Soon, the inspector resigned himself to the fact that he would be baby sitting me for the day. The first building, a multi-story brick apartment block in the city's seedy South End, from the outside, looked almost too creepy to enter. The inspector, undaunted, knocked loudly on a badly decaying first floor apartment door. "Go away mother-fucker," a voice from within bellowed. The inspector identified himself but received the same answer repeatedly despite demands that the door be opened.

Not one to be deterred from doing his duty, the inspector put in a call for police assistance. Minutes later "Biffer" Johnson, a barrel-shaped old veteran of the street wars, rousted from his fire station "dugout," arrived and assessed the situation. With almost automatic decisiveness he quickly resolved the stalemate. Short on patience, Johnson grunted, "Stand back!" and with that and a running start, he rammed the huge oak door with his shoulder, sending it flying off its hinges and across a bed in the room where it landed atop an emaciated black man.

"OK mother-fucker, I'm in. Now lets see some identification," the old Swede growled, his foot heavily atop the door as he tapped it authoritatively with his lignum vitae billy club.

Several naked women scurried for cover in every direction. Only then did we realize we were in a whorehouse. The building inspector, meanwhile, was methodically moving from room to room checking electrical wiring, cockroach population, broken windows, and other code violations, ignoring completely the sepia feminine side show performing for us. In one last act of defiance, "Sweet Sally," a nubile prostitute, stood before me, her thighs undulating and youthful breasts giggling seductively as in a native dance. Then with a look of utter scorn, she stalked into a bathroom and slammed the door.

Back at the News Room at the end of a long, exhausting day, I wrote the story straight: just another profile about a city employee and his job, something to fill up a news page. Several months later, much to my surprise, the paper was notified that the story of the building inspector had won a prize—the New England Associated Press News Executives Association prize—the first of many for me.

From that one experience I learned how the game was played: every time at the plate, go for the home run. Swing from the heels. Make each future story of award-winning quality. But my exile dragged on, as practically every conceivable feature story idea was milked and the journalistic well ran dry.

In time, I was transferred to the suburban beat where I was responsible for news in four contiguous towns: more coffee, dry town clerks, stuffy selectmen, volunteer fire departments, and hick cops. I was given a cast off company car, previously run into the ground by the Circulation Department. Because annual safety inspections were not yet state law, I wheeled around in a car with a cracked windshield, one headlight, almost no brakes, rusted out floorboards covered with hunks of sheet metal, and a driver's door that would not close unless slammed repeatedly. It also had a mobile phone connected to the photography department, ostensibly, so that editors could alert the suburban reporter to breaking news. I considered it a tether, so I routinely reported it out of order. However, the assignment was not all "Dullsville," for again it gave me the freedom I needed to perform my work away from the scrutinizing eyes of desk bound editors. Eventually, as the rusted out, cast off hulk I was driving continued to fall apart and I could watch the highway whizzing by between my legs, I refused to drive it. I was reassigned to the News Room, because it was more cost effective to take me back than to repair the car. It was junked.

Soon afterwards, the decision was made to test the waters at Police Headquarters, to see whether, after four years, all was forgiven or I was still persona non grata there. But, as any newsman or woman who has ever had the police beat can attest, cops have long memories. They never forget or forgive an alleged misdeed. On my first day back at the station, with my back pocket stuffed with folded copy paper to serve as a scratch pad, and my shirt pocket loaded with freshly sharpened pencils, I set forth to slay the dragon.

To say that I was remembered for my miscreant action of four years earlier would be a gross understatement. The word was out that I was back! My entry into each office, those that were even open to me, produced a litany of street language at worst and menacing looks at best. I smiled confidently at each tormentor and vowed, then and there, to kill each one of the unforgiving bastards with patience and kindness. I exhibited bon vivant cheerfulness on the surface, but was seething with resentment on the inside. Instantly, each insulting blue shirt became an entry on my shit list. I vowed, one day, to extract a price from each of them. Even several months after my return to the city's version of law enforcement, the vengeful silent treatment showed little sign of abating. But, at least, most of the vile, obscene name calling had stopped. The fearless protectors against evil were just reassuring me that my acceptance back into the police world would be agonizingly slow. I was still in for some very rough times.

Time heals all wounds, it is said. Gradually, this proved true, at headquarters. But, no sooner had conditions improved somewhat, than I learned that the City Hall reporter had his chain yanked by both the City Manager and municipal labor negotiators to write an expose on how much each officer in the department made performing off duty pay jobs. The idea was to show that police did not need a pay raise, that, in fact, they could support their families quite well by moonlighting. Quickly realizing what effect such a story would have on my future, on the police beat—the only reporter in history to be thrown out of headquarters twice—I argued against the story. I knew quite well what parading, before the public, the earnings of 450 city police officers would do to what little remained of my relationship and reputation at the cop shop.

I was right. When the paper hit the street, I was again frozen out with the silent treatment, even though the story by-line was someone else. I surely did not need this repeat performance. Again, I noted those who, some day, would have my brand of retribution meted out. Resembling many cops, I too, had a long memory and an inability to forgive easily. Each time the department turned against me, my skin became a little thicker and my resolve, a little firmer.

working conditions

THE FOUR-YEAR EXILE WAS NOW BEHIND ME, AND I WAS RETURNING to police headquarters for a second tour of duty. The pressroom that greeted me was a dank former cellar storage room. The walls had not been painted or even wiped down, it seemed, for nearly half a century. The floors had not been swept, washed, or waxed during that same time, and loose asbestos showered down whenever a heavy passing vehicle rattled the building.

The pressroom had not changed at all. Two opaque glass windows had remained unwashed during my absence, and decades of dirt on the brick foundation walls had turned the badly peeling pea-green paint to an almost sooty black. Tattered shreds of asbestos still hung from baseboard and ceiling steam pipes. In the corner, additional stuffing from the Salvation Army lounge chair was piled up on the spit-stained floor. The dark green metal clothes locker was even more dented from hundreds of playful truncheon raps by cops sleeping their relief away in the pressroom after midnight.

The two- and four-blast Klaxon horn over the desk still blared out announcements that the Cadillac ambulance or the paddy wagon was rolling, in case the reporter on duty wanted to run at breakneck speed to hitch a ride to cover the incident to which they were responding.

Traditionally, the teletype machine was out of paper because the night reporter, who had not spent a sober day at headquarters in more than 30 years, was generally too soused to order paper. An antiquated manual typewriter with a jammed carriage return and broken roll bar was a permanent fixture, as was the typing chair that had not boasted a padded cushion in years. To complete the depressing scene, two huge, half-rusted steam radiators hissed, scalding everything carelessly placed too close to them.

A bare light bulb was suspended from a single frayed wire drooping from the ornate, cobweb-laced, 14-foot-high sheet metal ceiling. Hundreds of cigarette burns camouflaged the original color of the metal drop-leaf desk, a relic of the 1920s.

The philosophy at the newspaper, I was told by a city editor, was not to waste a penny on the police pressroom. Management thought it was a municipal building, consequently, it was the city's responsibility to spruce it up and furnish it. Conversely, the police department assumed that if the newspaper was privileged to use it, the least it could do was maintain it. As a result, there had been no maintenance by either party since the building was constructed in 1918.

But I refused to accept this fact of life and set about rectifying it. After all, there are limits to how much filth one has to endure in the workplace. Wielding a trusty 4x4 Speed Graphic camera—police reporters in those days doubled as photographers—I took pictures of the room from every unfavorable angle possible. Then I affixed cutlines about a "Nazi torture chamber with blood stains (tobacco juice and grease)" clearly showing asbestos dropping onto desks and chairs oozing stuffing in the foreground, and sent them to the newspaper's executive editor. There was no going through channels for this boy— straight to the top, with no stops in between. This was the most direct route to get the fastest action, I reasoned. The words "channels" and "protocol" were not even in my vocabulary.

In those early days this was an extremely dangerous move, but I was young and cocky and good judgment was not yet on my "important to use" list. Besides, how much farther could I be exiled? I was already relegated to a converted broom closet in a depressing, antiquated police station manned by blue-uniformed strangers who did not like or trust me in the first place.

My tactic worked. The next morning, company-hired painters swarmed over the pressroom with paint buckets and drop cloths while a cleaning crew scrubbed the walls, floors, and ceiling. When I returned several hours later, the place smelt of fresh brindle-brown paint, but it was at least clean. However, the asbestos was never removed, the typewriter never repaired, nor was the dilapidated metal typing chair replaced—not until 14 years later when a new headquarters building was built and the pressroom relocated there.

Eventually, I settled into the old building, gradually accepting the fact that out-of-sight, out-of-mind police reporters were the absolute lowest rung on the newspaper's importance list, an opinion that persisted throughout the ensuing years.

Police reporting in those early days was athletic. When a Klaxon horn split your eardrums, it meant drop everything and sprint through narrow, dimly lighted, sweating corridors, across an open courtyard, through a battle-scarred Cell Room booking area, and out into a garage where you lunged at the rear door handle of the paddy wagon or the rusted-out, low-slung Cadillac ambulance. This all had to be accomplished before the doors of either were slammed shut by attendants as the vehicles pulled away from the station. The race each time went to the swiftest. Whenever the reporter did not make it and was left panting in the street, he became the butt of sarcastic police humor.

More often than not, the wagon or ambulance run was a waste of time, for the majority of the calls were uneventful or false alarms. I soon learned to differentiate between "garbage calls" and emergencies whenever the raucous buzzer over my desk sounded. Ambulance calls usually meant news. You just took your chances on whether a call was a story or a dry run.

When the "meat wagon" call was to a fire, motor vehicle accident, or a deranged "sky diver" performing on the roof of a three-decker, the police reporter in the ambulance was there at the outset to cover it, often ahead of patrol route cars. The drawback, however, was that when the victim was whisked away to the nearest hospital, the police reporter was left behind with a fistful of notes but with only his legs to get him back to the pressroom. Improvisation was the name of the game. The better the improvisers, the more accomplished were the reporters. And these got a $2 pay raise annually if otherwise they kept their noses clean.

A phone booth call to the paper from the scene, a few dictated sentences to a rewrite man, followed by coffee at the nearest luncheonette or drug store, and the reporter was ready for his daily jog back downtown, always trying to beat a deadline. These extended journeys spawned the name "leg men" for police reporters. The death knell in the manner of a desk assignment or, worse still, of an editorship usually occurred when the police reporter could no longer conceal from management the fact that his legs were giving out, indeed that he was slowing down.

The police chief at the time, a far-sighted, brash, 30-year veteran of the street trenches, was the most vociferous champion for new police headquarters. Month after month, he was on everyone—the City Manager, the City Council, the newspapers—about the "deplorable monstrosity" in which his men had to operate while "serving and protecting." Repeatedly, he ridiculed the City Manager and Council for "shadow boxing" and "window dressing" regarding the problems of the antiquated police facilities and working environment. He accused administrators of "looking at shadows behind trees" when discussion started about possible sites for new headquarters.

The police department operation was split: half, located downtown where there was no parking; the other half, located in a cramped, two-story squad room squatting on top of a garage two miles from the city's business district. There, cruisers fought for street parking with the residents of the neighborhood's three-deckers.

Repeatedly, the chief implored the city to bring his department into the 20th century. Impatiently, he took the initiative and had architectural plans drawn up himself for a $1,359,600 modern three-story building with one third more working space for the projected police departments of the future.

But, man of vision that he was, he should have realized that local hind-sighted politicians and administrators of that era were reactionary rather than anticipatory, capable only of applying band-aid methods to patch up the deficiencies of the past. His suggestions for a new station wound up collecting dust in some remote City Hall closet.

Fire and Health Department inspectors uncovered 105 building defects, safety hazards, and code violations that, if found in a non-municipal building, would have led to a condemnation order. A subsequent inspection detailed 62 additional safety violations, enough to give the inspection team writer's cramp.

Some of the defects and sanitary violations were: inadequate exits on upper floors of the building; non-existent ventilation in a squad room adjacent to the pressroom; staircases lacking handrails; no hot water; peeling, water-saturated walls; cracked floors, walls, and ceilings; falling chunks of ceiling plaster; inadequate lighting in interior passageways, corridors, and stairways; a rear door cracked and rotting away; a leaking roof with buckets everywhere to catch rain water; warped window sashes; cracked and broken floors; a leaking skylight; and detention areas without wash facilities.

Inspectors reported filthy, dingy locker rooms; inadequate exits; an unsafe, cable-operated passenger elevator; stinking urinals; radiators emitting scalding steam; overloaded and deteriorating electrical wiring; water from holes in the roof leaking into fixtures and outlets, causing them to shoot sparks and smoke whenever it rained; contaminated water bubblers (they were ordered shut off immediately); broken and dangerous concrete stairs; toilet bowls that leaked urine-tainted water onto floors, and escape doors that would entrap people in the event of fire.

A plumbing inspection was made and 53 more defects were listed. The building was described as a "severe health hazard" by the fire department and "deplorable" by plumbing code inspectors.

This "happy haven" was the place I obediently called home for more than 16 years, a dilapidated relic the city had neglected for decades and would allow to further deteriorate for many years to come.

In August 1978, a citadel-like station, totally devoid of architectural character, was opened at Lincoln Square. A few weeks earlier, I toured the construction site. With no windows on the lower two floors, it was an aesthetic nightmare. Although neglected and dilapidated, the former station with its beautiful original brickwork, marble stairways, and ornate interior appointments, had been a charming, classic reflection of a previous era. It had character.

The new station had nothing: four sterile walls of masonry block; ugly, gun-slit windows on the top floor; and a flat roof, a feature that any knowledgeable architect knows is not feasible in New England weather. The first sprinkle soon proved the folly of the roof design. A mop-and-bucket brigade was recruited to man the top floor every time it rained.

During a tour of the new building, I asked where the pressroom was located. The floor plans were unrolled and studied. There was no provision for a pressroom. Original plans, the dream of a previous chief, had provided for a two-room suite—a pressroom and a linking conference room. A subsequent chief had eliminated the conference room. The current chief, in turn, had wiped out the pressroom completely. It was a perfect example of how each chief interpreted the importance of the newspaper function in relationship to his department.

I howled long and loud at the chief. Finally, apologizing for what was called an oversight, an 8x10-foot utility closet off the main lobby "close to everyone and everything" was offered. The proposed press-room was flanked on one side by the women's toilet, on the other, by the men's. I was doomed to hear toilet flushes in living stereo every few minutes for the next eleven years.

fire

PROBABLY NOTHING DEVASTATES A PERSON, FAMILY, OR COMMUNITY more than being the victim of fire. Fire snuffs out life in the most violent, terrifying manner, leaves the deepest emotional wounds and reduces possessions and heritages to mere memories. To survive a fire is to carry the shattering experience for evermore.

For a police reporter repeatedly witnessing grotesquely cooked bodies, especially those of children, and then laying bare before the world the torment of the victims, leaves indelible emotional scars, much like those gained in a war. In three decades of reporting an estimated 4,500 fires, only a small percentage involved loss of life. In the fires that did involve deaths, however, the totals were often staggering.

I sat in my drafty office one snowy, bitter cold morning during my early years on the beat, grateful that the events of the day consisted merely in monitoring the radio call "squawk box" rather than plowing through snow drifts chasing news stories. But suddenly a box alarm sounded for a dwelling fire in the Green Island section of the city. Then came the firefighter's nightmare: an elderly resident was trapped inside.

Damning the fortunes that drove me out into the immoderate weather, I ran, slipping and sliding for my car parked a half block away. City streets were ice-glazed and poorly plowed, but even under these adverse conditions, I almost beat apparatus from three fire stations. While simultaneously sliding around corners, we converged on the scene.

The nearly 100-year-old house, hardly more than a two-story shack, was almost enveloped in flames as the first fire companies connected to hydrants and started pouring water through the flame-belching front windows. "There's a 92-year-old man still in there," several people on the sidewalk screamed almost in unison, gesturing wildly at one of the windows.

"Search team, hit the front door," a fire captain yelled at rubber-coated men jumping from an arriving fourth fire company and awkwardly sprinting toward the building. The crowd of bystanders fell silent as the drama unfolded.

One fire company drowned the front of the building with water as another threw up a protective water curtain between the now-flaming side windows and a multi-family apartment block only a skinny alley away.

Police officers frantically pounded on locked front and rear doors of the other houses on the block, eventually kicking them in. Moments later, some reappeared carrying bundles of children cocooned in blankets and coats; while other officers led occupants by the hand to safety. Invalids and the infirm elderly were carried from the block by additional police officers brought to the scene by the second alarm. On the perimeters of the fire scene, police sergeants, having gone through the procedure many times before, routinely canvassed the neighborhood looking for temporary shelter for the fire evacuees.

Fire lines were quickly thrown up as spectators and traffic were rerouted. Acrid smoke crept along the ground and billowed across the street, causing emergency workers, reporters, and others to gag violently as fresh air became precious. Because I had to observe the story details personally, I could not retreat from the brownish-yellow, soot-filled smoke.

The search-and-rescue team members practically swallowed up by sheets of flame were almost knocked off their feet by torrents of water as they battered their way into the building. Moments later, a fire-fighter stumbled from the inferno and slumped onto the sidewalk. Instantly, he was grabbed under the arms by hose men and police officers and dragged to a nearby ambulance, an oxygen mask held tightly against his face. His Scott air pack had malfunctioned and he had been smoked by the first few breaths of tainted compressed air gulped inside the burning building. With siren shrieking, the ambulance lurched around a corner, wheeling the semi-conscious firefighter to a hospital where his lungs could be purged with oxygen.

As a district chief placed additional hose lines at the rear of the building, the search team located the elderly resident unconscious on a pile of smoldering rags on a front room floor beside a glowing hot pot-belly wood stove. The man's body was covered with blood-festering boils that stained his rescuers' rubber coats as he was carried from his burning home and into the arms of another police-manned Cadillac ambulance crew. As the back door to the ambulance was slammed shut, portions of the burning building rained onto the sidewalk.

When most of the flames were extinguished, I tagged along as Fire Prevention Bureau investigators and police detectives combed the debris-littered shack for a fire cause and point of origin. As we poked through the rubble, streams of icy water cascaded onto us from the saturated, water-logged ceiling above us. Slogging about in ankle-deep water while crawling through charred partitions and burned-out stairwells, we soon determined the cause of the fire. The only heat in the building for the elderly occupant was the wood-burning stove, fueled by broken, discarded broom handles supplied by the landlord. The handles, too long to fit completely inside the stove, had burned down and flaming pieces had dropped to the floor, igniting it. Later, probing room-by-room through the fire-ravaged structure with city Health Department inspectors, we found no electricity nor water in the house and an inoperative second-floor toilet bowl heaped to over-flowing with dried defecation.

Detectives informed me later that the slum-lord had taken for rent each month most of the old man's monthly eighty-three dollar rail-road retirement pension check, leaving him to scrounge the streets for food. Neighbors told me that women brought him soup or bread whenever they could, at least a couple of times a week. It was a lower-class section of the city where the poor shared what little they had with others.

On Page One, editors gave the story the moral outrage display it deserved while I stormed into the Health Department, threatening more publicity if the building was not condemned as unfit for human habitation and razed that same day. When they complied, it was the first time I had seen bureaucratic red tape cut so fast! The indigent fire victim died a few weeks later in a city-run nursing home without even a newspaper obituary to signify his passing.

FIRE OFFICIALS CAN DO ONLY SO MUCH IN THE AREA OF FIRE prevention. After a two-week rash of tenement fires that injured eight fire fighters and left 79 people homeless, the Fire Department cracked down on landlords for not promptly removing rubbish from their properties. A frustrating aspect of the attempts by police and fire officials to protect people from themselves were the deficiencies in human nature and an almost inherent resistance, it seemed, by many to change or improve their living conditions. No sooner were properties cleaned and vacant lots scoured that they were again inundated by trash and rubbish left there by careless and slovenly people with no interest in maintaining their clean and safe sur-roundings. One top fire official summed it up: "It is a truism that some segments of our citizenry are recalcitrant slobs who often breed future generations of the same genre."

IN AUGUST 1965, MY ENDURANCE WAS TESTED AGAIN BY A MID-night "three-bagger" ravaging a block-long warehouse complex in South Worcester. By the time I pried my eyes open, grabbed a Thermos bottle of my wife's hastily-heated coffee and barreled through several red lights on Route 20 into the city, I could see the whole western sky before me lighted up by the glow of flames raging unchecked.

As I parked my car near a football stadium and ran toward the orange night sky, acrid smoke from burning bales of wool waste broiled to ground level, covering a two-block area with damp, yellow haze. Like a halfback loose on a broken-field run, I jumped over a spaghetti maze of fire hoses, some of them soaking me with showers from leaking couplings. Huge balls of embers hurled into the night sky like a mammoth fireworks display. Dodging them, I groped my way through the smoke, eventually finding Fire Chief Ed Hackett who was coordinating the efforts of his men along a two-block fire line. Nearby, heat build-up explosions and flash-backs blew out win-dows, punctuating our conversation while the burning fireballs illu-minated the note pad on which I was trying to scribble observations and details. As more fireballs fell to earth, I continued to duck and jump away from one position to another, trying to avoid being burned. While the chief filled me in on details of the fire, sections of a three-story brick and metal wall collapsed, showering flaming debris toward us. At the height of the fire, officials estimated that flames were shooting more than 100 feet into the night sky.

Despite the almost constant cascade of burning fire balls, the chief had a job to do, which prevented him from backing away. I could not back away either. We both stood our ground. My limp, water-soaked notebook soon made it necessary to commit fire details to memory. During winter months or while being sprayed with hose water one learned that neither pencils nor ball point pens function very well on water-soaked paper.

Civil Defense volunteers were stationed on nearby roofs, preventing the burning embers from igniting the three-deckers clustered about the inferno. Vibrating pumper trucks, their engines loudly rumbling in concert as water was sucked from nearby Middle River behind the warehouse, drowned out my questions to officials working the fire. Exhausted fire fighters soaked the building as dozens of hot spots defied the network of hoses strewn across adjoining parking lots. Torrents of water poured through the night, drenching a railroad boxcar parked against the burning warehouse. It contained ethyl bromide, a highly explosive liquid used for manufacturing anesthetics. For six hours the fire roared out of control, but by daybreak the neighborhood was declared free of the danger of being enveloped by flames. As I checked the time by the headlights of a fire truck and headed for the pressroom to get a jump on my workday, only a grotesque twisted shell of metal siding and burned-out, windowless brickwork remained of the warehouse. Damage was estimated at $500,000.

DURING THE EARLY STAGES OF MY CAREER ON THE POLICE BEAT, I learned to predict the unpredictable. Never was that more true than one noon in mid-April 1968. The day started out routinely, while I occupied my time with a few "give-'em-eight-hours-for-a-dollar" stories. Then, the police dispatcher's voice intoned over the air: "Attention all rolling stock. The Worcester Expressway bridge at College Square has collapsed. I repeat, the Worcester Expressway bridge at College Square has collapsed. There are multiple casualties. Ambulances and the Fire Department are on the way. Who's rolling?"

One by one, as fast as they could grab a second of air time, route cars throughout the city responded. I shot a fast glance up at the wall clock and grimaced. It was 12:40 P.M., more than ninety minutes after deadline. Regardless, I had to try for the edition: you *always* had to try for the edition.

Heading toward the scene at breakneck speed, the sky in front of me was already darkened by billowing black clouds of burning oil smoke. No matter how long you are on a police beat, there is always that foreboding, gnawing, almost frightening doubt and apprehension in the pit of the stomach when responding to incidents of major violence or tragedy. Fire lines obstructed traffic two blocks from the collapsed bridge. While running the remaining 400 feet, I was overwhelmed by the carnage. An entire span of the bridge which was still under construction—sixteen 135-foot long steel girders—had fallen like dominoes onto three cars, two trucks, and a van. One of the trucks, an oil tanker, was burning furiously. One of the crushed cars contained the corpse of the driver, a 68-year-old man. His wife, a passenger, had barely been able to extricate herself from the wreckage with chest injuries. A fourth car, passing underneath the bridge as the collapse occurred, was struck by one of the falling girders but the driver managed to ram his way forward out of danger, with only minor injuries to himself and a passenger. Three were known dead and eight others already hospitalized.

Sketchy, initial testimony from witnesses recounted the instant that one girder crushed onto some of the vehicles. When construction workers and the contractor rushed to their aid, fifteen more girders fell, trapping most of the workers under countless tons of steel. The contractor and a hoisting engineer were killed instantly. Preliminary information from police indicated that the steel beams had been temporarily secured on only one end. Rescue workers could not remove the corpse of the elderly driver until the oil tanker-truck fire was extinguished. Monstrous twisted girders towered over the scene, and huge blocks of concrete were piled like ancient ruins wherever I looked.

Towering oil-fed flames mushroomed above both sides of the bridge construction site. Fire fighters and police worked perilously close to the flames to remove the body from the crushed car before it was incinerated. At times, emergency workers were obliterated as were most of us by the lung-clogging black smoke that continued to build up faster than it could dissipate into the atmosphere. Almost as if in a huge cycle, the heat generated by the raging fire re-attracted the smoke and, a second time, sent it rushing into the sky with renewed ferocity. Everywhere, police, fire fighters, EMTs and volunteers ran with hand-carried stretchers bearing victims to a fleet of waiting ambulances. It was as close to a battle scene as could be recreated.

One arriving back-up reporter yelled to me, "They're holding the presses." Then I knew we had a good chance of making the edition. As detectives and uniformed officers crawled through the maze of twisted girders and concrete debris searching for more possible victims, I was right in their shadow filling in the details that would ensure a more complete story in the few extra minutes we had been given by the City Desk. A death-gray face stared up at us from a crushed car. He could wait. There was nothing that could be done for him. Eventually, fire fighters removed the body with hydraulic tools. By shouting over the din of sirens, roaring flames, fire apparatus, and emergency radios, I was able to dispatch other reporters to local hospitals to obtain the names of the dead and injured.

When deadline finally passed, I drove slowly back to headquarters trying to collect my emotionally-shattered thoughts. I was still learning how completely draining such momentous tragedies could be. But, for a police-fire reporter, there was satisfaction in knowing that only a bare-bones rewrite was left for the opposition newspaper the next morning.

FIRES, INVOLVING DEATH, SHOCK AND SADDEN A COMMUNITY, BUT none more so than when the tragedy involves the young and especially if the deaths come at Christmas time. One such fire stunned the city when a raging, gasoline-fed flash fire turned a two-story, make-shift log clubhouse in secluded woods on one of the city's seven hills into a death trap. By the time fire fighters clawed their way up the ice-encrusted hill on their knees, dragging pumper truck hoses behind them, five teenage lives had been snuffed out and three other youths had been critically burned. The dead were all 16 or 17. Silently, shaken rescue workers strapped the charred bodies onto toboggan-like stretchers to bring them, slipping and sliding, down a hill to waiting ambulances. Later, investigators said the cabin was an inferno even before rescuers could struggle to the site, as the victims tried desperately to break their way out through walls, even as the heavy roof collapsed upon them. Survivors told investigators the fire exploded when the group attempted to ignite a fire with gasoline in a trash burner. One survivor, already a human torch, was pulled from the building and rolled in snow as his companions threw themselves on top of him to smother the flames. Dental charts were used to identify the bodies.

The next day, I trudged through snow with police fanning out across the city in search of clubhouse-like shacks. Several were found and destroyed. But for five grieving families, the preventative effort came one day too late. It was the first multiple-death fire I had covered. There were be many worse ones yet to come.

A NORTH END THREE-DECKER TOOK A DIFFERENT HAZARDOUS twist a month later. Eleven occupants, many dressed in flimsy night clothes, were driven to the street in sub-freezing weather. Women tugged at fire fighters' arms imploring them to re-enter the burning building to rescue parakeets, cats, and other pets. Children wrapped in ambulance blankets wailed hysterically as police tried to calm them in warm cruisers.

It appeared to be just another building fire until fire radios suddenly blared, "pull back. pull back," to fire fighters still inside the building, producing a scramble of helmeted men running from doors. As they ran for safety, three burning front porches pulled away from the house and a huge section of roof collapsed with splintering violence onto the street, barely seconds after police had aggressively pushed spectators back across the street. Quickly, fire fighters played their hoses on nearby parked cars and fire apparatus, some covered with burning debris. In a matter of moments, the porches were reduced to hissing steam. Then, without warning, loud explosions came from within the still burning tenement building. "Flashback blowing out the windows?" I asked a sweating fire captain beside me. "No, a cop lives there. That is ammunition going off." There were a few anxious moments, however, for spectators and rescue workers alike until the cartridges had expended themselves.

EVENTUALLY, THE WINTER STARTED TO EASE—AND FOR THIS, STREET reporters are always grateful. Fire chasing in the dead of winter consists in huddling against throbbing fire apparatus engines trying to find some heat, shivering in police cruisers seeking warmth, or massaging numb hands before trying to teletype a story back at the pressroom. I was not to enjoy the season change for long when another multiple-death alarm was sounded, this time for a raging "five-bagger" in an aging six-story brick, commercial, downtown building, only a block from the newspaper. It was a case of another middle-of-the night "rapid response" call.

I dropped my car near the newspaper offices and sprinted toward the floodlights eerily illuminating the night sky. Flashing roof lights from more than a dozen police cruisers, ambulances, and fire trucks created a psychedelic melange against towering office buildings. Initial police reports indicated that multiple deaths were involved. Before the flames were finally brought under control shortly before dawn, six were dead and twenty others hospitalized, including eight fire fighters and police officers. To onlookers, the scene was chaotic, but for emergency workers it was a well-rehearsed pattern of search and rescue. They had done it countless times before. One by one, bodies were carried laboriously down aerial ladders, the figures silhouetted against the still flaming building façade. Silently, soot-covered, grim-faced fire fighters loaded body bags into waiting ambulances for transport to the morgue.

Every few minutes, fire fighters and police officers, hacking and spitting from the smoke, came out of the building escorting or carrying elderly residents from their dingy rooms. As they emerged from the smoke whirling along the ground, more teams of fire fighters rushed past them to replace them in the building search for more victims.

At times like this, an experienced reporter does not pester fire chiefs for details. I had plenty of time before deadline. I could be patient as I continued to chronicle another unfolding tragedy.

More than a dozen surviving residents wandered silently off into the night, perhaps to escape the violent agony of having lost a friend, to find another flop house shelter, a reassuring bottle of cheap wine, or just another beginning somewhere else. As I watched the exodus of what one former police chief had called the "flotsam and jetsam in the harbor of life," I was suddenly startled back to reality when, without warning, with a deafening roar, the massive roof of the building collapsed onto the upper floors. I ducked back into the protection of a doorway across the street to escape a torrent of falling bricks and the accompanying fireball of burning debris showering onto the street, almost at my feet.

Scurrying backward, I bumped into a police officer, also in the darkened entryway.

"You're slowing down Rock," he teased. "You used to move faster than that."

The legs are first to go with age," I retorted.

"Not according to my wife," he shot back.

Desperately, fire fighters struggled to contain the flames before they could wipe out an entire city block of connected aging buildings. Built-up heat continued to blow out upper-story windows, propelling glass onto those laboring below. Even as flames licked from glassless window frames, Fire Prevention Bureau investigators began probing through the building, as always, searching for a point of origin and a cause of the deadly blaze. As they did, the room-by-room search for more victims continued. Initial investigation indicated the fire had started in rubbish beneath a rear first-floor porch. Exterior points of origin generally indicated that fires were arson, or at least of suspicious origin. Due to the high loss of life, an accurate determination was imperative.

My two-page story was embellished with seven pictures. Twenty-four days later, it was announced the fire had been set. Now the Police Arson Squad and detectives would take over. The city's homicide totals were now bloated by six more murders in the city, none of which was ever solved.

THERE ARE MANY TYPES OF FIRES: DWELLINGS, COMMERCIAL buildings, vehicles, explosions, and forests. But, perhaps the most hair-raising type, one that demands that fire personnel, police, and even reporters walk a very fine line between life and death, is a natural gas fire. Such fires always carry the potential for explosions of such intensity and concussive force that whole neighborhoods could be wiped out in one blinding flash.

It was a quiet, rather uneventful day, the type that gives a reporter's adrenal glands a rest, when the antiquated police building was shaken by a blast that rattled windows. It was much more than the occasional cherry bomb exploded by pranksters in the building. A sonic boom? Too loud. This was the real thing. As sirens split the air, a mushroom cloud rose slowly over the East Side, several blocks from headquarters.

Frantically, I called the City Room for photographers.

"Tell them to look for all the smoke," I shouted, slamming the phone down and legging it three blocks to the scene.

Vehicular traffic quickly became snarled in every direction. The natural gas blast practically destroyed several of the twelve units at a low-income housing complex units. By the time I arrived, dazed and bleeding occupants were crawling out from under the collapsed walls and small mountains of scattered debris. Police cruisers and ambulances were zigzagging across sidewalks and yards trying to get some of the eleven injured to a nearby hospital. Walls on the north and south sides of the three-story brick building bulged menacingly, and threatened to collapse at any moment. Burning construction materials, window frames, clothing, glass, shattered furniture, bedding, and shredded curtains littered the ground, making it more difficult for rescue workers to enter the building. Bricks and concrete had been hurled more than forty feet. Police quickly ordered the area evacuated of spectators and those not needed in the rescue operation. For several blocks around, windows in homes and business establishments had been shattered by the explosion. Gas company workers quickly shut off supply lines for several blocks around to prevent further fire and explosions while fire fighters freed three men and a woman from the rubble.

It was later determined that a construction backhoe had ruptured a gas service line, allowing the deadly gas to seep into an apartment where it eventually exploded. Within two hours, the crisis had been resolved. Building inspectors said that the badly damaged structure could be salvaged. Miraculously, none of the injured died.

THE DOWNTOWN SCENE OF THE SIX DEATHS IN THE FLOP-HOUSE complex, an area known by police as "Nightmare Alley" or "Death Alley," soon claimed more victims. I had been awakened at two A.M. by my wonderful professional friends in the Worcester Fire Alarm Division and told to "Get to Irving Street fast. Heavy loss of life." The spectre of death which always hung heavy over the area had pounced again.

A four-story apartment block, only a stone's throw from the previous killer conflagration, had erupted in flames and within a matter of minutes three men and a woman had been pronounced DOA at the city's municipal hospital. One of the men had jumped in desperation from an upper-story front window to escape flames bellowing into his room with scorching ferocity. He landed headfirst on a sidewalk and was killed instantly.

Speeding through early morning blinking amber traffic lights, a very somber fire chief informed me that four were already dead with the possibility of more to come. As fire fighters scoured the inferno for more victims, ambulance crews confirmed that ten other injured occupants had been transported to local hospitals, mostly with severe burns.

One fire victim had climbed to the building roof and had hurled himself over an alley to the roof of a smaller dwelling next door. He survived.

A sobbing woman, sprawled on a sidewalk gushing with hose water, was in emotional agony. To anyone who would listen, she spilled out horror stories of trapped occupants screaming in the smoky blackness, hurtling bodies, and the terrifying confusion of survivors frantically milling about searching for loved ones. It was as though she was transferring to me the horror in her mind. I could only wince in sympathy. Other survivors, overcome to the point of emotional numbness, told of panic-stricken occupants who, when offered escape routes, had instead run back and perished in the flames.

Exhausted after an hour of logging all the information and descriptions, I slumped on the nearby retaining wall of a church lawn and washed down a Salvation Army doughnut with luke warm coffee. The hysterical stories I had recorded in my notebook took their toll and I felt smothered by so much death and suffering around me. My head was bowed by fatigue when I became aware of angry voices rising across the street. Almost emotionless, I watched police detectives hustling away in cuffs one of the building residents. He was charged later that day with four counts of homicide by arson and was committed to a state hospital for psychiatric evaluation.

A Roman Catholic priest had finished the grim task of administering the last rites to each green body bag being loaded into waiting ambulances and was now silently leaving the area. Fire fighters waved to him. It was a scene they had seen only too often before. In time, the last police and fire vehicles pulled away, leaving only discarded Styrofoam coffee cups floating down the gutter like so many small sailboats going nowhere.

ONE OF THE FEW TIMES I WAS ALMOST FORCIBLY RESTRAINED FROM an emergency scene was when 200 propane gas tanks exploded in a suburban town, scattering 100-gallon tanks like missiles for more than 250 feet, forcing the closing of a major inter-state highway. Fortunately, no motorists had been passing the gas storage center when the tanks came raining down. A nearby elementary school was quickly evacuated of 580 students and twenty-nine administrative personnel. The ensuing fire sent shock waves that were felt in neighboring towns. Witnesses told of an estimated forty explosions within five seconds of the fire eruption. Acting with bravery I had never witnessed before, local fire fighters inched their way close to the main 30,000-gallon gas tank, all the while pouring tons of cooling water on it to prevent ignition from nearby burning tanks. For more than an hour, the fire fighters stood their ground until flames showed signs of burning themselves out. Had the main tank exploded, most of the nearby town might have gone with it. The gas explosions had brought the town to the brink of total disaster for at least four hours. Finally, luck and the heroism of fire fighters made the difference.

OF THE MANY FIRES TO WHICH I RESPONDED DURING MY CAREER, it seemed that most occurred during the winter months and in the middle of the night. After a few months, I began to feel hexed by the elements. A fire alarm call jangled me awake me at three A.M. one January morning. "A five-bagger on the East Side. You can't miss it. Just follow your nose. You'll smell it."

The dispatcher was right. While with wheels whining I tried to navigate an ice-slicked hilly approach to the city, the sky before me glowed orange, a sure sign that I had a big one on my hands. It turned out to be an industrial complex, one block long, the site of a former metal stamping company. It was really going, or as fire fighters would say, "It was REALLY cooking." The flames, originating in rubbish at the rear of the building, had spread to several propane tanks and instantly the building was enveloped in flame.

I slid to a stop just short of the fire hoses strewn across the street and bolted out of my car just in time to witness the entire roof collapse with the roar I had heard so many times before. I had not taken three steps from my car when I was flat on my back painfully bruised from a sliding fall. I had tried to sprint across an ice field of frozen fire hose water! From the ground, I looked up and watched several rubber-booted fire fighters, arms and legs flailing, trying to escape from debris showering down on them. With a slow, grating groan, steel-beam roof girders buckled and almost majestically lowered themselves to the ground. Released from their confinement, and in almost violent beauty, flames now billowed more than seventy-five feet into the dark sky. More fifty-foot sections of the roof eventually gave up and collapsed while huge bales of scrap cloth fueled the raging flames on the second floor.

As multiple alarms were sounded 250 hastily-summoned off-duty fire fighters began arriving at the scene. Police reinforcements cordoned off the entire neighborhood, and quickly established circuitous detours away from the fire scene for the early morning commute traffic. The nose-pinching cold made it almost impossible to interview fire officials and then transcribe information onto a note pad. Nothing worked. Pens would not write, wet paper would not take ink, and numb hands with unbending fingers could not hold a pen, even if it did work.

Hundreds of stalactites saw-toothed the roof line or what was left of it. Layer upon layer of ice continued to build up as fire fighters stubbornly poured water at resistant flames shooting from dozens of smashed windows. Walking became almost impossible without grabbing onto something and pulling one's self along, legs sliding in every direction. To keep from falling, fire fighters manned hoses from a kneeling position, usually one man supporting and holding another against the pressure of the water stream.

Ballpoint pens, one after an another, froze and refused to make even an indentation on a wet note pad. All information and descriptions had to be committed to memory, a task easy enough after some practice.

The interior of the building was still an inferno radiating considerable heat through the corrugated metal walls, and I repeatedly sidled up as close to it as I dared without becoming the target of some hose man with a misguided sense of humor. That night, I sought warmth wherever I found it, even pressed against the hood of idling ladder trucks which, in fact, throw off the most heat; just one of the survival tricks learned on the police–fire beat.

At the rear of the building, added crews tried to keep the fire from damaging the adjacent Penn Central railroad tracks. With the coming of dawn, Fire Prevention Bureau investigators started poking through steam-hissing debris, searching for a point of origin and cause. When the fire was finally announced as under control, not much remained for the investigators.

Nothing looked, or felt as good as the asbestos-dripping steam pipes back at the pressroom. When hands thawed, the story was completed and on the wire even before the rest of the news staff woke up.

FIRE FIGHTERS AND POLICE REPORTERS SHARE THE SAME QUESTION: "When will the other shoe drop?" When will the next major fire hit the city? It surely will, fire fighters claimed. Such fires were inevitable and could not be prevented. Would it be a high-rise office building towering above the reach of the department's 120-foot aerial ladder, or a crowded nursing home or a hospital? Fire officials concern themselves with such fears. Before long the city found out.

Again, in the middle of the night, a violent fire broke out in a five-story brick apartment block in the city's South End, a decaying section, rapidly becoming known as a slum. By the time I arrived, the fire had claimed four lives. More casualties were inevitable. When mop-up operations began and hoses were laid out to dry, the death toll had risen to ten, the highest total, officials claimed, in the city's history.

Every available piece of apparatus was at the scene and mutual aid apparatus from surrounding towns were "covering" the vacant stations throughout the city. Four blocks of the city's main thoroughfare were grid-locked with fire trucks, police cruisers, ambulances, and hundreds of silent spectators. I spotted the police chief at the scene and latched onto his coattails. I knew he would be briefed regularly by his unit commanders and, therefore, he would be my best source of information. However, this was no time to question him or his subordinate officers, all of whom were battling one of the major fires in their careers.

A fleet of ambulances, flanked by wheeled gurneys, stood sentinel around the perimeter of the clogged street, transporting dead and injured to area hospitals. By daybreak, sixteen occupants of the building, seven fire fighters, and eight mute body bags had been carted away from the macabre scene. The tailgate of every fire truck held slumped-over, exhausted fire fighters with their soot-covered, heaving, sweating faces carrying tightly clamped oxygen masks. Four of the hospitalized fire fighters had been knocked off a ladder and buried by bricks cascading down on them from a collapsing wall. One man's face had been practically crushed.

Two police officers valiantly entered the burning building and rescued several occupants before being forced to flee the inferno. By the time other officers arrived, the third, fourth, and fifth floors had disappeared into swirling, acrid smoke. The officers, visibly shaken, said that "people were hanging from windows screaming for help, and others had already jumped into an alley on the north side of the building. We yelled for them not to jump, that they would be rescued, but they jumped anyway. We could only stand there helplessly. Then we picked them up and got them to hospitals or to the morgue." Some occupants from upper stories tried to slide down ropes and bed sheets tied together. Some made it to the third floor and then let go. Four aerial ladders at the front and rear of the building plucked more than a dozen scantily-dressed, terrified occupants from upper-story window ledges.

Lightly falling rain and a sudden shift in the wind propelled dense clouds of smoke swirling along the ground like an advancing tidal wave, scattering hundreds of spectators. Momentarily, a massive shower of burning embers and debris illuminated the drizzly sky as the roof collapsed onto the fifth floor, sending it in turn crashing onto the fourth floor, and then onto the third, almost like dominoes. Unable to withstand the added weight, exterior walls separated and buckled, as massive cracks appeared at both front corners of the building. Apparatus drivers hastily pulled back. More than one hundred people were evacuated from an adjoining apartment building, separated from the fire by only a fourteen-foot wide alley.

The familiar sight of dead-weight corpses, silhouetted against piercing emergency floodlights and sullen gray smoke as they were being lugged from the building, continued as the grisly search continued. The total collapse of the building made it nearly impossible to find further victims. As each floor, room, or pile of rubble was searched, voices on fire radios apprised the fire chief of the progress. On and on it went throughout the night: unidentified, eerie voices from inside the building, somber responses from the street, wailing sirens of ambulances evacuating the scene, the heavy, throbbing pulse of fire apparatus pumps, water spray everywhere—and the smell of death.

After the ferocity of the fire was eventually conquered, searchers found in an alley the body of a woman, who apparently driven by fear and desperation, had jumped from an upper window. She died of her injuries several weeks later.

I retired to the City Room to file my story, almost totally overwhelmed by the enormous loss of life. Most reporters are usually able to detach themselves from a tragic story; but not always. By the time the presses rolled, nine deaths had been confirmed and nine other people were still unaccounted for. Afterwards, searchers told me that practically everywhere they turned there were pieces of dismembered bodies or remnants of bodies reduced to chunks of charred meat beneath the debris. Each step they took in the collapsed building was precarious. All stairwells and most floors had collapsed. Fire fighters with walkie-talkies were stationed on roofs of adjacent building to monitor the search. Finally Main street was closed for several days as wrecking balls smashed out of existence one of the city's older landmarks. Only a vacant lot remains today.

ALMOST WITHOUT EXCEPTION AT FIRE SCENES, THERE ARE INCIDENTS of heroism by emergency personnel, especially when it comes to harrowing rescues. Usually, the above-and-beyond goes without notice by spectators, the media, and even the performer's superior officers. When questioned, fire fighters usually mumble something about "it is just part of the job; it is what I am paid to do." One such uplifting event occurred at a multi-alarm fire in a housing complex for the elderly, four blocks west of the downtown business district. The elderly often become disoriented when confronted with fire or smoke. They refuse to budge or to attempt escape. They resist even when police or fire fighters resort to carrying them to safety. Scooping them up and carrying them does not always work. Rescue workers say that the elderly can be very stubborn.

One search team, feeling its way along a corridor wall, found a woman cowering in the dense, pea-soup smoke in her bedroom, obviously stunned by the blackness. She resisted all attempts to evacuate her. The rescuer whipped off his compressed air mask and placed it on her face. With the first gulp of fresh air, the woman calmed down and, with the mask protecting her all the way, she was brought to the street for medical attention. Officials said later that the air mask procedure was repeated several times by two other fire fighters, thus saving lives. I made sure these three rescuers—all of whom had been "smoked" and later treated for smoke inhalation—were recognized in a news story. You never saw three more embarrassed and shy heroes when the news photographers showed up. The trio were commended by the department. Officials said that even a few minutes of breathing lethal, toxic fumes from burning plastics can be fatal to the elderly. Later, one fire official described that it was the worst interior smoke he had seen in twenty-six years on the job. Mask swapping is not uncommon for fire fighters. They are trained to swap masks with other fire fighters who have run out of air, much like the procedure used by SCUBA divers. It was always part of my regimen, if possible, to find an off-beat angle to a story in order to take it from the mundane "page filler" class and into the "best-read-story-in-the-paper-today" category. Sometimes it was easy, more often it was not.

A FOUR-ALARM, MULTI-STORY APARTMENT BLOCK FIRE IN THE SOUTH End provided just what I was looking for. Six injured occupants had been hospitalized, and seven fire fighters treated. Fire hoses bouncing streams off exterior walls seemed to have little effect as flames spread upward, seemingly fed by some invisible accelerant. This race by the flames to reach the roof almost cost a firefighter his life. Only an act of desperation saved him. As a member of the search team, the firefighter had cleared the first four floors and was working his way, mostly by feel, along a fifth-floor corridor. He checked his air supply, only to find he had barely enough for a quick search if he did not tarry long. He put his shoulder to what he thought was the last apartment door. Suddenly, he was jolted by a sudden release of air from the room erupting into a wall of fire behind him. His escape route was blocked.

He lunged into the apartment room, slammed the door shut behind him and staggered to the room's only window. Frantically, attempts were made to position aerial ladders beneath the window while the stricken man was slumped over the window sill trying to find air to breathe. Slowly, he was asphyxiating. As he slipped into unconsciousness, his motionless body was framed by the glow of flames filling the room. His would-be rescuers could not get the ladder truck into position to help him and the height was too great for ground ladders.

It was the classic nightmare that every firefighter dreads: a comrade trapped in a flame-filled building and rescuers unable to get to him. Already, eight other fire fighters had been evacuated from the rapidly spreading flames when the building roof collapsed around them.

With the last surge of desperation, the trapped firefighter somehow removed his gear, climbed out the window and hurled himself at a nearby tree. As flames mushroomed out the window behind him, the man blindly wrapped his arms around the tree trunk and managed to hold on. With belching flames still threatening to roast him, he weakly shinnied, limb-by-limb, down the tree to where others could grab him and carry him the rest of the way. He was treated for severe smoke inhalation and eventually returned to the job. When retelling the incident afterwards, some department members said the man had been dubbed, "the flying squirrel," a name that apparently stuck for I heard it repeated for some years afterward.

FATAL FIRES ARE ALWAYS EMOTIONAL. SOME LEAVE LONG LASTING scars and haunting memories. Year after year, the middle-of–the-night calls kept coming. One for a four-alarm blaze in a three-story dwelling threatened to wipe out an entire section of the city's South End. When I arrived to "paint a picture" for my readers, I soon realized I was again witnessing multiple deaths. During my thirty-two years on the job, no matter how many times this scene was repeated, it never became easier. In fact, as the thick skin developed by police reporters gradually wore away with advancing age, the emotional shock at each fire became more difficult to accept. When the burning building came into sight, brilliant orange flames illuminated the black void of night where a roof once had been. The clammy weather did nothing to dispel the ominous feeling, and the warmth of standing near a flaming structure was also missing. Walking into a fire scene had become like walking into an icebox, both physically and emotionally.

The scene was always the same: cops pushing back the curious; the dancing red and blue psychedelic lights; the throaty rumble of idling fire apparatus; choking, acrid smoke; orders barked by fire officials; patient clergymen anticipating the worst and waiting to administer the last rites of the Catholic Church; the friendly Salvation Army coffee venders; and sometimes, even the City Manager. And the Angel of Death always seemed to be hovering over us, as police often said.

Spotting me writing notes on my pad, the Fire Department chaplain, a bloated, rather obnoxious priest, wisecracked to police and fire fighters nearby, "Hey look. The vulture is here," pointing in my direction. It was difficult at that moment, watching charred bodies being carried from the building, to restrain myself from lashing out at him, even as those within earshot winced in disbelief at the hurtful remark. But, from that night on, whenever our paths crossed at fires, I merely snubbed him with dead-pan disdain.

As we stood helplessly below, a woman appeared at a window screaming, "Get me out, Get me out." Then, inexplicably, she disappeared back into the wall of flames. We learned later she was an eight-month pregnant mother. When the woman's body was recovered, the baby could not be saved.

As air-born balls of fire exploded over the street, every firefighter's nightmare unfolded. Children's screams could be heard. As soon as one ambulance pulled away with a fire victim—dead or alive—another took its place. Five occupants were known dead and six others, critically burned, were clinging to life. Miraculously, nine others, mostly small children, managed to escape without injury. As residents fled, leaving doors open behind them, the resulting drafts accelerated the fire. As I somberly watched the tragedy unfolding before my eyes, a police ambulance driver came running from the building, tears running down his face, with a small baby girl cradled in his arms. I could see that her arms had been burned off to stubs above the elbow. In a moment, she was whisked to a hospital. I had to keep a death watch on her at the Boston Shriner's Burn Unit for more than a month. Mercifully, she eventually gave up the struggle for life and without a sound "little Lisa" became a statistic, the fire's sixth victim.

It was a night of terror, a horrible, shattering experience. To this day, every time I drive by the fire scene, my eyes are drawn to the grass-filled vacant lot, once the home of three families. The image of this frail, little girl will forever be burned into my memory. Covering a fire with fatalities is what separates a police-fire reporter from all others on the news staff. I covered many multiple-death fires but none have clung to me like "little Lisa." But, at the time, regardless of my personal feelings, the story—hard-hitting, factual, descriptive and complete—had to be written. Later, police impounded a Fire Alarm Division tape on which a teenage voice bragged, "I just lit a big one. It is going like hell. You better hurry." Police bull-dogged the case for weeks. They really wanted this one. Eventually, two youths were charged and tried. One beat the rap, the other, a retarded teenager, was convicted and imprisoned.

OCCASIONALLY, THERE IS COMIC RELIEF IN A FIRE. IN A SIX-WEEK period, fire fighters had been creating a trough on a South End street where they had responded to fifteen fires, mostly set, sometimes two and three a day at one certain tenement building. As soon as one floor was damaged, the occupants moved in with another family on a different floor. As the fires continued, the whole building was eventually living in one apartment. A couple of days went by with no fires reported and the neighborhood quieted down. Suddenly, a letter carrier on his route saw smoke billowing from a first floor window. He sounded the alarm and rushed into the building, pounding on doors to alert the occupants. Within minutes, he was joined by fire fighters who took over. Minutes later, fire fighters came stomping out of the building, their boots flapping on the pavement, some swearing, others laughing. The only victim they found was a pig being barbecued over a flaming bathtub being used as a roasting pit. The letter carrier's reaction was not recorded—at least not in the "Paper That Goes Home." The snail-paced wheels of city government eventually condemned the building as unfit for human habitation. It was only when the wrecking ball finally started demolishing the front wall that the occupants were pushed out the back door.

FIVE PEOPLE WERE MURDERED ONE SPRING MORNING IN A THREE-alarm, six-family dwelling conflagration in the Union Hill section of the city. Investigators said the fire was set by a revengeful teenager in a dispute over a girl. One of the victims was a simple-minded young custodian at Police Headquarters who spent most of his time crocheting comforters to give away to cops who put the arm on him for freebies. Two other victims were handicapped elderly, unable to flee the building unassisted. By the time fire apparatus arrived, the building was beyond saving. Repeatedly, police after being told there were still others inside the burning building, tried vainly to penetrate the smoke. Eventually, some of the officers, on the verge of also becoming victims, were rescued by fellow officers. The intensity of the flames precluded further searches for victims by fire fighters until the water hoses took their toll on the broiling flames. Only when the flames were brought under control could another grim search recover more victims. As each corpse was brought out, tentative identification was ascertained by police and neighbors, according to which floor each victim was found.

GATHERING IDENTIFICATION AT FATAL FIRES WAS PRETTY MUCH A set routine. One technique that usually worked was grilling the fire chief's driver and the top police official at the scene for the names of the dead and injured. Conditions and extent of injuries were obtained at various hospital emergency rooms. Cause of the fire came from the Fire Prevention Bureau, a highly-trained and experienced group of investigators. Without friendly contacts in both departments, people upon whom one could rely for accurate and fast details, the job would have been far more difficult and the monster "deadline" would have won far more often.

IT WAS A WINDY, BITTER COLD MID-JANUARY WINTER DAY WHEN THE serenity of the pressroom was shattered by a box alarm coming in shortly before noon, then, there was another, and another, and another. They were for a fire five blocks east of Police Headquarters. To assess more accurately the severity of various fires and also to determine as quickly as possible whether the alarm was real or false I generally used the police parking lot to look for smoke in all directions. In this case, the entire sky over the East Side was black and getting blacker by the moment. Already past deadline, I opted to leg it out rather than use my car and then be boxed in by cruisers and apparatus when I needed to return quickly to the pressroom to file an after-deadline story. Minutes were crucial.

Arriving at the scene, barely able to breathe after chugging up a long, steep hill, I was surrounded by women screaming hysterically in Spanish. In those days, few, if any, police officers spoke Spanish and they were having trouble controlling the crowd. Fortunately, Spanish-speaking PSAs (Police Service Aides) responded and quickly informed fire officials of the situation. There were small children still inside the cellar apartment of one burning multi-story building. As a search team entered the building, two adjoining structures ignited. Quickly, before the whole neighborhood of closely-packed dwellings could erupt, the fire effort was concentrated on all three buildings.

With a feeling of foreboding, I knew that people would die that day. Moments later, the screaming intensified as fire fighters carrying two small limp bodies ran clumsily toward waiting ambulances. The soot-covered bodies seemed so small and fragile in the arms of burly, rubber-coated fire fighters. As one of the fire fighters ran past me he shook his head. He did not have to tell me. When I saw the badly-blistered faces with globs of burned skin hanging down, I already knew. Although a hospital was only a block away, nothing could save two little brothers.

A sudden updraft propelled the flames into the sky. The fires were into the roofs and now nothing would stop them. Both three-deckers were dying before my eyes. With the help of the Spanish-speaking PSA, I was able to obtain the names of the small victims from the hysterical mother, a job I did not relish. I raced back down hill to head-quarters, and filed my grim story. The neighborhood was saved but nine families were left homeless and one mother, childless.

ANOTHER NIGHT'S SLEEP WAS ABBREVIATED WHEN MY BEDSIDE phone alerted me to a violent natural gas explosion, leaving a pile of kindling wood, where a two-family home once stood on the city's East Side. The stench of swirling smoke and dust still had not settled when I arrived. Police and fire fighters picked their way through the rubble looking for possible victims as ominously-silent spectators watched. They were neighbors and they feared the worst.

An elderly man, trapped under a chair in the cellar was extricated in a dramatic rescue. One wall of the building had been blown, mostly intact, sixty feet across the street. Several nearby cars had been buried by debris and a section of two-by-fours had been impaled like an arrow into the side of a nearby home. Nothing recognizable remained of the demolished home.

In the cellar, investigators recovered a sixteen-gauge shotgun, with one expended shell, and gave it to police. An occupant of the building informed police that he had lighted a match and when he did so, "I saw a big flash of light and the refrigerator door blew right by me and the whole roof caved in." Investigators zeroed in on a section of gas line in the cellar that appeared to have a bullet hole in it. Neighbors told police the elderly man had a habit of shooting at rats in his cellar. The bullet-punctuated gas line was removed and taken for evidence if criminal charges were ever brought against the man. I never heard that they were.

"YOU HAD BETTER GET ON YOUR HORSE, BLUNT. ALL OF SOUTH Worcester is going up in flames," a late worker at the opposition paper tipped me off in a pre-dawn phone call. I quickly dialed the Fire Alarm Division private number and Stephen "Yogi" Connole, one of the division's "Mighty Servants Who Never Sleep," blurted out, "General Alarm, Rock. Go in from Camp Street," and then he hung up abruptly. That was all I needed. Fire Alarm Superintendent, Ralph Thomson, a leading authority on emergency radio installation, had trained his men well.

At the time, it was the third general alarm in the city's history, I was told later. Before it was over, a lumberyard, a trucking terminal, several warehouses and an entire city block had been wiped out. Also, seven multi-family dwellings were in imminent danger of destruction.

Like spokes in a wheel, traffic was snarled for a mile in every direction from the fire. I drove over sidewalks, through back yards trying to avoid the most complex networks of fire hoses I had ever seen. Visibility was already down to zero and the white smoke of burning wood clung to the ground, held there by the chill of winter. I worked my way deeper into the smoke bank, feeling my way along a sidewalk chain link fence for direction. I had been smothered in the dense smoke for barely a few minutes but my eyes were already smarting and tearing. I placed a handkerchief over my face. As the white smoke turned to gray, I knew I was getting close to the fire itself. I followed the fence around a corner and suddenly I felt the heat of the fire on my face. For a moment the disturbing idea hit me that perhaps I was too close to the flames, that I had inadvertently gone beyond the fire lines. I had encountered no one since entering the smoke bank and I had no idea where I was.

As I continued feeling my way along, I laughed to myself when the thought crossed my mind, "You will know where you are soon enough, dummy, when you get a puss full of fire hose." But, the humor of the situation dissolved rapidly when I started gagging on smoke and realized I was on the verge of being asphyxiated and still had no idea where to find clear air to purge my lungs. I cracked my knee against a parked car without seeing it. Suddenly, possibly due to a slight shift in the wind, I was in a pocket of fresh, breathable air. Right before me were two fire trucks and a company of men kneeling on the ground manning a water cannon at a reddish glow in front of them. I gulped the good air as if I could not get enough of it.

"Good morning Rock. Nice to see you. Welcome to the party," joked an old Irish firefighter friend, a Pearl Harbor survivor. "Barney" had perhaps the nicest disposition of anyone with whom I worked in all my years on the job.

"Where's up wind, Barney," I asked.

"Over there, I think. Take your pick," he joked, pointing to a denser smoke bank.

The sounds of a major fire are difficult to describe. No two are the same. Some, fueled by wind or thermal updrafts whistle or roar like thunder. Others, allowed to burn unimpeded by contributing outside elements, crackle and snap like crinkled cellophane. I still could not describe how close I was to the fire or whether I was in any danger. I had only the crackling and the roaring to guide me. I probed one way, then another. As the threatening fire sounds got louder and the soot-saturated smoke darker, I paused momentarily to reorient myself.

"We've got to stop meeting like this, Rock. Our wives aren't going to like it," a voice challenged me out of the cold, wet gloom. It was Fire Chief Jim Nally, whose eyes apparently could penetrate smoke better than mine. Greatly relieved to find him with walkie-talkie in hand, I learned an entire city block had been lost, that five fire fighters were already hospitalized, and an estimated 150 people evacuated from their homes on four neighboring streets.

Despite the desperateness of the situation, it was not uncharacteristic for the chief to crack jokes when under the severest pressure. But, his main concern was saving the neighborhood. Mutual aid apparatus had been called in from seven towns to cover vacant fire barns. Every piece of equipment the city owned was at the fire. No matter which way I turned, burning walls were collapsing onto the street, burying fire hoses and sending fire fighters scurrying for safety. Gradually, I became aware that smoke billowing into the sky had turned reddish-brown as different materials were being consumed.

"It's touch and go right now, Rock. You might consider pulling back where it is a little safer. This area can explode at any minute."

I nodded in silent agreement, but I knew I could not. I seldom exercised that much common sense.

Ice buildup on men, equipment, apparatus and streets compounded almost unbearable conditions as crews threw up water curtains to save nearby homes. I was told later that smoke covered all of the city's South End and even the core city two miles away, halting traffic on numerous streets. Much of the city's sky was tinted red by volumes of volcanic-like ash, towering higher and higher by sudden bursts of flame released from confinement from dozens of burning buildings.

Finally, the fire chief was able to "circle the wagons," and position his aerial ladders and scopes around the conflagration to battle the fire from all sides. The grit and determination on the faces of the fire fighters I observed reassured me they would never allow the fire to extend beyond the defensive lines they had established. Soon after the fire was confined and consuming itself from within, the air quality and visibility improved. This enabled me to move about more freely, recording my observations. The carnage before me was almost unbelievable. I had never seen such devastation at a fire scene before. Usually, fire consumes a building, sometimes two. Here, the destruction was almost as far as I could see.

Due to congestion, I was forced to take a circuitous route back to the pressroom, probing first one street, then another, trying to find a yard or driveway, a ball field, anything to free me from the maze. As soon as the story was filed and photographs identified, I headed back to the scene. There was still plenty to write about. Damage had been estimated at $1 million, a considerable sum in those days.

After days of digging and sifting through the destroyed buildings, Fire Prevention Bureau personnel determined the fire had been caused by improper disposal of smoking materials in the carpentry shop of the lumber yard. I never was able to figure out how they could find evidence of a single cigarette butt in an area of destruction that resembled a World War II incendiary attack on a city. When the final tally of IODs (injured on duty) reports were in, thirty-six fire fighters had been hurt. By the time all investigations had been completed and the book closed on the fire, I had written eight stories covering practically every aspect of the lumberyard blaze.

The final chapter was written when the series was chosen by the International Association of Fire Fighters for a national award, the first of two I received from them during my career.

THE MIDDLE-OF-THE-NIGHT PHONE CALLS NEVER SEEMED TO CEASE. A tip-off call from Fire Alarm Division jangled me awake another time. "Get going, Rock. Five-bagger, Franklin and Salem. There are going to be fatalities." He was right. Before dawn there would be two dead and fifty-one others left homeless. I knew the block, more of a flop house, well. I had covered eight previous fires there, one of which, eight years before, had cremated "Crazy Frank," a 70-year-old elevator operator at Police headquarters. The first police officer I encountered was Stan "Red Eye" Niedzwiecki, later to become a detective, who somberly stated that the rapid spread of the fire assuredly would produce fatalities.

"I've never seen such flames. We couldn't even get close to the building," he said.

As occupants wearing only nightclothes stumbled onto snow-covered streets, they were bundled in blankets and taken to a nearby YWCA. Suddenly spectators groaned as a woman, her clothing ablaze, ran screaming from the burning building and into the arms of EMTs.

Upon arriving at the scene, the fire chief called for more manpower and apparatus. Flames, relentlessly eating their way to ground level, wiped out a beauty parlor, barber shop, and florist shop as fire fighters struggled to salvage whatever they could. The heat from the fire could be felt on Worcester Common, several hundred feet away, spectators said.

After I had logged a description—a so-called word picture—on my note pad, I accompanied "Red Eye" to the YWCA to compile the names of the homeless huddled there for shelter. The most difficult part of the fire was not describing it, but getting the surviving victims to stand still long enough to be interviewed and then to decipher their names.

Shortly before dawn, the walls groaned and buckled, an indication of imminent collapse. A demolition crew was quickly summoned. As portions of the building gave up to the flames, a wrecking ball was already at work. Floodlights tried to penetrate the smoke and dust now heavily blotting out the scene at ground level. While wreckers worked on the front of the building, firefighter search teams scoured the rear, searching for more bodies. By early afternoon, the remains of another badly-charred body was found. The cause remains of undetermined origin. I had an unofficial agreement with the Fire Alarm Division personnel to "call out the varsity" only after five, six, or seven alarms, or those involving loss of life. I jokingly accused them of conspiring to schedule every major fire after I had gone to bed. At least, it seemed that way.

THREE MONTHS AFTER THE SALEM-FRANKLIN FIRE, I WAS AGAIN awakened, this time by a fire dispatcher who said only, "Get up to 811 Main Street. A real bad one. They're pulling bodies out of there every few minutes."

The address was only two blocks from the horrific fire that claimed eleven lives a decade earlier. By the time I arrived, flames had been reduced to orange fingers creeping along the roof eaves on two sides of the ramshackle building.

"Seven already," a somber-faced fire chief informed me. "My driver has the names. Tell him I said it's OK to give them out."

The building was a half-way house to acclimate those released by a state mental facility back into community living. Fourteen who had been able to flee the flames were given temporary shelter nearby.

Geraldine Collier, an award-winning reporter on the *Evening Gazette* staff, came flying around the corner as I interviewed the fire chief in soaking rain and intermittent snow flurries.

"Sit on the hospitals and I'll cover the fire," I instructed her. This was the most expedient manner in which to cope with the magnitude of the fire. Also, she had solid contacts at the hospitals and the State Department of Mental Health. We both exercised our individual strengths. If the paper figured I needed help on this one, Gerry was the best with whom to work. She was a real pro, and one of my favorites. It was readily apparent that the community home death toll would be the second largest in city memory. Four of the dead were found in their third-floor rooms, two in a corridor and one had jumped or fallen from a third-floor window, knocking off a ladder a firefighter who was trying to reach him.

As I sat in a police cruiser trying to dry out, "The Angel of Death," a detective lieutenant, swung by and plopped an agitated Hispanic male next to me.

"Talk to this one. He has quite a story to tell," the detective recommended. Half in English and half in Spanish, the witness blurted out a tale of terror as the memories of the initial moments of the fire flashed back in his mind. His voice became louder and louder. Soon, he was shouting. "She kept screaming over and over, 'Help me, help me, please help me!' but there was nothing I could do. I couldn't get to her. Even the firemen couldn't. She's dead now.

"I ran to the front door. There was a woman there screaming. I told her to run away. The smoke was terrible. I kicked in a door. A naked man came stumbling out. I gave him my coat and told him to run. He was taken to the hospital. I was able to get to the second floor, kicking in doors and yelling and yelling for everyone to run. A woman was on the third floor screaming. I couldn't get to her. Everywhere, people were screaming," he stuttered.

Police credited the man with saving several lives. He did not want to be called a hero, so I merely reported the facts of his involvement without comment. After a two-day investigation, the cause was listed as careless smoking by one of the victims.

Six months later, the New England Associated Press News Executives' Association (NEAPNEA) granted Collier and me a joint award for our coverage of the fire.

ON THE POLICE BEAT, NOT OFTEN, THERE ARE RELAXED DAYS—AND there are spectacular days. On those, you are glad to be a police reporter because it entitles you to stick your nose into all sorts of bizarre incidents.

The Thermos of tomato soup was hot and filling. As I sipped on it for lunch, I suddenly was jolted upright when the pressroom "squawk box" blared, "Attention all units. Attention all units. A house has just blown up at Institute and Schussler. I repeat, a dwelling has been destroyed by explosion at Institute and Schussler. Use caution. Fire teams and ambulance are on the way. All units, all Code 17s (lunch breaks) are cancelled. Who's responding?"

I grabbed a phone and yelled for a photographer. This time I did not object to any assistance I could get. It was already ninety minutes past deadline, but the magnitude of the event meant I still had to give it maximum effort and perhaps still make a delayed edition. Pausing only momentarily for red lights, I focused on the black smoke in the sky west of the downtown business district. In police reporting fires or gas explosions one never needed to consult street directories—just look for the smoke and go, go, go!

Sheets of flame obliterated one wall of the two-story dwelling as I wheeled up to the site. Parking a block away to avoid the inevitable traffic snarl, I sprinted up a hill to the fire. Gerry Collier was right on my heels, a reassuring sight, for she was a proven asset at any catastrophe.

"I'll cover the fire. You find a phone somewhere and get the details to the desk," I yelled to her. She nodded and, instantly, we were a team performing a well-coordinated, extremely difficult, high-pressure job.

This time I broke my own rules about not pestering fire officials while they were busy extinguishing fires. I attracted the chief's attention by raising my arm and pointing to my wrist watch. If at all possible most chiefs recognized my sign language and gave me the needed information. Most often, there was not sufficient urgency to interrupt them. After all, they were dealing with lives and property.

I was told a meter reader had thrown a cellar light switch and a spark in the switch triggered the blast. The reader was blown into a kitchen but miraculously was not seriously injured. The house was blown off its foundation by the blast, described by neighbors as a bomb going off, and a thirty-foot long by six-foot high gash had been ripped out of the foundation. A rear porch was thrown more than seventy-five feet into a neighboring yard. A front porch was severed from the main structure. Despite flames broiling furiously from the front windows, firefighter search teams entered the building checking for victims, only to emerge several minutes later declaring the house "all clear."

After considerable scrambling, Collier and I were able to get a detailed story, four pictures and a location map in the afternoon edition. We both shared a satisfying feeling of victory, of a job well done.

IT HAS BEEN CLAIMED BY SOME GENERAL ASSIGNMENT REPORTERS—
better described in the vernacular of the Fourth Estate as jacks of all
trades and masters of not much—that once you have seen one fire,
you have seen them all: the voices of inexperience speaking. No two
fires are the same and, conversely, no two can be covered and reported the same way.

Several months later, the point was proven by an incendiary, pre-
dawn, five-alarm fire that drove more than one hundred people to the
street, from twenty-two apartments in a century-old Victorian apartment block. Half of the evacuees had to be removed—many of them
forcibly—from the burning building by police and fire fighters. When
a five-alarm fire breaks out, experienced police reporters scrub out. To
hasten a departure they do not have brass poles on which to slide
down, but, by permission of the previous three police chiefs, I had
been given a privileged parking spot near headquarters, and that was
almost as good.

Four minutes after the alarm sounded, I arrived to find sixty-foot
flames obliterating a stack of five wooden rear porches. A fire
perimeter had already been established and water from aerial can-
nons was inundating the building from three sides. Due to the known
heavy occupancy, air-masked searchers were already inside to ensure
no casualties had been left behind during the evacuation.

As balls of fire battered the five-story brick façade of an adjacent
block separated from the fire only by a narrow alley almost too narrow to walk through, 120 residents from that building were also
hastily ordered from their homes as a precautionary measure.

For almost a block, sidewalks were jammed with barefooted fire
victims wrapped in blankets or sitting dejectedly on curbs holding
meager possessions or pets in their laps. One elderly women held an
empty parakeet cage she insisted on saving before leaving her apartment. Another occupant fought off fire fighters, determined to
change a baby's diaper before leaving her smoke-filled apartment. A

cop grabbed the baby and ran toward the street, the woman right behind him screaming curses at him in Spanish. A Spanish-speaking PSA at the front entrance laughed as he told the police officer, "Boy, you would not want to know what she was calling you."

Another officer, still breathing heavily from the exertion of carrying people from the fire, described his harrowing few minutes inside the building: "When we went in, the fire was above us. A few minutes later when we tried to get the people out, it was already below us and moving fast. In three minutes, everything was gone."

Despite flames consuming their apartments, several occupants threw blankets over their heads and ran back inside for unexplained reasons, cops right on their heels chasing them. Again and again, people were carried back to the street, screaming, kicking, cursing and struggling.

A flurry of excitement erupted on the east side of the building. An aerial scope had been swung quickly into position and fire rescuers were smashing an upper-story window. Moments later, Capt. Dennis Budd (later chief) of Rescue Squad 1, appeared, lifting a 70-year-old woman into the bucket. She was not breathing. Feverishly, he tried to administer CPR as the bucket was lowered to EMTs waiting with oxygen. Minutes later, her eyes started to flutter and her labored breathing resumed. The hospital where she was admitted to the Intensive Car Burn Unit with throat burns and smoke inhalation, was only six blocks away. She died several weeks later.

A man, his wife, and small child were airlifted from a fourth-floor rear porch as flames erupted from a corridor behind them. On the top floor, fire inspectors found a rabbit hutch in one apartment and cabinet doors removed and replaced with chicken wire to create a pigeon aviary in another. Chief Nally, shaking his head in disbelief, muttered, "My men tell me there are rabbits running all over the place up there."

The apartment block was well known to Health Department inspectors. At the time of the fire, an arrest warrant was in effect for the out-of-city slumlord owner, charging him with failing to appear at a code violation hearing. Two days before the fire, inspectors had found no water in the building. Spanish-speaking police officers herded the large crowd of occupants, many carrying small babies, to a near-by Salvation Army facility for food and shelter. Exhausted fire fighters drinking coffee offered by the "Sallys," many too drained even to talk, sat on truck tailgates surveying the blackened apartment building. "Close, too damn close," one offered. "We were sure as hell lucky on this one," another added, his fire ax leaning against his booted leg. It was an observation I had heard expressed so many times before at major fires. More than 100 had battled the blaze for nearly four hours and, as always, they had won.

WITHIN MOST FIRE DEPARTMENTS THERE IS A GROUP OF DEDICATED fire fighters who do not fight fires, who do not climb ladders to brave flame-filled rooms in order to rescue people. Generally, they do not even slide down brass poles when the alarm sounds. In fact, they do not even go to fires at all, unless specifically invited. These are the men of the Fire Prevention Bureau. They are inspectors and investigators highly trained and skilled through experience whose sole purpose on the job is to prevent, whenever possible, injuries, death, and loss of property to fire. If they fail in this endeavor, they use their instinct and training to find where, how, and why fires are started, so that perhaps the next time they can be prevented from happening. In cases of incendiary origin (arson) fires, FPB personnel join forces with a Police Arson Squad to ferret out who was responsible, and why, so that judicial processes can begin.

Finding a cause, especially of a major fire that causes great monetary losses or deaths, is a slow, dirty, smelly, meticulous process requiring assistance from the public, instinct born of experience, gut feelings, and a dash of pure luck. Determining a point of origin usually involves many variables.

The first fire companies to arrive at a fire scene are questioned on what they observed or smelled, the color of the flames and smoke, the burn pattern, building security, the number of separate fires found upon arrival, the possible smell of gasoline or other accelerants, all of which offer investigators important leads in determining a cause. The minutest detail can sometimes provide direction for the probe and provide time-saving avenues to explore and even to prevent possible poor judgment or errors in determination.

Fire fighters are trained to watch for suspicious-acting spectators at fires, familiar faces, cars seen driving away suddenly as apparatus arrives. Those who discover the fire are questioned. The smallest details are not overlooked or ignored as the brains of witnesses are picked for information. Methodically, the "wheat is separated from the chaff." When field interviews are completed, physical evidence is analyzed, even sent to State Police or Fire Marshall laboratories where expanded facilities are available.

The deeper the char on wooden beams, the closer to origin. Degree of charring shows the path of flames. Flames can burn laterally, or up or down, depending on obstructions and heat-driven air. Location of furniture in damaged rooms may be recreated. Wiring inspectors are called in. Worn electrical circuits, wiring conduits, frayed extension cords, antiquated fuse boxes, heating systems, chimneys, portable heaters, faulty stoves, oil or gas boilers are all checked. Cigarette smokers are noted. Insurance policies are studied for expiration dates, changes in amount of coverage or changes in beneficiaries. Flammable vapor detectors are used to detect hydrocarbons from petroleum products. Veteran FPB commanders agreed that the best detection device they had was "nose and experience." Police Arson Squad members "work the crowd" at practically every fire, mingling out of uniform with spectators in case any of their street informants— "snitchers" — have anything to pass on to them.

Fires can be set for a variety of reasons: arson for profit, drug-related retribution, boyfriend-girlfriend fights, gang rivalries, disgruntled employees seeking revenge, husband and wife domestic squabbles, pyromania, insurance fraud, diminished mental capacity, excitement. More commonly than is generally known is the "hero syndrome," a person suffering from an inferiority complex who wants to be portrayed as a hero for alerting or rescuing occupants of a burning structure he has just set ablaze. He seeks publicity, a story, maybe even a picture in a local newspaper. Police check out such "heroes" closely. Disturbingly, inter-service rivalries and jealousies have been known sometimes to derail fire investigations, or at least hinder them. Detectives have sometimes described FPB investigators as "amateurs," while FPB investigators privately have called detectives, "self-important, arrogant know-it-alls."

FIRE FIGHTERS, WITHOUT ANY DOUBT IN MY MIND, ARE THE unsung heroes of society. They are seldom paid enough literally to put their lives on the line every time the alarm sounds. The heroic acts they perform, usually at great risk to themselves, is most often taken for granted by the public. Why? Fire fighters, as a group, minimize what they do and never brag about themselves and would not be caught dead dealing in self glorification. Theirs is a thankless job. One firefighter confided in me once, "If any fireman ever tells you he is not scared when responding to an alarm, he's lying to you."

During three decades, while reporting nearly 5,000 fires in sweltering heat, bitter freezing cold, blizzards, and torrential rain, I formed a rock-solid opinion that it has been a privilege for me to work beside and live with fire fighters. They are the champions of the poor, the saviors of the rich, and the hope of any community.

Worcester Cold Storage Warehouse
A City's Tragedy

Date: December 3, 1999.

Hour: 18:13.

Fire Box: 1438, Franklin and Arctic Streets.

Alarms: Frantic 911 call followed by five alarms
struck in rapid succession.

Weather: bitter cold with Christmas season in
full swing.

Victims: Tim Jackson 51, Ladder 2 (promoted to
Lt. posthumously);

Jay Lyons, 34, Engine 3 (promoted to Lt. posthumously);

Lt. Tom Spencer, 42, Ladder 2;

Joe McGuirk. 38, Engine 3;

Jerry Lucey 38, Rescue Squad No 1;

Paul Brotherton, 41, Rescue Squad No 1.

It is a date that forever will be branded into the memories of an entire city. It was the night that six of the city's "bravest" died tragically in a raging, unrelenting fire in an abandoned former meat packing warehouse. It was a scant three weeks before Christmas, the season when tragedies cut the deepest.

As word crept through the second largest city in Massachusetts that six of its bravest cadre of fire fighters were unaccounted for, a silent migration of onlookers formed to line the streets, many with heads bowed in prayer. Those who the day before had been strangers were now brothers and sisters in shared sorrow. Everywhere they looked, an army of black-helmeted men and their throbbing apparatus stood their ground, furiously battling an unforgiving conflagration, all the while feeling one the department's greatest fears that they were losing comrades. Most knew from gut instinct what was happening to their ranks, but they uniformly refused to give in to the ultimate, eventual outcome. A firefighter's credo is, "Never give up hope."

Fire department radios crackled plaintively through the bitter cold, but were only answered with dreaded silence from within the building, still belching acrid gray smoke that within minutes had smothered the city's nearby downtown business district. Sixty fire fighters battled intense flames that reached almost to a nearby overhead expressway.

Upon arrival, fire officers had been told that homeless derelicts frequently inhabited the cavernous warehouse as a make shift flop house shelter and it was feared some were still inside. A first response search team had penetrated its way into the multi-level building but now could not retrace its steps through the cavernous labyrinth, a veritable maze, of former meat packing rooms.

It was every firefighter's nightmare. They could not have known that all the transient derelict street people had escaped the fire and had dissolved without detection like shadows into the night. Subsequent investigation revealed that a mentally deprived teenage girl and her simple-minded companion had argued by candlelight and the candle had been knocked over, igniting their meager belongings. Both were able to feel their way through the darkness to an unboarded door. Mentally incapable of assuming their responsibility to report the fire, they sought refuge for warmth, in a downtown mall music store, two blocks away.

Emergency floodlights ringing the macabre scene, changing night into day, illuminated an army of brawny, helmeted fire fighters moving almost in unison atop a mountainous monolith of rubble, like so many shadows in the night. An estimated 440 exhausted, on duty and off duty fire fighters sifted through the ruins for their fallen comrades. Hour after hour, day and night after day and night, the pace of the recovery teams never slackened. Working around the clock, the men continued to fight off mental and physical exhaustion. Many searchers, driven by strength derived from desperation dug through the rubble by hand alone, searching for their former companions. These dedicated men wanted their brothers back and they wanted them at that time, determined not to allow their former station house companions to spend another night in the still smoldering warehouse rubble.

Over their shoulders, they saw the anguished families of the victims standing in a vigil of grief, watching the search intently. Many tears of deep sorrow streaked the soot-blackened faces of the searchers. Men worked their shifts and then refused to quit, sustained only by food brought to the scene by many individuals and organizations.

A day after the fire was put out, Jackson's body was finally recovered. An agonizing two days later, Lyons was found. Still another two days and Spencer and McGuirk were found together, apparently working as a team. The search continued unabated in its desperation. Forty eight hours later, Lucey's remains were uncovered and finally, a day later, Brotherton's.

Eight days of intense search, a week and a day, and the physical ordeal, the recovery task was over and the fallen fire fighters were finally returned home for proper and decent burial. It was time for the troops to rest and grieve and fight off their nightmares. The empty beds back at the station houses would haunt them for years to come. Fire fighters, past, present, and future of every city will pause silently each year at the precise moment of the tragedy and reflect back upon the moment and the event that ripped at the soul of the city. They will each year honor their fallen brothers with quiet meditative memories and prayers.

For the memorial observances, an estimated 35,000 brotherhood fire fighters from Australia, Ireland, England, Canada and every state of the union and other countries responded. In parade formation they solemnly marched the half mile parade route past black shroud-draped Fire Headquarters. The crowd of thousands of spectators lining the route stood, heads bowed in prayer and in total mute silence as the almost endless uniformed brigades of fraternal brothers filed by. Along the way, only the soft, muted cadence of the marchers could be heard accompanied by the wailing refrains of Amazing Grace and Going Home by bag pipers from Worcester, Boston, Connecticut, Cleveland, Ohio, and other caring states and cities.

At the city's municipal civic center, memorial funeral services were held, observed, and listened to by thousands crammed into the center and throngs of more thousands lining the streets outside, in mourning and respect for their heroes. President Bill Clinton and Vice President Al Gore also attended the services to console the grieving families of the six victims in their time of emotional need.

Never again would the city see fire fighters as those who just polished the brass or played checkers between alarms. Every time a fire station is passed today, the thoughts of many return to that December night of horror when the city lost so much. The scenes of that night were branded into the city's memory and soul forever. Never again will these public servants be taken for granted.

AFTERMATH: AS SOON AS THE SHOCK OF THE KILLER WAREHOUSE fire hit the city, officials began formulating plans to prevent it from ever happening again. Demands were made for owners of empty and abandoned buildings to give detailed floor plans of their properties to the fire department.

Orders for thermal imaging cameras were placed. The city now has ten, seven on the city's ladder trucks, and three at the department's Rescue Squads. The night of the warehouse fire, the city had none and hurriedly had borrowed one from a suburban town department to aid in the search. The cameras penetrate even the densest smoke and show images on a screen within the camera detecting varying degrees of heat. Displaying different colors, the camera can detect bodies, other persons, and objects radiating heat in varying degrees. Intense flame activity will overwhelm the camera and warn the viewer, perhaps to retreat. The cameras offer fire fighters a sixty-foot viewing range.

Large Area Search Lines, nylon ropes that tether fire fighters entering a burning building to a stationary object outside the building are now in mandatory use. This, fire fighters say, ensures they will, in most cases, be able to escape safely if need be.

Highly trained Rapid Intervention Teams (RIT) now stand by at every fire in the event of a "May day" call from within the building that a firefighter has fallen, has run out of Scott pack compressed air, or has lost his bearings. RIT members move swiftly.

Commanding officers at every fire are now provided daily and instantly with lists of all firefighter on duty that day or that night. Roll calls, if needed, can be taken at the fire scene, looking for anyone who might be missing from the ranks.

Could the tragedy occur again? Firefighting is listed as one of the most dangerous of all occupations. No amount of equipment, training, or experience can alter that fact. Each community can only hope.

feature stories

Cops face violence, cruelty, sordid filth, tragedy, and death practically every day they are on duty. Often, they resort to humor—sometimes sardonic—to shield their emotions, to preserve their perspectives, and perhaps even to help maintain their sanity.

Living in the same environment, practically their whole existence, police reporters also need to hide behind a buffer to keep their emotions from being twisted out of reason. One way for them is to create a fantasy world where there is no pain, no suffering, no sadness. And, if the reporter can bring his readers into that same fantasy world, then he or she sheds light where, otherwise, there would be only darkness.

During my journalistic career, I spent considerable energy transporting my readers underwater on archeological expeditions, traveling hundreds of feet aloft in hot air balloon gondolas, into the cabs of train locomotives, onto the back of lumbering elephants, into the center ring as a circus clown, and in just about every conceivable situation. And, perhaps selfishly, the spectrum of feature stories permitted me to join my readers in this escape from the realities of life. As a sidebar, the stories also gave me the excitement that was such a strong motivating force in my life.

As a cub reporter learning the business in a county bureau, I had ridden drilling trains in tunnels digging for water aqueducts through solid
rock 385 feet underground; had informed the world of the plight of an
elderly, sole operator of a saw mill destroyed by highway-construction
progress; had tracked sheep-killer wild cats; had crawled with a camera
into a 200-year-old, collapsing storm drain culvert; had hobnobbed with
Hollywood celebrities; had hung on in seat-of-the-pants aerobatics in a
crop dusting bi-plane; had written a series on prisons; and had dined privately with a governor. I always thought that if stories were to be truly
informative, first they would have to be interesting. Holding the interest of the reader to the last paragraph was the name of the game.

Writing about police officers, about what they say, think, and do, in
their cruisers, was easy. I soon found out that there are two kinds of
cops: those who would do just about anything to get their name in the
paper, and those who fight just as hard to keep their names out of print.

Through the years, I walked many foot beats prowling down dark
alleys under all sorts of conditions. I posed as a cop to guard prisoners,
sat in as a police dispatcher, engaged in juvenile offender counseling,
served as a Training Division instructor, as a ghost writer for top police
officials, and even as a decoy during a male prostitute sting. Whatever
the situation called for, I tried to do. The job, to say the least, was
never dull. Sometimes, despite the best of intentions, attempts to
develop a feature failed. As the time I rode with Sector Sgt. Bob
Freeman, later a captain, and one of the rising stars in the department.
A Vietnam combat veteran, Freeman was a quiet, laid back man,
meticulous in his approach to the job, and highly respected by the
troops. The weekend night we crisscrossed the southern and western
sectors of the city turned out to be the quietest night in recent memory from a news standpoint. Up one darkened street and down another,
Freeman's cruiser poked at speeds hardly faster than a walk. He parked
in the center of Main Street where he could observe nearly a mile
toward the center of the city. There was not even a pedestrian in sight.
Then, without warning, an oncoming car, swerved off the travel lane,

rammed into a tree, backed up, and wiggled its way past the cruiser. A young female driver offered Freeman a dirty look as she drove past the cruiser. Activating the "gum ball" blue roof lights, Freeman pulled her over. She was operating past curfew on a learner's permit. After a fatherly lecture, he sent her home . . . hardly a newsworthy event.

Not one to miss much, Freeman pulled behind a tire store where he found a parked cruiser with lights off. Easing up to within inches of the driver's door, the sergeant shined his flashlight on a sleeping route officer. Wrapping on the man's window, Freeman said, "Hey sleeping beauty, I'm real proud of you. Keep up the good work." And then, without another word, drove away. For the rest of the night, "Sleeping Beauty" was seen answering every call, and was usually the first to arrive at the scene. Throughout the night, the sergeant provided an even hand over his troops. Back to prowling, the stillness of the night continued. Asked why it was so dead on a Saturday night, Freeman responded, "Maybe they heard I'm out here tonight." I used the quote in my story, causing him to endure numerous good-natured jibes from fellow officers.

Back at headquarters—I pulled one of my frequent double-headers—my notes offered very little about which to write. I improvised as best I could. You win some, you lose some. As a parting shot before going off duty, Freeman offered, "Slowest night I ever remember. You brought us luck, Rock. Come back anytime."

A year later, thinking I would have better luck, I tried a different Sector Sergeant, Bob Rich who had done it all: street cop, Auto Theft Squad investigator, undercover investigator, department armorer, SWAT team sectional commander, training and weapons instructor, and highway law lecturer. Rich, departmental officials said, had it all together: intelligence, good looks, military appearance, awesome strength, desire, impressive size, and street-honed wisdom. In the locker room, he was known as "Super Cop."

During our midnight patrol stint, Rich responded to two dozen calls, cited several motorists for moving violations, investigated a torched stolen car, answered an in-progress break-in call, stopped ille-gal motorcycle activity, directed traffic at a downtown theater fire, and broke up a potentially dangerous bonfire around which twenty teenagers were frolicking at a drinking party. This time I had a ream of notes from which to draw for a story. Rich eventually became a div-ing buddy and close family friend.

On another occasion, I was recruited by the Vice Squad to act as a decoy at one of the city's most prized monuments which had, over the years, become a rendezvous for the local homosexual community—an activity that kept City Hall and police phones ringing off the hook—irate residents were screaming that they no longer could take their children to the park for picnics. Disguised with dark glasses, I sat on a wooden bench with the squad's burliest officer—code named, "Stinky"—whispering sweet nothings in my ear. For an hour this went on. The bench became quite hard and uncomfortable. Finally Stinky whispered, "Let's reel the line, the fish aren't biting today, Rock. Incidentally, don't give up your day job. You're no good at this."

ON THE POLICE BEAT, YOU NEVER KNEW FROM MINUTE TO MINUTE what to expect. Shortly after my arrival at work one morning, as I was preparing to make my first early rounds of the building for news from night shift officers going off duty, I heard loud yelling from an upper floor, "Get the SWAT team! Get the SWAT team!"

Not waiting for the elevator, I sprinted up the rear stairs two at a time. I knew a news story was breaking and I would have an eye-wit-ness account. Officers were pouring out of the Traffic Division and sprinting in every direction, some with revolvers in their hand. I sidled up to the door and inched my head around the corner for a look. It had to be a hostage or sniper situation. I tried to nudge my way closer. It resembled a scene from a Keystone Cops film.

One cop was yelling, "Stay cool! Stay cool! No guns!" Another pleaded, "But, I can get him. Let me get a shot at him." I peeked around the corner and saw a desk clerk ducking one way, then another.

Then I saw it, a small black bat swooping and zooming against walls and office enclosures. The clerk grabbed a waste basket and feverishly tried to scoop the frightened rodent. The faster the bat flitted, the faster the clerk scooped empty air.

Another cop continued to brag, "Let me shoot him. I can get him with one shot," waving his gun around menacingly. Still another officer with lightning reflexes managed to whip off his eight-sided cap and net the bat as he zeroed in on the officer. But, he did it with such force, the stunned rodent bounced out and again became somewhat shakily air-born.

A long-haired female officer happened by in the corridor, just coming off duty, and was grabbed and forcibly pushed into the traffic office. The grabber yelled, "Bats love long hair. You're being sacrificed. Go get 'em." With the first bat pass at her, she was last seen heading south, her hair flowing behind her. "Seal off the floor. Don't let it get away," another cop, doubled over with laughter, was yelling.

Two other officers stationed themselves at opposite ends of the traffic office, wielding baseball bat-like (no pun intended) night sticks. With each swing and miss, witnesses were yelling, "Ball three. Low and outside." I had never seen such a carnival-like affair at the staid headquarters. One officer continued to swing wildly, more in self protection than in baseball form.

"Someone close the belfry," I yelled. "We don't want any in there." This brought some laughter and a couple of patient glares.

One officer whipped out a radar gun. "Someone stop 'em. I just clocked him at twenty-seven miles an hour in a fifteen-mile-an-hour zone." More laughter. All present were having a hilarious time. Someone offered to call in a fellow officer nicknamed "Batman."

A custodian, attracted by the commotion, sized up the situation, ran to a broom closet and returned a minute later with a weapon. With one mighty swing, he dispatched the winged intruder. The weapon? What else? A bat. As everyone holstered their guns, someone suggested the janitor be awarded the Purple Heart for meritorious performance. The medal might have been more apropos for the bat.

NOT TOTALLY UNEARNED WAS MY REPUTATION AS A "DELIGHTFULLY and refreshingly disrespectful" personality. It was hung on me by a former city mayor, generally known as an astute judge of people. I always considered it a compliment.

I was invited to participate in a State Police staged media event on Interstate 290. It was to be V-shaped formations of State Police cruisers—"Operation Roadblock"—holding back the pack of would-be speeders at precisely fifty-five miles an hour. When I arrived at the carnival a few minutes late, as usual, the operation starting point was clogged with TV vans and police cruisers, resembling a used car lot. I parked some distance away, grabbed my coffee Thermos, and at the same time divorced myself from all the thrill-seekers milling about. As I did, the female assistant of the state Commissioner of Public Safety came running toward my car.

"You're Rockie Blunt aren't you? The commissioner wants you to ride with him."

"Tell the commissioner that I don't ride with politicians," I answered. The young woman's mouth fell open in shock.

"No one speaks to the commissioner that way," she stammered.

"Well, I do," was my response. "Tell him he is on my turf now, that he is working my side of the street." When she ran back to the pack, I could see the commissioner laughing in the distance. Flying back again she came, breathless.

"The commissioner said to tell you he was a Boston cop for twenty-seven years before retiring as a lieutenant."

"Tell the commissioner I'll ride with him." I said. The whole time I was in the back seat, his State Police corporal driver kept glancing at me in the rear view mirror with a puzzled look on his face.

To some degree, writing features was taking over my life. I was spending more time working double shifts than I was at home with my wife, but this was the style of reporting that set me apart from other reporters at the *Evening Gazette*. It was getting to a point where I gave up family holidays to pursue a feature, constantly on the lookout for something different, something imaginative. My home had become a "dugout" for dozens of cops. FBI agents and even police chiefs ate at my table. To the children of the lake police boat operator, my wife was the "cookie queen." Now, in retrospect, I realize I was living and loving my job and blurring the distinction between career and home life. I had become a workaholic. My wife, ever proud of my accomplishments, never voiced a word of complaint for all she ever wanted throughout our marriage was my happiness.

Practically every day, a police reporter is witness to tragedy, but some tragedies touch a nerve deeper than others. One was the case of a 73-year-old widower, wracked so badly with emphysema and phlebitis that he constantly fought for breath and often was barely able to function. His age and medical condition made him an easy target for neighborhood teenage criminals.

For more than twenty years he had eked out a living by peddling automotive tools to garages and service stations. Motivated by eight break-ins into his walk-in tool truck, in slightly less than a year, and during which $17,000 worth of tools had been stolen, he started packing a gun and sleeping beside another at night.

"I carry a .357 Magnum every night and keep a twelve-gauge shotgun with double-O load beside my bed, and the next time those kids rob me, I'll use them. So help me, I will," were his opening lines when I interviewed him in his small kitchen. After months of no relief from police, the old man had reached his emotional breaking point and was reduced to threatening murder as a vigilante on the pages of a daily newspaper.

Finally, in an act of defeat, he had advertised his truck and meager remaining inventory for sale. Asked what police had done to help him, the wheezing tool salesman, dragging nervously on a cigarette, answered, "They came sometimes, sat in the yard in plain sight, kept the cruiser motor going to keep warm and then threw empty coffee cups in my yard. How the hell did they expect the kids to break in while they were sitting out there where everyone could see them. They never made any arrests."

The ailing man had floodlights installed to light up his truck, parked scarcely six feet from his back door. Compassionate neighbors even installed outdoor lighting in their yards to illuminate more of the old man's property. Still the burglaries continued, again and again. Nothing seemed to prevent them. Motion detectors and magnetic and sound alarms systems were installed in his truck. The thefts continued.

"I've been driven out of business and the cops have done zilch, zero to help me. If the police were out there, they have the best system of disappearing I've ever seen," complained the old man, struggling for breath.

About a year later, the issue was brought to a head violently. The bankrupt tool salesman, overcome by despair and illness, finally got to use his shotgun to commit murder as he had threatened. Tragically, it was on himself.

MANY HOURS OF SLEEP WERE LOST WHEN I SOUGHT TO TURN around what appeared to be a biased anti-Registry of Motor Vehicles editorial policy, at the newspaper. The best way to accomplish this, I thought, was to highlight the positive side of the department's activities: one of which was late night anti-sobriety road blocks.

I had worked closely with the Registry dozens of times in the past on highway fatalities, union negotiations, bootleg safety inspection, sticker investigations, holiday safety campaigns, department policy changes, and in publicizing the functions and duties of each Registry division with informational feature stories. But, anti-drunk road blocks offered a whole new approach to image building.

Almost habitually, I began spending long, boring hours standing around trying to ease the discomfort of aching leg muscles, bathed in the illumination of cruiser headlight glare, blue flashing roof lights, and the dampness of early morning, drinking luke warm coffee and taking notes. When I wrote one story, I dubbed it "Operation Johnson," to poke a little fun at a Registry friend in command of the operation. It was promised payoff for a caper some months earlier in which Johnson had snookered me into showing up at an annual Registry banquet. When I begged off, saying I had a band engagement that evening, he cajoled, "Just pop by and say hello." I agreed.

Upon arriving, I was motioned to the head table. As I bent over to hear what he was saying to me, he grabbed a microphone and proceeded to present me with a large, ornate plaque naming me as the Registry's man of the year for "outstanding journalistic professionalism, fairness and objectivity in all matters pertaining to the Registry." Stunned almost speechless, somewhat of a rarity for me, my acceptance speech was brief, only seven words long. I took the mike from him and said, "Thank you all. I'll get you, Donnie." The audience of Registry inspectors, many with whom I had worked before, roared.

From the wide grin on his face, he good-naturedly accepted the fact that I would keep that promise. Some months later, I did, with the roadblock story. I was told he became the butt of considerable teasing due to the "Operation Johnson" headline.

When confronted a few weeks later, I innocently argued there were two other Johnsons working the roadblock . . . that the caper had been named for them. The roadblocks, I should add, were always quite effective: multiple arrests, countless defective equipment violations, a few drunks and even a high-speed chase. In my story, I pointed out how expensive a DUI (driving under the influence of drugs or alcohol) arrest could be: a total of $2,300 for bail assessment, towing costs, court fines, attorney fees, insurance surcharges, loss of safe driver insurance credits, and $480 for a mandated state alcohol education program. "All because of a few beers," one inspector maintained.

THE QUEST FOR FEATURES CAN BE A ROLLER COASTER OF MIRTH, tears, suffering and zaniness, stark realism and fantasy, triumph and failure, tragedy and renewed hope. One mirthful story involved my becoming "Bosko," a Ringling Brothers, Barnum and Bailey clown. But, first I had to be initiated before running away with the circus, by riding an elephant in the traditional, grand processional animal parade from a railroad siding to the city center. It was a cold, drizzly, rather uncomfortable day as each pachyderm was prodded off railroad cars. With considerable exertion and two roustabouts heaving me upwards by the posterior quarters onto "Siam," the lead elephant, I managed to perch myself on the swaying, bristly gray beast. Almost instantly, I knew I was in trouble. I could not spread my legs wide enough to straddle the leathery old giant. When the handlers prodded the string of lumbering elephants along, it was all I could do to hang on. With each step Siam took, his monstrous haunch-like shoulders slammed into my groin, one pile-driving blow after another. Quickly, my body reacted to the painful punishment and both thighs knotted up in excruciating pain. Seeing my predicament, the handler stopped the procession and eased me down just as I was starting to fall off.

I was deeply disappointed that the squealing kiddies lined along the mile-long sidewalks would not see Bosko in all his glory, but I could no longer stand up, much less walk. I was unceremoniously given a ride back to headquarters by my son, Randie who had been taking pictures.

To compound the embarrassing failure, the entire police headquarters staff had been lined along the road to see their favorite police reporter make a fool of himself. Many were annoyed that they had been cheated out of their big "in-house" laugh for the day. The only redeeming aspect of the whole miserable episode was, I was told by *Evening Gazette* management the next day, that my account of the elephant ride was probably the best story I had ever written. Always fearful I might be relieved of my command on the police beat, even temporarily, I never told them that I was hobbled by the thigh cramps for nearly two months.

But, I had been scheduled to perform that night with Master Clown Glen "Frosty" Little. True to the old adage: the show must go on. Little met me at "Clown Alley," where he studied my face and decided I would be made up as a bum. Within minutes, bum it was. I mingled with the other clowns for the "bust out" run on into the arena, band blaring, audience applauding happily. Yelling, "Let's go clowns, let's go," Frosty led the pack with me limping along as fast as I could, sporting a big smile for the kids to mask the pain.

You wiggle, strut, jump over railings to "work the crowd," kiss a few babies, pose momentarily for proud parent picture snapping, cavort some more, bring joy to the hearts of the customers and then it is into the center ring where the serious (?) antics begin. Mine was to pratfall when slapped with a large powder-laced mitt, followed by more "sight gags." Carried away with the silliness of the whole "schtick," I pushed away the pain in my legs. Adrenaline is a wonderful pain killer. After ten minutes of frivolity, it was a retreat to a bathroom to remove the makeup with baby oil. My moment of glory had been just that— a moment in my life. I never told Frosty I had been a frustrated clown all my life and had, in fact, been rehearsing for that single performance for nearly a half century. I think he had already figured that out for himself.

SINCE EARLY CHILDHOOD I HAD HAD A CONSUMING DESIRE TO FLY, a yearning that tugs some people upward into the heavens, a pull that never really subsides. As a twelve-year-old, I wore a flying helmet and goggles to school. Later in life I obtained a pilot's license flying vintage fabric and wood Piper Cubs from a grassed pasture in a suburban town. I was meant to fly.

When the idea struck me to describe to my readers the joy of hot air ballooning, I was off and soaring. Ballooning was right down my runway. Resorting to the barter system, I negotiated a balloon ride for a news story.

The morning for lift-off was still and quite crisp, perfect ballooning weather. As my waving wife began to disappear from sight, we rose quickly to avoid electrical wires, trees, and other hazardous obstacles. Without a noise other than the burning propane gas sounds to keep the balloon inflated, we floated gently along, dipping occasionally to grab a fistful of leaves from passing trees. Motorists gawked, children jumped for joy, horses spooked and ran wildly in their corrals.

Ballooning is heart-pounding but still serene, silent, awe-inspiring, brilliantly beautiful, muscle-wrenching and invigorating. But, above all, it is fun, wild and uninhibited fun . . . until one tries to land. We maintained a 600-foot altitude and six-mile-an-hour forward drift. No sound filtered up from the ground below. The total sensation of detachment is similar to that experienced by scuba divers.

Soon it was time to land, hoping the chase vehicle would find us. Warned to brace for a hard landing, I grabbed the rim of the open basket gondola. We came down hard, jumping out to grab tether lines to act as ballast and prevent the balloon from being dragged. Even at that, the gondola skidded through bramble bushes and small trees. Aviators claim any landing you can walk away from is a good one. This was, all in all, a good one. Looking around, the deflated balloon had become draped over a nearby home. It was not supposed to be. Back at headquarters, an exhilarating sense of accomplishment at a new adventure turned to tired relief.

TOWARD THE END OF MY CAREER, I SEARCHED FOR A FITTING FINAL tribute to the Worcester Fire Department with whom I had worked so many fires, had walked so many miles, had suffered through so many tragedies, and had shared so much coffee and so many jokes. As

I looked back on the years, I realized I had spent almost as many hours in the company of fire fighters as I had with police officers.

They had enriched my life and I wanted to express my gratitude the only way I could, through the printed word. What better way, I eventually decided, than to research and chronicle the history of their department as a gift to them. Instantly, I recalled tales of the city's fading history told to me before they were dimmed further by time, stories passed on to me as a small boy around a campfire by my father. One of them was burned into my memory:

> "The drumbeat of their hooves on the cobblestone streets at night could be heard a half mile away. With their flared nostrils, their bulging eyes and their briskets straining against their traces, they were something to see. The shiny red and brass steam chimney belching smoke and sparks like a Roman Candle, the bronze bell clapping away, the trumpet blaring to clear the streets. There was nothing like it."
> —Roscoe C. Blunt Sr. (1890-1975)

These were the sights and sounds he had heard as a child, experiences he knew his young son would never see nor hear. They had to be preserved and passed on. In considerable detail, I told of the horse-drawn, steam pumper era from the Civil War to the 1920s when the city first started utilizing motorized apparatus, for they were faster and did not have to be fed. At the city's 106-year-old Cambridge Street station, I illustrated oats falling onto fire fighters from the still-existing hay loft whenever heavy trucks rumbled past. I resurrected antique alarm slats with long-forgotten names of neighborhoods and box designations. I climbed into dusty lofts where hose had once been hung to dry after fires. I crawled though fire house attics (fire fighters do not like the station houses to be called barns) to research dusty, yellowed construction cost sheets, dating back to the time when some of the city's earliest stations were built, several of which were still in use.

I wrote of "Eagle, No.3," the "Governor Lincoln," the "Rapid," the "Squad Wagon," the "Despatch," the "Hero," the "Tiger," the "Torrent," the "Extinguisher," the "Lafayette," the "General Putnam," the "Independent," the "Alert," the "S. E. Combs," the "Ocean," the "Yankee," the "Niagara," the "Protector," the "Parker," and the "A. B. Lowell," —the city's proud apparatus manned by valiant men in leather helmets armed with leather water buckets. Spirit ran high in those days and rivalry was keen amongst the old fire companies.

In 1919, there were still twenty-three horses pulling fire apparatus. By 1925, the number had dwindled to four. In 1929, the last stallion, "Black Beauty," was relegated to the ignominious duty of pulling the department's equipment and linens wagon. Two years later, Black Beauty was injured in a runaway accident and had to be put down. An era had passed on forever. Most of what remains today of those golden years: a bell, several fire houses, some horse oats, and a couple of restored pieces of apparatus are memories. But, those too shall always remain important.

Fire fighters are not ones to take without giving something in return. Without fanfare, the city's fire fighters' union submitted my story to the International Association of Fire Fighters for proper recognition. Somewhat secretively, twenty-five days before I retired, the union president and fire chief called me to Fire Headquarters and, before assembled fire companies, presented me with the national IAFF national award for "outstanding achievement and distinguished journalism."

As far as fire fighters were concerned, I was leaving the job with a distinct sweet taste in my mouth. The fire history story was the most extensive, in-depth coverage I gave to any feature during my years on the beat.

Features provided a niche through which I could transport my readers to another medium—one in which, for the most part, there were happy endings.

high jinks:
humor to break the tension

POLICE SAY A MACHINE, IF SUBJECTED TO INCREASED PRESSURE OVER a long period of time, runs the risk of exploding without warning. They also liken themselves to human machines who can erupt suddenly unless release valves for emotional pressures are found and utilized.

Some officers resort to adultery, booze, and drugs to release internal and psychological tensions that can build up over the long haul. Most, however, resort to humor—obscene, sardonic, often outrageous, or even almost cruel humor. It is not uncommon to observe, at tragedies, police officers joking among themselves, out of sight of the public. It is a defense mechanism, almost a way of life.

They feel they have to resort to such measures. There is only so much violence, death, depravity, squalor, and actual horror that a person can absorb emotionally, no matter how hardened by reality—and street life for a cop is surely that. Cops have feelings too. Deep feelings. They seldom display them, but they have them. They die a little inside, like anyone else, when confronted by a decapitated baby at a highway fatality, or an infant reduced to a chunk of charred, unrecognizable meat in a tenement fire, or a toddler abused to death by a depraved or dull-witted parent.

These sights and experiences can never be erased from memory, but sometimes they can be pushed aside a little by unbridled humor serving as a pressure release valve.

Police reporters, over the span of time, become partners with police in the tragedies of life. Subjected to the same sights, the same tortured emotions, the same nagging memories as police officers, they too endure the need at times to release steam from the pressure cooker.

Early in my journalistic career, I found myself employing a psychological cover-up motto: "You might as well laugh at life, it is going to kill you anyway." Through the years, I found myself participating in, and even precipitating considerable in-house police comedy antics.

Those early days were a period of uproarious laughter, outlandish horse-play keeping everything light, maintaining the violence, and suffering at arm's length. Usually, in-house humor was personal. Cops poked fun at and ridiculed one another. More often, they delighted in teeing off on me. The secret was to retaliate with as much as or more than you took. To do less was to be eaten alive.

Nicknames are prevalent in police departments. Some fit physical descriptions, some are ludicrous, others describe former exploits, many were just outlandish, and nonsensical to provoke a laugh. Worcester PD had its share. "Canvas Back," an officer renowned for his fighting ability. "Godzilla," a takeoff on an officer's name and strength. "Red Eye," description of a sleepless officer's bloodshot eyes at a civil, near riot, disturbance. "Moe," named after a sting operation undercover agent. "Angel of Death," a detective lieutenant called out on every murder. "Cabbage Patch," and "El Gordo," a popular, slightly portly lieutenant. "Bobbsey Twins," two inseparable, low-key officers, also known as "Mr. Anonymous" and "Sidekick Anonymous." "Earl the Pearl," "Early Go Slow," takeoffs on an officer's name. "Touchdown," spoofing an officer's athletic ability. "Shotgun," origin unknown. "Admiral," the lake patrol boat operator. "Commodore," the fill-in officer on "Admiral's" days off. "Action Jackson," takeoff on a name. "Superman," officer who rode the hood of a car, hanging onto windshield wipers, during a drug dealer's desperate getaway attempt. "Speedman," the department's fastest runner. "Fat Tommy," self-explanatory. "Blackjack," self-explanatory. "Cuckoo," self-explanatory. "Buzz," named after a silent-film cowboy hero. "Scoop," lauding officer's ability to make arrests. "Stinky," "Bubbles," "Flako" (Spanish for skinny), "Sgt. Crab," "No Neck," "Fido," "Fish," "White Knight," "Weasel," "Frog," "Belker," all high-security narcotics undercover names. "Kojak," takeoff on a name similarity. "Nasties," Vice Squad code name for themselves. "Pinky," abbreviation of an officer's name. "Boney," tagged onto a bald officer. "Krash," who wracked up an ambulance his first day on the job. "Porky," meaty officer with great disposition. "The Cossack," a play on the officer's name. "Batman," origin unknown. "The Man From Glad," officer with prematurely silver hair. There were also "Chipper," "Icky," "Herky," "Chesty," "Ducky," "Mitzie," and dozens of others, derivations all unknown. It was an honor to be saddled with a nickname, especially when the recipient was not a sworn member of the brotherhood. During three decades in the "Cop Shop," I earned seven such names: "Nutzy," reason unclear. "Monsignor," moniker given me by a legendary chief. "Plunkett," after a slurred mispronunciation of my name by an irate city manager, on a local radio talk show, after I refused to obey his gag rule on publishing police labor negotiations. "Capt. Nemo," because of my diving career, much of which involved police activities. "Crusader," after a series of eighteen stories about various deficiencies in the department, including its dilapidated, unsafe cruiser fleet. "Freezie Two," radio code name given me by the Juvenile Division's top investigator, my partner in orange Freezie soda drinking. "Bosko," after performing as a clown with Ringling Bros. and Barnum & Bailey Circus.

SOON AFTER MY AFFILIATION WITH WORCESTER POLICE BEGAN, stories began to surface about a living legend in the department, the master jokester of all times: Patrolman Ed Kenary. He truly was "King of the Jesters." His son, Paul "The Bird" Kenary, an officer in a suburban town, later openly admitted he would not dare pull the legendary stunts his father had perpetrated for fear of being fired. His handicap was that he entered the field of law enforcement one generation too late. By his time, the wild, outrageous high jinks within police departments were, for the most part, a thing of the past.

But, the elder Kenary had been more fortunate. Old timers still laugh about the time he "requisitioned" a huge stuffed polar bear from a department store window display, crammed it into his cruiser and brought it to headquarters in the still of night. The night shift supervisor, a crusty old sergeant, worked the booking desk in the Cell Room. On tip toes, Kenary carried the bear to the cell room door, threw it open abruptly with a bellowing, howling roar, and shoved the bear toward the booking desk. The sergeant, who was well-known in the department for his fear of animals, literally dove through a ground-level window and started fleeing across a courtyard. Only when he heard raucous laughter behind him did he return. The department chronicles did not record whether there was any reprisal against the comedy-bent officer. There was not much they could do to him anyway; he was already on the last half of the graveyard shift.

On another occasion, the same officer pulled a similar stunt on the same sergeant with the same results, only this time with a live snake. Other times, it was cherry bombs. Police brass readily admitted the prankster was an excellent cop, but he had an undisciplined sense of humor for horseplay and practical jokes. One night he argued with his partner over who was the better pistol shot. The disagreement climaxed when both officers jumped out of their cruiser in a huff, pulled their sidearms, and peppered a telephone pole fifty feet away, at three A.M. Behind the scene, the switchboard at headquarters was flooded with calls from awakened residents reporting a possible massacre in the Lake View section of the city.

By the time other cruisers responded to the calls, the Wyatt Earp twins were long gone. The passage of time wiped out everyone's memory of who was the best marksman.

Before being assigned to ambulance duty in the Cell Room, the legendary officer walked a foot beat downtown with a partner. Sometime after midnight, they came across an open door at a funeral home. Cautiously, the two men separated and with flashlights started searching the darkened building for a possible burglar. Upon entering the casket display room, Kenary climbed into one, laid down, folded his arms and waited for his partner. When the other officer passed by the casket, the supposed corpse sat up, tapped him on the arm and asked, "Hey fella, got a match?" If the story has survived accurately, the partner was last seen heading north, his feet barely touching the ground.

HOWEVER, THERE WAS A DISTINCT OTHER SIDE TO KENARY, A DEEP sense of compassion for others. In the early sixties, when I arrived in the department, the biggest unsolved internal mystery was what had happened to the old pot-belly wood stove at the Lake Station.

While patrolling the Lake District one bitter cold winter night, the affable officer came across an elderly man half frozen in an unheated apartment. Without a moment's hesitation, the route officer drove to the Lake Station, dismantled a cast iron stove, wrestled it into the trunk of the cruiser and drove back to the man's home, where he reassembled the stove, filled it with wood—also pilfered from the station—and made a fire.

A few of us knew where the stove went, but we were all mysteriously afflicted with memory lapses. Furthermore, the incident never made the paper, even though it would have made a great feature.

I am not sure the chief, at the time, ever found out either who drove the lake patrol boat half way up the steep embankment to the

Lake Station, missing the boathouse completely, only because the boat jockey—guess who?—could not remember fast enough how to shift the gears into reverse.

Back in the early days on the police beat, it was customary for reporters to hitch rides frantically on the meat wagon when it went out on a run. Kenary was the driver I seemed to get most often when later he was assigned, through seniority, to the day shift in the Cell Room. I loved to accompany him, for each trip was a roller coaster, thrill-a-minute adventure, like seat-of-the-pants flying in the rear cockpit of a crop dusting bi-plane. But, while in the rear patient compartment I was hanging onto grab rails for dear life as he resorted to careening across front lawns to avoid turns at intersections to save a few seconds, I began thinking that it was time for me to start begging off and walking back to the pressroom. I cared for my life, even if he did not value his.

OFF-THE-WALL HUMOR NEVER SEEMED TO CEASE IN THE EARLY days. It became one of the most endearing aspects of working those years within the confines of the police bastion.

One night, the Precinct 1 commander, a tall rangy lieutenant who leaned toward perpetual crabbiness, received a phone call full of hissing sounds, simulated crackling static, and a faraway muffled voice.

"This you, lieutenant? This is George. I'm calling on a ship-to-shore telephone from a fishing boat stranded in the middle of the Atlantic." There was more hissing and static, increasing and decreasing in waves, right on orchestrated cue.

"I can't make it to work tonight. Can somebody cover for me?" the muffled and somewhat slurred voice inquired.

"Get your 'gawdamned' ass in here in fifteen minutes you drunken faker or you won't have a job tomorrow," the night commander bellowed back at the man-made phone static.

We all stood around counting off the minutes. Sure enough, just under the time limit allotted by the night commander, the purported stranded deep-sea fisherman came wobbling unsteadily around the corner of the building and reported for duty. His ship-to-shore phone call came from a barroom two blocks from headquarters. After a few cups of black coffee, the alleged fisherman was able to work his relief—or at least put in his time.

THIS WAS THE SAME OFFICER WHO, WHILE WORKING AS PART OF THE ambulance crew, was blowing up a plastic air splint on the broken leg of a woman being transported unconscious to a hospital from a car accident. The inflation valve was located at the upper end of the splint. Well, George was huffing and puffing on the valve when the woman regained consciousness and saw this huge officer with his head stuffed up almost to her crotch.

Instinctively, she screamed. Her vociferous reaction to what she thought was going on could be heard, I was told, two blocks away. The upshot of the incident was that the woman arrived at City Hospital with a deflated splint on her leg and one police officer sulking in the ambulance front seat.

On a police beat, you learn to differentiate between news and incidents of only comedic value, but which would be told around police campfires for years to come.

ONE MORNING, KENARY CAME INTO THE PRESSROOM GRUMBLING about a "$@#%!&* stupid male nurse." At a highway fatality, the nurse reportedly insisted on shaking the corpse, demanding insurance information, until the attending officers pulled him off and then drove away with the cadaver, leaving the nurse stranded at the accident scene.

The in-house humor was not always self-deprecatory. Often it was used to teach someone a lesson, police-style. Usually, it was a lesson that remained with the recipient for a lifetime. Such a lesson was taught when Captain Jim "Chesty" Sullivan, police training academy director, was faced with a rookie trainee who never failed to fall asleep during classroom lectures, probably because of a full-time job on the side. Sullivan was a red-faced former foot-beat officer who possessed the brains, experience, talent, foresight, and personality to become one of the city's truly outstanding chiefs. His age prevented him from eligibility before the Civil Service promotional examination list expired.

After repeated warnings to the rookie, Sullivan resorted to more drastic measures. The next time the officer candidate fell asleep in class, Sullivan put his finger to his lips for silence and motioned for the entire class to tip-toe from the room. When everyone was evacuated silently to another section of the station, Sullivan pushed the hands several hours ahead on clocks in the classroom and his office. With the stage all set, Sullivan stealthily rolled a lighted cherry bomb beneath "sleeping beauty's" chair. The explosion rocked the station, practically lifting the thoroughly frightened recruit off his chair. When the ringing in his ears subsided and his voice returned, he rushed into the training office where Sullivan was casually shuffling papers. Pointing to the wall clock, Sullivan, completely straight-faced, looked up at him, and said, "Classes are all over young fella. You slept right through them all." For the remainder of the fourteen-week course, the droopy-eyed "sparrow" slept on his own time.

NOT LONG AFTER RETURNING TO THE STATION AFTER MY FOUR-year exile due to an unflattering story I wrote about the department, the city experienced its first sprinkling of winter snow. The dusting was not even on the ground before there was a fifteen-car pileup on Interstate-290, a few blocks east of headquarters. Every year, like clockwork, the first sign of a snowflake produced the same results. I sat in the Communications Division sipping coffee, watching, and listening to the confusion in the radio room caused by the chain-reaction accident. After about fifteen minutes, the officer assigned for the day to the dispatch board became tired of trying to draw cars from all over the city to assist on the Interstate. Without a word, heavy under-arm sweat stains soaking his blue shirt, he stood up and stormed out of the radio room, leaving the board unattended. From every direction voices over the air squawked for instructions. As I sat listening, transfixed by the confusion, the radio calls, as police would say, were "stepping all over each other." When no one made a move to rectify the situation, I quietly eased myself into the radio chair and started assigning cars to the accident. After several broadcasts, my radio career was cut short by the voice of the chief breaking in on the radio.

"This is car 100. Whose voice is that on the air?" His question was met with dead silence. I could not answer and I could not avoid answering. Several minutes later, I hastily evacuated after Communications Division personnel in an adjoining room became aware of the conundrum I had created and rescued me by sliding an officer into the seat.

"This is Officer Rourke, chief. I'm a little hoarse today." Just more high jinks.

IN DECEMBER 1978, FOUR MONTHS AFTER THE DEPARTMENT WAS transplanted into the new station in Lincoln Square, I found that the police code of silence, the unwritten credo by which police officers protect one another from the chief, from supervisors, ranking officers, and the public, also applied sometimes to insiders not protected by a uniform: people such as myself. A biker with whom I sometimes shared breakfast invited me, on occasion, to ride shotgun on the back seat of his motorcycle for what he promised would be a short joy ride. Never one to pass up an opportunity for a laugh and lark, and always crazier than smart, I accepted the offer, not bothering to inquire where we were going.

In a flash, someone, on a pre-arranged signal, held open the massive front glass doors to the station lobby and in we roared, revving the two-wheeler's throttle into deafening reverberations that thundered throughout the building, rattling what few windows it had. Just as fast as we wheeled in, the black-jacketed biker gyrated into a "wheelie" in the lobby with me grabbing him in a bear hug, his gun belt crammed into my gut. The fun-loving, blue-helmeted traffic cop careened back out the door again, deposited me like a sack of potatoes in the police parking lot, and was gone again before anyone could figure out what had transpired. I walked calmly back into the station with a "Who me?" expression on my face and then bolted into the sanctity of a locked pressroom.

My thrill-seeking benefactor had the entire city in which to hide, while I had only a six-by-eight foot former broom closet cubbyhole in which to make myself invisible. The chief's internal investigation was immediate. But muted lips were the only response, almost in unison, "Gee chief, we didn't see or hear anything." Sightless, deaf friends were good to have, especially on the police beat, where the high jinks of the "good old days" were rapidly becoming extinct and less tolerated. At the time, the chief was a quiet, rather gentlemanly sort who was never known for a sense of humor. Therefore, it seemed only natural that what in-house gags still persisted should be perpetrated during his six-year tenure as chief.

A YOUNG, FEMALE CLERK FROM THE BUREAU OF RECORDS STOPPED by the pressroom to visit one morning on her day off. Cradled in her arms was a cuddly pet skunk. Struck by a lightning opportunity for a gag, a diabolical idea came to mind.

"Can I borrow him for a few minutes? I want to visit someone," I asked.

"Sure," she replied, handing the furry black and white animal over to me.

I perched the skunk on my shoulder, took the elevator to the third floor and sauntered past the deputy's office and wide-eyed clerical staff and entered unannounced into the chief's inner sanctum.

Startled, he stammered, "I hope that's not what I think it is," in total disbelief, while jumping up from his desk.

"Sure is. Isn't he pretty," I grinned, feeling more mischievous by the minute. With that, the agitated chief bolted into an adjoining conference room, slamming the door behind him. I have no idea how long it was before he cautiously reentered his office, but as I retreated to the pressroom, I received admiring smiles from the secretaries and thumbs-up signs from the deputies.

In an apparent forgiving mood, the chief called me a few days later and invited me to a coffee party at the federally-funded Impact Program office in the former Precinct 2 station house in "Scalp Town." Police reporters, like any self-respecting cop, will go anywhere for a free coffee, so I accepted. When I arrived, everyone started applauding. The chief, by now smiling, presented me with a plaque for promoting the program with "fair, impartial and accurate journalism." I had written a series on the department's saturation enforcement to reduce crime in one of the city's most crime-ridden neighborhoods.

Once described by a managing editor as a "good leg man," I had daily taken time out of my usually hectic work schedule to visit the Impact office for chit-chat, camaraderie, coffee and possible feature material, something that less motivated reporters seldom did, preferring, instead, to remain planked in their seats in the News Room.

As I left the party the chief had thrown for me, I could only surmise that the plaque had been inscribed and the cookies baked before the skunk incident.

ONE OF THE DEPUTIES WAS, IN HIS YOUTH, A DRUMMER WHO COULD still beat out a mean paradiddle. I had been a jazz, show, and big band drummer for nearly half a century. We were kindred spirits. It was toward the end of my career and a what-the-hell-can-they-do-to-me attitude was shaping my personality. Knowing precisely at what time every morning (8:05 A.M.) the deputy came chugging into work—as a former U.S. Marine he was very punctual—I lined up at attention the entire complement of officers in the Services Division and we lay in wait for him in the headquarters lobby, a rotunda-like setting. I piped him aboard with a smart, snappy military marching beat on an over-sized street drum slung over my shoulder. As I did, the troops "shot him a highball."

Even though the almost constant in-house jocularity and practical jokes, the zaniness of earlier years was insidiously giving way to the almost grim, all-business mood of the 1980s, occasionally we still cut job tensions with silliness. It was our way of stripping away some of the authority and austerity in our lives, even if only for a few minutes. It was a pressure cooker relief valve that allowed us to laugh at ourselves, something we sorely needed.

the oldest profession

ORGANIZED BAWDY HOUSES, FOR ALL PRACTICAL PURPOSES, WENT
out of existence in the city in the early fifties, due partially to the inau-
guration of City Manager government and society's post-World War
II increased mobility.

Whorehouses in Worcester in the forties and early fifties were like
daisies in a broad, sunlit meadow in springtime: they were practically
everywhere. Many sported bars, live jazz band music, dancing and
even food. The better known brothels—no one spoke about them out
loud—were in the black "East Side" district; and in a two-block circumference around City Hall. Also, there were a few where Police
Headquarters are located today; and reportedly, a couple more in the
so-called "West Side" along the city's primary north-south boulevard.

When the city's first city manager was hired to replace the strong
Mayor and the back-room, politics-ridden Board of Aldermen, one of
his first edicts on March 19, 1951 was to clean up the city's bookie
parlors, after-hour speak-easies, and houses of horizontal refresh-
ment. Shakily, but steadily, police tried to comply. Veteran foot beat
cops, those who most closely kept their finger on the pulse of the public, knew exactly where the games and the girls were, how many there

were and how to eliminate them if orders were to be followed. These street-savvy old timers led the charge against society's two most sought after vices.

But, one thing in life is certain: neither prostitution nor gambling can ever be eradicated. Neither were back then, nor have they been yet.

Betting parlors, the infamous bookie joints ran wide open all along the main thoroughfare extending east from City Hall before the crack-down was mandated. When the much-publicized enforcement started, the bookies merely went underground, but kept right on operating with phone banks in their homes, far removed from police scrutiny.

Houses of prostitution, on the other hand, were more subtle. At least they did not advertise their wares openly as they do today. Yet, everyone knew where they were. During the effort to clean up the city, the whorehouses, like horse races and numbers pool bookies, did not go out of business. The demand for their services was too persistent. The girls just dressed a little more warmly, or peeled a little more off, depending on the season, before working their turf.

There is an old adage in business: if you want to promote business, go where the customer is. That is exactly what the hookers did in the city. They migrated to the streets, mingling with prospective customers. Provocatively, they sold their wares, exposing themselves on the street in skimpy mini-skirts, leather pants, or boots. They leaned against decaying buildings or loitered in darkened doorways into which they could quickly duck if an approaching police car was spotted in the slum neighborhoods in which the girls—and sometimes boys—operated. Prostitutes reacted to the city's clean-up order in a way diametrically opposite to the way the bookies responded. Now, whoring was out in the open for all to see.

Each hooker staked out her own territory and fought viciously if it was invaded by other prostitutes. Hard-liners moved in from Boston; Providence, Hartford, and Springfield on weekends, the high volume days. Everyone wanted a piece of the sour, sordid pie.

I watched as whores from Boston were arrested in some of the East Side dives. Their faces covered with festering, open syphilis sores, they were booked in groups in the police Cell Room after each police "swoop and scoop" operation. In ancient police cells they suffered the agonies of the disease overnight before being arraigned the next morning in Central District Court. I listened to them howling in pain as heroin withdrawal wracked their bodies. Even grizzled veteran cops winced when some were brought in with swollen, bleeding faces after being savagely beaten by their pimps for minor infractions of his rule, like holding back some of the proceeds or performing a "freebie" for a friend.

Perhaps the most tragic aspect of this local sub-culture of hooking in the city is, according to police sources, that practically every woman who sells her body does so to support a drug habit, one that almost inevitably leads to a violent end. It is a career whose only work benefits are to be worked over by pimps or dissatisfied "johns" (customers), to overdose on tainted "smack" laced with poisonous additives, to contract terminal diseases, and the ultimate pay-off, to wind up as an unidentified, unclaimed torso in some neighborhood dumpster or litter-strewn dark alley. At one time in my career, about a third of the city's homicides were victims plying the world's oldest profession on the streets.

Those who manage to survive the personal violence live in a world of cruel deception. Johns seeking sex are often lured into alleys, dingy bedrooms, even cars, where an accomplice—usually the pimp—is waiting to rob and assault, even stab, the unsuspecting mark. What was supposed to be a twenty dollar trick results in an empty wallet, a swollen head and, if the customer is not lucky, loss of his life.

Riding with the late night "hooker patrol," it was a common scene to see prostitutes writhing in pain in the gutters of the South End, unable to turn a fast trick for a fast heroin fix. An addict undergoing withdrawal pain is not a pretty sight to watch. Sympathetic cops, in these cases, send for the patrol wagon and the women are brought screaming, kicking, cursing, biting, clawing, scratching, struggling to a hospital, where they face only more cold-turkey withdrawal. For some of these wretched souls, the answer was methadone, a temporary relief at best from these agonizing spells. Drug addiction, and the pressing need to support it, often strikes early, even in the teen years. When addiction strikes, it becomes a desperation born of weakness and defiance.

There are calls from liberals far and wide for the legalization of prostitution and drugs, with the claim that they are harmless, victimless social problems. These people should spend a few nights on the streets, the so-called front lines, of most cities. Police, sitting in the front row as these vices infect society, strongly dispute this premise. They point to the woman ravaged by venereal disease, spreading it to others. Police point to home owners and business concerns, victims of shoplifting and burglaries by prostitutes supporting their heroin or cocaine habits. And then there are those, police say, who are viciously mugged on the street by hookers and their male accomplices in need of a fast heroin fix, not to mention the inestimable damage to the community's moral fiber as a whole.

Traditional methods of arresting hookers when a patrol or vice car actually sees a trick going down, were largely ineffective. A seasoned whore has a cunning, built-in radar that can detect a police car—marked or unmarked—three blocks away. In the old days in the city's cloistered "cat houses," there was no real need to develop this instinct. The madam stationed at the front door was the only detection device needed to shield her from the law.

Today's vice cops, I feel, have the dirtiest, lousiest, most debilitating assignment of any police job. Their lives, like those of drug addicts and prostitutes, are also spent living in the shadows of a world inhabited by the lowest of the low. They perform their duties daily knowing fully well that they stand no chance whatsoever of eradicating these terminal vices. All they can do is hum the old vaudeville tune, "Me and My Shadow," as they push the flourishing prostitution market from one neighborhood to another, trying to offer law-abiding citizenry of each neighborhood some relief from the filth proliferating on their doorsteps. Wherever the girls go, the vice boys provide their shadow. Vice Squad Lt. Alexander Donoghue, one of the best ever, explained, "We just keep 'em moving, moving, moving, rolling, rolling, rolling."

When prostitutes blossomed onto the streets, they created neighborhood resentment. Wives became incensed when their husbands were propositioned while working in their yards or sat on their front porches. Fathers became fighting mad when their tender-age daughters returning home from school were propositioned by johns cruising the neighborhood in cars looking for a score. Husbands were poised to do physical combat when johns accosted their wives when they walked to or from neighborhood markets, or waited for school buses to deposit their children back home. Women reportedly were reduced to tears by the degradation of their neighborhoods.

Some jokesters threatened to set up toll booths for johns' cars, estimated at more than 100 a night on weekends. Then, the counteroffensive turned ugly. Men started taking pictures of these cars, had police friends run license plate numbers through the Registry of Motor vehicles and then mailed the snapshots to the families of the vehicle owners. Even that did not diminish the volume, especially on warm summer nights.

Neighborhood watches were formed. City Council meeting were bombarded with moralistic screaming of the citizenry from infested sections of the city. Politicians, as they usually do, jumped on bandwagons. The newspaper began listing the arrests and court results of johns. The irrepressible problem persisted. Minimum court misdemeanor fines did little to help.

Nightly, Donoghue and his men carted patrol wagons full of prostitutes and their customers. Cops rode in the rear of the wagons to watch them even there on the way to the police lockup. I wrote a regular series of stories describing the nagging problem. Even that had little, if any, effect. As fast as they were busted, bailed, charged, and fined with a slap on the wrist, the girls were back on the street, this time hustling even more vigorously to make up for the lost time and lost wages. Night after night, the same hookers were scooped by Vice Squad officers. Eventually, hookers and arresting officers were on first name terms. Cops were playfully offered "freebies" as the musical chairs routine kept rotating month after month.

Police met with residents. So did politicians, who, at the same time, were conferring with police. Everyone was meeting with everyone. Even local clergy became involved. The so-called sign of the cloth did nothing to deter johns—some imported from other New England cities and seeking anonymity while the hooker legions mushroomed. The police effort was like whistling in the wind: lots of intent and effort, but no noticeable results. Donoghue added the element of "anticipatory expectation" to his planning. "We want them to keep their eyes peeled on every manhole cover to see where we will pop up next," he commented with determination. The articulate lieutenant was one extremely dedicated cop who did not like to lose many battles.

Police concentrated on sex customers rather than on the suppliers, hoping to spook them away. The sex queens splintered their solicitations into a network of "lone eagles," more difficult to detect, harder to eliminate. I watched many Vice Squad commanders come and go in the department but Donoghue brought a whole new vigorous perspective to law enforcement with unique approaches to combat drugs and sex, and innovative, sometimes unorthodox strategies. He studied the peak hours of sex solicitation when the johns wanted to fulfill their needs. Then, he rallied his manpower accordingly.

Always one to watch crimes in progress, if possible, I rode many nights with the vice officers. These nightly excursions invariable produced highly-readable feature stories.

On one such night, the Vice Squad commander—he most always rode with his men—silently coasted his unmarked command car into a darkened parking lot a short distance from where he could "pike" (survey) the landscape, a high volume spot for cruising johns. A rather voluptuous female dressed in tight buckskin jacket, jeans and black boots sashayed back and forth provocatively, remaining always within the confines of street light illumination. It was easy to see why horny males would zero in on her. She was the queen of the streets that night. She was also "Bubbles," a vice cop decoy whose bite would be painful.

Staked out across the street, crouched low and out of sight in the front seat, were two of the squad's burliest partners, waiting to pounce at the first sign from the decoy of violence or trouble.

As we watched in silence, Donoghue said under his breath, "These johns are like moths flitting around a candle flame. Around and around they go, slower and slower until they are consumed by the flame. Watch." Not for even a moment did anyone allow himself to be distracted from eyeballing "Bubbles."

Two young teenagers approached the decoy. "Chase them home to their mothers," a voice from another silent cruiser ordered. An unmarked car eased up to them, said a few words and drove away. The two underage prospective customers, looking for their first adventure skedaddled.

"Bubbles" had two prearranged signals for her backup units: "Move in fast and scoop 'em, guys," after a proposition had been made, and "I need help fast," when a customer became too aggressive, made a threatening move or pulled a weapon. All eyes remained riveted on "Bubbles." Under Donoghue's direction, the anti-prostitution team was a finely tuned operation. Every detail was worked out in advance and every officer followed his responsibility to the letter.

Before the decoy hits the street, she is photographed so a court judge, can view what her street uniform was at the time of the arrests, before the eventual procession of johns congregate before his bench.

The modus operandi is simple. The decoy walks an abbreviated foot beat, sometimes loitering to look around fetchingly. She says nothing. She does not entice nor entrap. The customer must initiate the conversation when he tries to dicker a price for sex. The pre-arranged signal is given and "the moth gets burned." Cars swoop in and in a matter of minutes, the patrol wagon parked discreetly in some darkened area is full and on the way to headquarters. Customers are given the opportunity to sit in the unlighted, odoriferous wagon, contemplating their future, until a full load is assembled.

Customers come from all over for a cheap thrill. But, the thrill is not cheap, Donoghue explained. When the court costs, fines, bail fees, and car towing are factored in, the cost can be excessive. In addition, the customer gets his name in the paper, his marriage is destroyed, his reputation is tarnished, and his career or job goes down the drain. "It's difficult to understand," the lieutenant murmured, his eyes still on "Bubbles." At headquarters, the errant Romeo is given his phone call (seldom to his wife), processed, photographed, and jailed, despite heartrending pleas for leniency.

"Hey, look who's back. The guy in the white car," someone laughed. "Maybe the judge will give him a two-for-one price." The driver, an out-of-town businessman, had been busted an hour earlier for soliciting at a different stakeout location. He was now cruising again to see whether his luck on this roulette wheel had improved. It had not. He was grabbed a second time. "Slow learner," someone whispered. A holiday reveler approached "Bubbles" and offered her a Christmas poinsettia plant. She declined the gift. Cops could be heard laughing. The push-'em-here-push-'em there" game went on month after month with no appreciable results. "We're their best travel agent," one vice cop quipped.

It was perhaps the dirtiest of all worlds, for the girls were predominantly addicts carrying a double monkey on their backs. The only future they had was more violence, crippling disease, more suffering, and almost invariably death. For vice cops, the only future was translated into endless cups of lukewarm, rancid coffee; lost sleep; and the tolerance of numbing cold and boredom—hours and hours of boredom.

ON OCCASION, TACTICS WERE ALTERED. A DIFFERENT DECOY WAS used—a male cop shadowed by Sgt. Phil "Sgt. Crab" Dussault canvassing the "Portland 500," across the street from City Hall. A growing proliferation of male prostitutes, some as young as twelve, had staked out their turf in the heart of the business district, spawning complaints to police from merchants whose righteous indignation would eventually spread to the newspaper. Dussault's patrolling, often accompanied by a feature-seeking police reporter, drove the male prostitutes off the streets and into phone booths to advertise their product. The clandestine rendezvous migrated to parkland on the fringe area of the city and eventually, under more police pressure, out of the city.

Vice cops had really imaginative disguises and code nicknames. There was "White Knight," "Sgt. Crab," "Weasel," "Fish," "Flako," "Belker," "Stinky," and "Frog." I spent so much time with them—the best source of reader-interest features—I was eventually dubbed, "Capt. Nemo," a reference, I always thought, to my hobby of scuba diving. Patrolling with them was always fraught with subversive danger. The element of surprise when arrests are made by individuals who do not look like cops can trigger violent responses.

How urgent is a hooker's existence? One emaciated hooker once told me she was supporting a $650/day heroin and cocaine habit—ten to fifteen thirty dollar "smack" bags and $200 in coke. "I boost (shoplift) during the day, do B&Es (burglaries) or hook at night." Needle marks ("chicken tracks") covered her arms and legs. Her legs were bloated and her hands and arms twice their normal size. As we talked, she repeatedly dozed off, only to jerk upright again, screaming, "I need a fix NOW!" She then wandered into an abandoned building to await her supplier, hopefully in time before the withdrawal howling began.

"Bubbles" once told me that there is comic relief in decoying johns. People who knew the fake prostitute as a young girl stop and start lecturing her. Former school mates ask, "What are YOU doing here?" Clergymen had been known to drop by to bless her. The elderly had expressed concern for her safety, alone at night. One woman sicked a dog on her. Others threatened to call police. When she explained who she was and what she was doing, most left her alone, walking away nodding their head approvingly.

Today, the battle still goes on, police on one side, druggies and hookers on the other, neither side willing to concede a single city block. The eventual outcome? Hard to tell. The addicts, drug pushers, and whores have numerical superiority, outnumbering police by a wide margin.

The struggle for supremacy has yet to be decided or won.

drugs

THE ELUSIVE EUPHORIA, THE PILL, CIGARETTE, OR POWDER-induced high constitute the artificial world of destruction into which so many feel they must flee. All can be induced by drugs, the scourge of society. Mind-altering narcotics in varying forms have been used in most of the civilized world since the beginning of time as we know it. Drugs offering a temporary respite from reality are used throughout the world, in Asia, the Orient, the Middle East, Africa, parts of Australia and, to an epidemic degree, now in the United States. It was not always so. Never before has the scourge of drugs cut through such a broad cross section of America, destroying the poor, sociologically affecting the middle class, and providing enjoyment with sometimes tragic consequences to the wealthy.

More than half a century ago, marijuana "reefer" cigarettes were smoked behind closed doors, mainly by the daring, the uninhibited musician, actor, and other free-spirited souls. The key word here is individuals, and not the masses that experimented with the drug in the sixties and seventies. "Bennies" (Benzedrine pills to stave off fatigue or drowsiness) were popular with the "hep cat" set in the late forties and early fifties. Black and white movies made mention of "reefers," or

"tea," in gangster films. As with everything else it seems, each succeeding generation had its own name for the weed and these names
became part of our culture: "grass," "Mary Jane," "hashish," "sticks,"
"joints," "loco weed," or "gage." But, in the sixties, other changes came
about. Youngsters started emulating what they saw and heard on television. They experimented, they dabbled, and, tragically, they became
hooked. The first rumblings of a drug problem in a metropolitan
area—it is almost laughable, in retrospect—was when police, in the
summer of 1965, found six boys and girls, ages fourteen to sixteen, hiding secretively behind a local school sniffing airplane glue. They said
they had tried the old saw about an aspirin in a bottle of tonic to produce a mild drunk, but the giddiness they desired had not materialized.
They tried swimming in deeper water: they resorted to glue-sniffing.

Police investigators, troubled by the potentially harmful effects of
glue vapors, could not even envision words like "smack" (heroin) and
"nose candy" and "crack" (cocaine). In those days, police considered
glue sniffing a serious offense, especially when it involved children.
The practice became a misdemeanor offense in late 1966. Warnings
to parents about the pitfalls of glue sniffing were issued citywide.
Police canvassed stores in the city selling model-making glue, advis-
ing them of the law, and the penalties for selling the glue to children
without registering their names. Frequent purchasers were logged
and questioned.

Juvenile investigators fanned out with aggressive prevention programs into churches, schools, parent-teacher associations (PTAs),
service clubs, and police departments throughout Worcester County.
Medical authorities joined the anti-sniffing program, warning that
glue vapors were harmful to kidneys, liver, bone marrow and the brain,
and could cause slurred speech, body instability, and unconsciousness.

"Like alcoholism and narcotics addiction, glue-sniffing has become
the refuge of maladjusted or disadvantaged teenagers who find the
practice a means of escape from reality," authorities preached to the
public.

Despite police efforts, stronger drugs soon swept throughout the city. Glue-sniffing became a harmless childish pastime compared to what was on the horizon with more potent mind-altering, drug-induced trips to never-never land. During the sixties, illegal use of amphetamines, barbiturates, ergot, and hypnotic or sleep-inducing drugs were considered misdemeanors in Massachusetts. Felony offenses included the illegal use of marijuana, heroin, lysergic acid diethylamide (LSD), morphine, Demerol, codeine, cocaine, opium, and several other narcotics. Concerned police, finding that the age of those arrested was steadily becoming younger and the drugs being used were of higher potency, especially those injected and highly addictive, turned to police reporters to spread the alarm to the public.

A narcotics squad was formed. High school and college administrators met regularly with police trying to find methods to slow the on-rushing tide of drug abuse in the city. Members of the Interfaith Clergy Association also met with police, who asked them to issue warnings on the subject of drugs from the pulpit.

In early February 1968, I confronted police and school authorities in a suburban town with information I had picked up on the street that pot smoking was widespread at the town high school. After trying every means possible to stop publication of that fact by vehemently denying it, attempting to stonewall my questions and even threatening to have me fired, they finally caved in and admitted the information was correct.

The story was given an eight-column banner headline that shocked the town and made me quite unpopular in many circles. Indignant, threatening phone calls were made to the paper from parents screaming about the disservice I had done by telling the world about their little darlings' social activities.

During the next few days, I hammered away in the same vein at one of the city's high schools, one that was decorated with eight-foot high graffiti "pot" on its brick walls. The school superintendent quickly issued a statement that no student in the city's school system had ever smoked pot. It was the most blatant, laughable cover-up attempt in the city's academic history, veteran teachers maintained.

Keeping the drug series going, I exposed a similar drug problem at another bedroom town high school. Police there, more realistic generally than academicians, admitted that marijuana smoking in that town had become a serious problem with kids of all ages and in all schools.

The chief at another contiguous town called me to say he was rallying the support of selectmen, the clergy, parents, and school officials to set up an anti-drug educational program with authorities in an adjoining town because of the growing problem of marijuana smoking in their regional high school. Known users were as young as fourteen, he said.

In some towns, school administrators refused to allow police into the schools to investigate drug usage or to interview students, claiming students would be embarrassed and their constitutional rights might be violated. For police, it was an uphill battle every step of the way. When parents threw further roadblocks in the path of the police effort, well-meaning but naive school administrators or publicity-fearing selectmen gave in to parental pressures.

It was ironic that as the use of narcotics increased everywhere, it was always the police who first recognized it and led the way in attempts to eradicate it. One town faced up to its growing problem so squarely that selectmen doubled the size of the police department by appointing its first full-time officer.

Various school departments continued to pressure the paper, demanding that I abandon the school drug series. The paper's answer was to run a story I had developed: an interview with a sixteen-year-old pot pusher, the son of a socially prominent Worcester family, who bragged of selling $200 worth of grass to fellow students and skimming off twenty dollars for himself before passing the remaining profit on to his distributor. The classroom pusher described a New York drug network that filtered down all the way to local classroom smokers in rural towns.

This, I informed my readers, was not a big time, hardened criminal. It was a typical teenager, one who did not even shave yet, but who was already well along the road to a destroyed life in a jail cell. The enterprising teenage pusher closed off the interview by saying he considered his new business better than slinging hamburgers in a fast-food outlet. The series concluded with a comprehensive analysis of what marijuana was, where it came from, how and by whom it was transported into the city, and the effect it had on the community. The series of news stories had taken a relatively obscure narcotic, unheard of in most families, and made it a household word around the supper table. No matter what street name it went by, it was still marijuana, and for thousands, it became a stepping stone to the hard stuff— "horse," "H," or "smack,"—heroin, the "maker of happy dreams."

Police tried every means possible to find something positive to say to counterbalance all the disturbing stories I was printing about drug use in the city and county. Police revealed that fifty-three drug arrests were made by a newly-created special narcotics squad the first seven months of 1968, quadrupling the thirteen busts during the same period the previous year. In trying so hard to show what a good job police were doing, all they did was illustrate that the problem was accelerating at an alarming rate every month. It also showed that the youngest on the drug-arrest list were getting younger, while the oldest reached almost into the geriatric set. More disturbingly, the special unit found that heroin was rapidly replacing marijuana as the drug of choice on the streets.

In the late sixties, an attempt was made to promote closer liaison between various police agencies by forming a Central Narcotic Drug Reporting and Information Bureau through which each of the suburban towns could funnel information about drug use in their areas. Records were kept of all known narcotics users, drug pushers, and routes used to ferry illegal drugs into Central Massachusetts. Eighty-four police officers from ten towns attended an eight-week drug education course. Area police fought back against drug traffickers and attempted to formulate a better understanding of the octopus-like problem whose tentacles were spreading in every direction. Even though it was common knowledge in police circles that there was considerable drug traffic and distribution between the city and several surrounding towns, free exchange of drug intelligence never really got off the ground. The barrier always seemed to be concerns about autonomy. No one wanted to share turf.

On July 3, 1970, Sgt. Tom Leahy, supervisor of the special drug unit in the city and an instructor at the Southern Massachusetts Police Training School, invited me to accompany Worcester Vice Squad and State Police drug enforcement undercover agents on a massive raid to clean out drug dealers from the rapidly decaying South End, believed to be the center of most drug distribution in the city. It was the first and largest such crackdown up to that point.

For several days, a strict veil of secrecy was thrown over the planned operation. I had picked up whispers in the corridors at headquarters about a large scale caper going down but had been unable to confirm it. Only the commanders of the planned raid knew the purpose behind a secret meeting at the police department's satellite precinct away from the porous walls at headquarters. The raiders were told what their assignment was only fifteen minutes before the actual jump-off time.

Precisely at 1410, the task force trooped from the briefing room and loaded into a caravan of van trucks, police marked and unmarked cruisers, the patrol wagon and a command car. The vehicles fanned out and approached the target site from several divergent directions. All marked cars and wagons were concealed two blocks away from where the raid was focused.

The time was 1413 when several vehicles quietly moved to cordon off side streets, establishing a one-block, escape-proof perimeter. Slowly, cruisers and trucks inched their way forward. Suddenly, on signal, twenty-five State Troopers and a similar number of Worcester cops sprung the net. In an instant, they were everywhere and moving fast. The largest drug raid ever attempted in the city, before or since, was under way.

What minutes before had been a tranquil summer scene of women pushing baby carriages in the hot sun, and people hanging from apartment windows to catch a breeze or talk to neighbors, and children playing ball in the street, was transformed into a war zone. Dozens of suspects were wrestled against building walls, frisked methodically for weapons, and then handcuffed. Pockets were emptied and sizeable quantities of white powder packets and marijuana blocks were confiscated.

Grubby, long-haired men scooted frantically in every direction trying to escape the police net. Wherever they ran, invariably there was a police officer waiting for them with open arms, or another right on their heels with arms flailing to lunge out and grab or tackle them. Suspects and police struggled and fought as they crashed through hedges and hurdled fences in escape tries. Punches were thrown while women screamed and tried to pry cops off their men.

"Leave my husband alone, you bastards. He didn't do nothing," one woman screamed as she struggled with the arresting officer, physically trying to pry her man free.

"Get back, lady. I'm warning you. It's all over. Back off or you're going too," the officer threatened over his shoulder as the struggling suspect was dragged to a police van nearby.

Stoically and unemotionally, about seventy-five people watched from tenement porches and windows, none wanting to get involved. When the cortege of police wagons and cruisers moved in, more than forty suspected drug users and dealers were crammed into them. From pool halls, ethnic stores, restaurants, and several nearby three-deckers, police, armed with search warrants, confiscated huge quantities of heroin, marijuana, and cocaine. Shrieking women protested in two languages while others continued to scuffle with police. As the prisoners were driven away, several women ran down Main Street after them, shaking their fists and bellowing threats at police. In fourteen minutes the raid was over and the neighborhood returned to its normal activities, now with something to talk about. People resumed hanging out tenement windows and talking to passers-by. Eventually the street stickball game resumed. Processing arrest complaints and "pedigree sheets" (mug shots, fingerprints, and physical descriptions) in a squad room took hours, and most of us did not get home until late that evening.

My Page One story of the South End raid made the opposition paper's rewrite account read like a junior high English composition. There never was nor will there ever be a suitable substitute for on-scene reporting. It was the first of many raids I would view first hand, but none would be of such wide-spread scale. What made it particularly newsworthy was that such raids were new to the city crime scene and offered newspaper readers an insight into matters far removed from the average family's interests. It also served notice to the city's drug subculture that police meant business and would be back again and again.

POLICE BOASTED THAT THEY HAD BROKEN THE BACK OF DRUG operations in the city, but they were a little premature and not very prophetic. After more hundreds of drug arrests, numerous drug-related street gun battles, scores of raids and battering-rammed doors, dozens of murders, and buildings torched by rival drug factions in drug-retaliation, narcotics traffic continued to explode every year. Today, it continues to boom in a magnitude of which pushers back in the sixties could scarcely dream. One Vice Squad official back then summed it up: "Hippies are very democratic people. They will sell (marijuana) to anyone, even to us. They don't even ask for a birth certificate. They hold grass-blowing and mind-blowing parties in their pads and when they reach a state of euphoria or well-being, they love everyone, even us."

Through the years, police became more sophisticated, establishing direct links between narcotics abuse and resulting related crimes:

prostitution, burglary, shop-lifting, purse-snatching, fencing operations, safe-cracking, armed and unarmed robberies, arson, and car
theft. In a more odious mode, police pointed to a staggering increase
in drug overdoses (ODs,) some on "hot shots (bad quality heroin),
others on doses "spiked," laced with poison, still others on heroin that
had not been "stepped on," (diluted) and too potent for ingestion.
Drug merchants employed all sorts of methods to increase their profits while expending the least quantity of drugs. Heroin was often
diluted with flour, sugar, baking soda, anything to preserve the powder's appearance—and sometimes taste—while duping the addicts,
most of whom were considered not smart enough to know the difference. Narcotics-related homicides climbed and soon outnumbered
murders of passion, or jealousy, or those committed during drunken
brawls, or robberies.

NEVER ONE TO BE OUTDONE IN GRABBING A HEADLINE, THE LOCAL
district attorney came roaring out of his sequestered seclusion with
"Operation Dragon," during the early eighties. A hard-core politician, the diminutive DA, by grandstanding every effort he ever made
regardless of how inconsequential it was, gave a glitzy title to each
one. He had difficulty differentiating between law enforcement and
the Lala Land of Hollywood. But, a vote was a vote.

A seventy-member task force of state and local police, armed with
seventy-one indictments, had rounded up fifty-one prisoners, mostly
on narcotics violations. When I arrived at the National Guard
Armory where the processing was being held, it looked like a recruiting station during World War II. It was a long-established fact that as
soon as the DA spotted a reporter or photographer, he puffed up his
chest and bragged that his operation had never before been done on
such a grand scale in the history of the Commonwealth. After several
of his "operations," I was on to his laughable posturing in the limelight and I was convinced he had seen too many B-grade cops-and-

robbers movies as a kid. I treated his subsequent media events for what they were: large-scale arrests, not show business productions with a cast of hundreds.

BY THE EARLY 1970S, POLICE WERE USING A MORE INNOVATIVE approach to the local drug problem. Vice squad undercover agents donned hippie love beads, grew scraggly, unkempt beards, and long hair, and sported grubby dress. They talked the talk: street jargon understood by drug traffickers and addicts.

The ploy worked, for soon the Vice Squad "Nasties" were bringing in more and more confiscated drugs, weapons, illegal money, drug paraphernalia. Seized drugs and betting slips ran into the hundreds of thousands of dollars. Squad Commander, Lt. Alexander Donoghue, a legendary figure in the department for his astute ability to employ and direct strategic tactics always in the most effective and innovative course, was one of the most highly respected officials and street fighters throughout the region. His leadership ability was so defined that his men would follow him into Hell.

No matter how cunning the street criminal, Donoghue was even more so. For a decade, the battle against killer-drugs was fought. Sometimes the good guys won the skirmishes; the bad guys always rebounding and coming back for more. The street-toughened "Nasties" were always ready for them. Working in collaboration with vice personnel, I wrote a series of informational stories on the narcotics problem in the city. The premise was that the more educated the public became on the subject, the more they might team up with police to wipe out this deadly scourge.

AS REPORTS OF ELEVEN- AND TWELVE-YEAR-OLD DRUG ABUSERS began surfacing, area law enforcement almost demanded that parents, churches, educators, social groups, civic organizations, town administrators, industries, and even the government get on board in the war against the growing narcotics plague. Some did, most did not.

Many city and town factions dragged their feet or buried their heads in the sand in the off chance that the problem would go away by itself. Obviously, it never would without massive effort and resources used against it. Deep-rooted apathy crippled drug education in some towns, fueled by an innate inability to admit that a social problem existed in those localities. The epidemic continued to spread, almost out of control.

For the most part, meticulously organized lightning raids proved to be extremely effective. Tons of drugs were seized each year by police but there never seemed to be a dearth of supply, almost as if it was coming from a bottomless pit. Obscene profits to be made lured otherwise law-abiding citizens into dipping their hands in the bucket of filth, the power of greed overwhelming their better moral judgment.

One of the major obstacles continually facing police was the almost lackadaisical court punishment of those charged with narcotics offenses, the perceived revolving-door policy, and fines hardly greater than those for parking violations. But smart cops never opened their mouths for they had to try to work with these same courts and it made no sense whatsoever to go there with one strike already against them.

In the South End, police sent out the message, "The heat is on." A fourteen-officer Neighborhood Task Force (NTF) was formed during my last year on the job, again with hand-picked officers, all with divergent talents. In one sting operation after another, undercover agents became drug pushers, selling cocaine and marijuana to unwary buyers on the street. Arrests went through the ceiling. In the uniformed branch, the glue that held the patrol operation together in the troubled neighborhood was Sgt. John "Freezie One" Harrington, again, one of the super cops on the department. Using "Freezie One" and "Freezie Two" code over the air, we frequently met at pre-arranged locations for our favorite orange soda drinks on sweltering summer days. Harrington, later to become a captain, touched all the bases during his distinguished police career. There were very few on the force for whom I had as much respect. Harrington's men, the first week the task force was in the beleaguered slum, made 108 arrests, one third of them drug related. In four months, the total rose to 872, fifty-five arrests a week, eight a day, sixty percent of them for narcotics violations.

Prostitutes became scarcer on the streets. Only a die-hard handful remained and they were always on the move. If they were still peddling, it was now fragmented and indoors as it had been forty years before. Open street drug sales all but disappeared also. The NTF was another opportunity for me to get back out on the street, back on my own turf pounding the pavement where any reporter worth his salt should be, for that is where the news was, and is today—one of the eternal verities of the newspaper business. My credo had always been: anywhere rather than behind a desk. During my years of reporting the human tragedy, I never felt closer to the people than I did when accompanying Harrington on his route. Other officers called him the best investigator in the department. After a few hours on the street, I knew why.

Harrington and I prowled through urine-stinking, garbage-strewn condemned buildings that addicts, crack-shooters, derelicts, drunks, drifters and street people called home. The stench in these building was overwhelming. Most were "shooting galleries" for heroin addicts. We followed tips of drug activity in strewn broken glass and syringe-littered back alleys, never knowing what we would encounter around the next corner. We talked to residents and merchants. We listened to their complaints, their compliments, their suggestions, their reports of criminal activities, and their fears. An hour with Harrington was an education into the realities of life.

One moment stands out in my memory: a greeting one morning from an elderly, somewhat shabbily-dressed black gentleman hobbling down a trash-strewn sidewalk, aided by a cane. As he approached us, he looked up, smiled broadly and said, "Good morning, Mr. Officers. Pleasant day isn't it? Thank you both."

Harrington and I glanced at each other and said nothing. How could you top that warm greeting? Gradually, a metamorphosis took place. Store owners again were seen outside their establishments. Women stood on porches and waved, pedestrians gathered on sidewalks, families reappeared in front windows. Deadpan, defeated facial expressions on so many gradually turned to hesitant smiles, thumbs up, and even applause as uniformed customers cuffed the troublemakers, and carted them away in cruisers and the patrol wagon. Children, seeking attention, ran up to officers, hoping for a friendly word.

Gradually, it became unfashionable to loiter and drink on the sidewalk, to openly peddle sex, to trespass or to rob or fight. Police intelligence flowed in as the neighborhood watched the police results. Sidewalk traffic increased. The mood and attitude of the neighborhood seemed to change and a pervading sullenness was turning to cautious optimism.

For a few brief hours of my life I was privileged to be part of it. The hour was rapidly approaching when it would be time to call it quits, to be put out to pasture, so to speak, to "pull the pin," as cops would say. But, I was determined to go out on a high, not with a whimper.

In a sort of going away present, I was allowed to accompany the "Nasty Boys" on a drug raid, one with all the components of a carefully-planned battlefield operation. In one sense, that is exactly what it was. A South End apartment had been "piked" (kept under surveillance) for five weeks. From this effort, vice officers had learned who was buying, who was selling, the volume of traffic, how many street dealers and addicts frequented the address, and when were the peak hours.

Affidavits had been prepared and a search warrant obtained. Command carefully scrutinized all the paperwork. Every period had to be in the right place, every T crossed. Also, the search warrant had to state specifically for what the officers were searching and in which section of the dwelling it was expected to be found. When raid planners were satisfied that all was in order a briefing was scheduled. With a layout of the building drawn on a display board, each officer—twelve on this raid—was shown where and what his assignment was: which officers would break in, who would act as the lookout, who was responsible for guarding alternate escape doors and windows, who would ram the door, and who would overpower those inside and make the actual arrests. All was meticulously detailed in advance: even who would carry the eighty-pound ram to the scene.

The jump-off time was set. The drug distribution center was busiest, surveillance had shown, right after sunset. The raid would go down at 1900. At 1815, the strike team assembled in the squad office, donned flak vests and reviewed last minute details. By 1835, everyone was ready. The squad crammed itself into a nondescript van with no police plates or other markings. It was a surveillance vehicle with darkened windows. Police cruisers are seldom used in such an operation for they take too long to park properly. The element of surprise is crucial in a drug raid.

The van coasted up to the building housing the drug office and waited and watched. Business was still brisk. Each officer checked his watch as the minutes ticked by. Those responsible for guarding possible drug dealer escape routes whispered into their radios that they were in place. Eyes glued to their watches, the command finally came, "GO!" and bodies scrambled from the door of each van, one officer struggling to carry the ram as fast as he could. The men hit the front entry. Surveillance had shown that the rear door was barricaded and was not used by customers or dealers. The barricade would slow the officers' entry and in a raid, seconds and precision counted for everything. With several officers crouched tensely on either side of the door with guns drawn, the eighty-pound cold rolled steel ram battered the door. It did not give. Again and again the ram battered the door.

Finally, on the third blow the door flew open and the "Nasties" poured in, yelling at the top of their voices, "Police! Freeze! On the floor! On the floor, now!" For one blurring moment, one of the dealers tried to muscle a cop out of the way so he could run barefooted out to the street. He did not make it. The cop was ready for him, and in one violent moment the dealer was overpowered and thrown to the floor and cuffed while another officer knelt roughly on his back.

At the other end of the room, a pig-tailed man was struggling violently with two other officers. Together, they picked him up and threw him to the floor. A third man huddled quietly in a corner, his hands folded over his head. He wanted no trouble. He too was cuffed and placed on the floor with the other two men.

The three blows it had taken the raiders to get into the building had given those inside the split-second warning they needed to react. As the officers exploded into the room, a blur was seen ducking into a back room. One officer dove after him. The dealer was heading for the bathroom. As he grabbed a "flush bucket," (a pail of water) to flush his stash of drugs down a toilet, the officer knocked the bucket from the dealer's grip. Water flew everywhere as the officer scooped handfuls of plastic-wrapped drugs from the toilet water. Without further struggle, the dealer spun around and bolted out the bathroom door, right into the arms of two other back-up officers who were moving in to assist the officer who made the initial pursuit into the bathroom.

When the four men were lined up on the floor, a Spanish speaking officer advised them of their Miranda rights. Practiced hands searched the men for further drugs or weapons. The surprise had been so complete none of the men had time to swallow the drugs they had been offering for sale. One reason cocaine and heroin was sold in small plastic bags was so they could be swallowed quickly in the event of imminent police apprehension. The packets normally pass through the human body in a matter of days, police explained. The apartment was in a shambles from the struggle. Damage to the door would be worried about later. As the patrol wagon pulled up to the front of the building—they had been alerted in advance that a raid was going down—the prisoners were loaded, accompanied by a member of the strike team.

Room by room the apartment was searched. BINGO! The first thing searchers found was a 9-mm Tech Nine, a fully-automatic, fifty-round weapon similar to a Uzi, both deadly weapons on the street. Before the search was completed, two pistols, a large sum of money, a sizeable quantity of heroin, cocaine, crack cocaine, and implements used to process drugs were seized. The raid was a major success and the list of charges against the defendants was long.

It was a fitting climax.

When I retired from the police beat in mid-year 1989, the war against drug use and prostitution had not been won—far from it. But at last police knew who and where the enemy was, and pretty much which strategies worked and which did not. At least, there was progress.

car theft

EVEN BEFORE THE ONSET OF PUBERTY, ONE OF THE STRONGEST urges of most boys is to rush the processes of nature: to achieve manhood and to experience the accompanying privileges. How best to accomplish this? One way is to shave. Another is to sneak a cigarette. But nothing better personifies manhood than sliding behind the wheel of a car—anybody's car—and zooming off into the big world. To a young male mind, an automobile is a ticket to independence. A youngster only has to look around. The kids with cars get the pretty cheerleaders in high school. The guys with the cars get the best paying after-school jobs. Jobs offer pockets full of money, and money opens up the world, a world where practically every sought after advantage is dictated by a car. Cars rule and control the country. Is it any wonder that kids steal cars as soon as they can see over the dashboard?

Car thieves fall into several categories. There are the pre-adolescent or adolescent teenagers who steal to experience the first thrill of power, or to teach themselves to drive after years of watching their fathers or older siblings. Police call these car thieves "joy-riders," who usually run the car dry of gas and then abandon it undamaged. The law they break in Massachusetts is using a motor vehicle without authority: a misdemeanor.

Some car thieves steal out of sheer viciousness with no ulterior motive other than to inconvenience or hurt someone. Often, this individual demolishes the vehicle, torches it, or submerges it in a river or lake. Still other car thieves steal for a fee—often as little as fifty dollars—to help their clients defraud an insurance company. Again, these cars or trucks usually wind up in a pond or burned in some remote area. Profit motive is the driving force behind a growing number of thieves who strip the vehicle of expensive, resalable parts and accessories, which are then fenced to clandestine "chop shops." These gangs—often highly organized—may be supporting drug habits or are just interested in a wallet full of easy money. In most cases, the prospect of prison is no deterrent to them, police say.

During a youth's middle to late teen years, another psychological change takes place: the male juvenile desires to flex his muscles. Often driven wild and fearless by booze, this thief wants a car he can enter into the gang demolition derby, where cars are repeatedly slammed against others in a four-wheel rodeo until they are demolished and no longer operable. These "demo derbs" are usually performed before a peer group audience, often attended by impressed and admiring girls. Thieves without the qualifications to enter these slamfests have to content themselves in many cases with just ripping off open car doors by backing at high speed through heavily treed areas. One such thief told police he loved to give his girl friend a "cheap thrill."

The most difficult cases for police or insurance investigators to solve are the well-organized, highly lucrative professional car theft rings, well protected from detection by street-smart cunningness. These rings steal on order, first determining what manufacturer, year, model, and color the customer wants. A car fitting the specifications is located, stolen, delivered to a secure destination and the thief disappears again into the night like a will-o'-the-wisp, a little richer. Car theft, police say, boasts the highest incidence of any major crime in the United States. For many years, Massachusetts was the car theft capital of the country. Car theft was seldom mentioned in the newspapers in the early sixties. It was basically a joy-riding juvenile crime, and juvenile crime was, by police tradition, seldom reported.

On one slow news day, I barged into the Juvenile Division—an area that reporters shunned because news never emanated from there—and confronted the commander: "Do you realize that the world doesn't even know that you and your people exist? How in the hell do you expect the people to know what a great job you do if you do not let me tell them?" A grizzled old captain stared at me in stunned amazement. He was not used to being addressed in that abrupt manner. With that, I walked out and the germination period began.

Soon afterward, the captain "leaked" a small story, just to test the waters. Suddenly, the flood gates opened and I found a whole new career for myself: writing about juvenile antics. A strange phenomenon developed as juvenile crime became public. Cops, often torn between laughter and anger when dealing with teenagers, found themselves intrigued by some neighborhood gang heroes, like the eight-year-old cat burglar who carried out his crime spree on a bicycle, or the smart mouth fourteen-year-old car thief who openly bragged about—and could prove—having stolen more than 500 cars since the age of twelve.

"Do something about it," he brazenly challenged investigators. This almost bigger-than-life thief eventually wound up conducting car theft seminars behind the closed doors of interrogation rooms, demonstrating to dumfounded police officers how fast he could break into a locked car, punch the ignition and drive away. His average time was fifteen seconds.

"If I want the car bad enough, nothing is going to stop me, not you, not burglar alarms, not nothing," the boy bragged.

Digging deeper into the nagging problem of car theft, investigators began finding underground chop shops, a new vernacular for police to learn. These shops were springing up, mostly unnoticed, in secure vacant garages and remote wooded areas where vehicles were being cannibalized for reusable parts and accessories. There always was a ready market for used car parts selling for a quarter on a dollar, police determined.

Stealing cars was no longer a teenage lark but a highly profitable business. The remaining hulks, after all salable parts had been removed and the vehicle identification number (VIN) filed off, was then torched beyond recognition. Street-savvy kids, some crime-hardened before puberty, boasted to police how they could dismantle, literally in minutes, and remove an automatic transmission from a car. It was, police quickly admitted, a whole new field of juvenile crime about which they would have to become more knowledgeable. Police admitted it was not easy to fight effectively juvenile crime when the criminal—even a fuzzy-cheek 12-year-old—knew more about the subject than they did.

What turns a fourteen-year-old boy from a good home into a car thief? Bad associations? Peer pressure? A distorted sense of values? A need for thrills? A lack of conscience? Inability to differentiate clearly between right and wrong? A cross-section review of stolen car arrest records showed that thieves were not always underprivileged teenagers from slums and broken homes. A case in point was made when a youth from a suburban town was charged with stealing thirteen cars in the city. While police clerks checked stolen car records, the boy claimed he had stolen so many cars he could not even remember where he had dumped them all.

The youth attended church regularly, belonged to two youth groups, was an average student, had never before been in trouble with the law or at school, was popular with his peer group and teachers, and was no problem to his parents. He came from a large family and had been given ample parental love and guidance. His credo, he told police, was that a crime was not to break the law but to get caught perpetrating it. This, coupled with an uncontrollable urge to drive, pushed him over the edge into lawlessness. His modus operandi was simple: wait until his parents were asleep at night, crawl through a bedroom window, retrieve a stolen car he had stashed in a remote area nearby, find another car he liked better on some quiet side street and he was gone. He avoided expensive, flashy cars that could attract police attention. When apprehended, he was totally without remorse. When his distraught parents asked police why, investigators were unable to give them a satisfactory answer.

In mid-summer 1966, I was invited to become involved in a program to combat skyrocketing car theft in the city. I was allowed to meet a six-man undercover team of investigators, and later with the FBI, Massachusetts State Police, the Registry of Motor Vehicles, National Auto Theft Bureau, and several Worcester County new car dealers. The sheer size of the assembled group promised the most concerted effort ever taken in the city to combat car theft. I was sworn to the strictest secrecy with the stipulation that the existence of the group could never be made known publicly without the chief's express consent.

The unit was commanded by Capt. Roger "Scoop" Mulhearn, the legendary toughest street cop in the city. This was the man who, by department legend, was jumped one night by five toughs. By the time the patrol wagon arrived, four were on the ground and the officer was working on the fifth. The assigned orders for the new unit were to bust up a reported professional, steal-on-order car theft ring, based in Worcester and operating throughout New England.

For several months, I mimicked the three little monkeys: see no evil, speak no evil, and hear no evil. I was sitting on the biggest story of my young career. I could not under any circumstances let the City Desk know what I was doing for editors were not bound by the confines of "police security," and might be influenced by the overriding compulsion to "scoop" the opposition paper.

Sitting on the story was a calculated risk, a gamble. I knew I was walking a tightrope as far as journalistic ethics was concerned, but if I pulled it off, it would pay back handsomely with one of the biggest news stories of the year. I also knew that if the existence of the unit was ever leaked, I would automatically be blamed and my tarnished reputation within the department would never be restored. I would also be severely criticized—perhaps even terminated—at the paper for not confiding in them. But, I could not trust possible loose mouths at the paper with the protection of my secret.

Six months after the unit was formed, Mulhearn called me at home, late one night, and told me to "hang loose." The lid was about to blow. Excitement took over. I had pulled it off, risking my reputation as a police reporter if the news editors did not understand or accept my motives. Expectation gave way to nervousness as I awaited through a sleepless night for the anticipated phone call.

"Get your skinny little ass up here and bring lots of paper and pencils," a gravelly voice barked. "This one's big." By the time I could fly to headquarters, the car theft unit was marshaling in a parade of sullen-faced, handcuffed prisoners shuffling into the Detective Bureau, surrounded by a phalanx of plain clothes officers and federal agents bristling with armament.

Police had documented 250 cars stolen, plus an attempted under-world bombing. As investigators sat with open ears, the weaker prisoners started to "weasel" on their accomplices. Thirty-five cars were recovered before they could be resold or shipped overseas. The "plea-bargain hunters" blabbed about the scope of the ring. Two dozen suspects from Maine, New Hampshire, northeast Massachusetts, and six Worcester County cities and towns were allegedly involved.

After the story was given the prominent display I had hoped for, I was summoned to the police chief's office. "Show up at the Coach & Six Restaurant at six o'clock and dress up. In fact, put on a tie. If you don't have one, I will lend you one. And, be on time. I'm going to feed you," he chortled.

When I arrived, the Worcester County New Car Dealers' Association was feting the unit for demolishing the car-theft ring and recovering many thousands of dollars in stolen cars. Before the dinner, my picture was taken with the Worcester officers involved and I was handed a telegram, my first. It was from my son, Roscoe III, a student at Phillips Exeter Academy. "There are still rewards for those who play the game the right way. Love, Rock," it read. I never was offered any special acknowledgment from the paper. To them, it was just another routine police story.

IN MARCH 1968, A FIVE-MAN AUTO THEFT SQUAD WAS FORMED, comprised of Juvenile Division investigators. Using a motor vehicle without authority, because it was a misdemeanor in the state and usually generated only a "shame-on-you-naughty-boy" attitude in Juvenile Court, had seldom been strictly enforced. The unit was the first step in what would eventually become intense enforcement by another auto theft team formed some years later.

I once rode with a Juvenile Division detective transporting a fifteen-year-old to Juvenile Court. He had been charged with stealing thirty cars. But, as usual, the boy was released before the cop could sign a court appearance slip and get back into his parked cruiser.

A few days later, I rode with the same officer delivering an alleged car thief to the state Division of Youth Services. Before hitting the road again, the officer paused to talk to a retired officer working there and saw the youth sauntering down the street with a grin on his face. Spotting us, he bolted through a back yard and was gone. "Screw 'em all. If that's how bad they want the goddamned kids, let 'em catch them themselves next time," the exasperated cop growled. And, with that, he drove to a neighborhood bookie joint where we had coffee.

The man's irate commander demanded a news story saying he was planning to file criminal charges against the DYS facility director and personnel who allowed juvenile offenders to escape while in their custody. Documenting eighty escapes from the local DYS building, the commander confronted authorities there. The confrontation produced an eight-column Page One spread. The DYS director countered that escaping delinquents were only stubborn children or runaways, troublesome perhaps, but no danger to the community. They were just misunderstood children, he claimed. Back came the Juvenile Division commander with documentation that the most recent escapee had previously been in court twelve times for rape, larceny, burglary, car theft, breaking into motor vehicles and malicious damage.

Waving another accordion-like rap sheet under my nose, the commander bellowed, "This one's been before the court twenty-two times since he was nine for four larcenies, seven burglaries, six escapes, five using without authority, two robberies, assault and battery with a dangerous weapon, arson, malicious mischief and court defaults. These are hardly harmless stubborn children. These are already hardened criminals. Print that."

The boiling controversy between police and the DYS produced a series of reader interest stories. Juvenile crime always seemed to be a hot-button issue of considerable interest to the reading public. During my next visit to the DYS facility with the Juvenile Division commander, the director of DYS seeing me, out of the corner of his eye, eagerly scribbling notes in the midst of all the screaming, was left sputtering apoplectically. He realized that an angry cop, especially one with a willing sidekick reporter, was too formidable an opponent. Threatened law suits and counter suits were dropped.

THE WAR AGAINST CAR THEFT WAS STEPPED UP A NOTCH WHEN THE chief instituted regional intelligence sharing and dissemination of "hot sheets," daily stolen car lists. This meant adding " hundreds of pairs of eyes looking for hot cars," he explained to me. However, nothing seemed to stem the tide. It was a craze that did not peak until sometime in the late seventies. In 1966, 1,794 cars were stolen. By

1974, car theft totaled 7,300 cars for the year—twenty vehicles every day, nearly one every hour. More drastic measures were called for. Police administrators across the state lobbied politicians for more stringent car theft laws. By the time I retired in 1989, stiffer laws had not materialized.

Stealing a car in Massachusetts was a felony only if the thief intended to deprive the owner permanently of his or her vehicle by destroying it, stripping it of parts or accessories, painting it, burning it, submerging it in a lake, river or pond, or reselling it. Much of the police concern was centered on the fact that car theft, even joy-riding, was a stepping stone to more serious crime. Police badgered Juvenile Courts for stiffer sentencing. When these pleas were ignored, police were forced to admit the fight was far from won.

Then, fifteen-year-old "Beatles" hit the scene. He was a legend in the department. He had been arrested twenty-three times before the age of seven, but, in most cases, he could not be charged because of his age. He had not yet reached the "age of reason" when, by law, he would know right from wrong! As he aged, he was charged with practically every juvenile crime imaginable. He was almost popular with police due to his resourcefulness. But, Beatles' weakness was cars, anybody's car, everybody's car, any model, style, or color. He did not discriminate. He stole them all. Police found out he was also wanted in two states as an escape artist.

Before the book was closed on Beatles, it was estimated he had stolen or ridden in 500 cars in Massachusetts, Rhode Island, Connecticut, New York, New Jersey and Pennsylvania. Police believed him. He willingly demonstrated for police the most efficient methods to steal cars. But, there is no honor among thieves. During an interview, Beatles told me his biggest fear was not police, but that other juveniles would steal his car. To prevent this, he removed the ignition coil every night and replaced it in the morning.

A STOLEN CAR ALWAYS HAS THE POTENTIAL TO CAUSE SERIOUS HARM to property or the public. A classic example of the carnage a car thief can cause came when, one morning just outside the core city, a police radar unit tried to stop a vehicle traveling 63 miles an hour in a 35-mile zone. When the radar officer started in pursuit, the teenager accelerated to more than 80 miles an hour in a thickly inhabited section of the city, narrowly missing a group of about eighty school children outside the city's Science Center. The getaway car careened all over the road, across lawns, skidding around a police cruiser blockade, knocking down street signs, and a utility pole. The pole landed on the roof of a nearby restaurant. For more than another half-mile, pedestrians and on-coming vehicles scattered all over the place to avoid the almost out-of-control stolen car. Finally, running on three bare rims, the car collided head-on with another in a rotary, the uninjured teenager running from the scene with several officers in pursuit. The youth was apprehended when a small boy pointed out to the panting cops where the juvenile thief was hiding in tall grass in a vacant lot.

IT WAS NOT UNTIL JANUARY 1976 THAT POLICE WERE ABLE TO STICK a pin in the car theft balloon with the creation of a still-existing Auto Theft Squad (ATS), a unit which eventually became a model for similar units throughout the state, including Boston. Again, the unit consisted of hand-picked officers with strong investigative credentials and proven dedication. The squad was given a dingy, closet-like office tucked away in the attic of an abandoned fire station; an office, if it could be called that, barely large enough to accommodate five officers unless they all stood up. The names of Bob Rich, Dick Cowden, George Orawsky, and Walter Murray, the backbones of the ATS, became known in law enforcement agencies in many areas of the state. They testified at the State House in Boston on methods used to stem effectively the tide of car theft in Worcester. Various agencies were being shown the battle could be won, especially with enough innovation. Dedication was the key factor.

I rode with them nights when, using their cruisers like tanks, they crashed their way through dense wooded areas to uncover and break up chop shops. Almost without fail, even though only bare hulks were usually found, the strippers left behind evidence helpful to the team. Team members continued to dig and dig. On several occasions, I assisted the team investigations by using an underwater sea scooter and scuba gear to recover, from area ponds, cars with VIN numbers intact. Over a period of months, every puddle large enough to conceal a stolen car was searched. Lists of hot cars dipped, gradually at first, then more drastically as the ATS took hold in the city. For the next thirteen years at least, car theft totals never climbed again substantially.

Gone finally were the "disposal technicians" of the early 1970s gas crunch years who, for as little as fifty dollars, would dunk or torch a gas-guzzler for customers bent on defrauding insurance companies. Between 1972 and 1977, one suburban teenage scuba diver, working closely with police, recovered more than seventy stolen cars from the city's numerous waterways.

Today, the ATS still works steadily, never for a moment forgetting that vigilance cannot slacken, even for a short time. As long as kids feel big behind the wheel and feel the need to rush the aging process, the ATS and hundreds like them across the country, will never be able to relax. The kids won't let them.

the silent victims

THE LIFELONG EFFECTS OF CHILD ABUSE ARE A NATURAL PARALLEL to the old adage, "As the twig is bent, so grows the tree." How children are treated in adolescence and earlier years molds their characters and personalities throughout their adult lives. If emotional and physical scars are part of a child's growing up process, those wounds may not fester on the surface, but they never disappear from the person's being. Child abuse manifests itself in many forms, the most common of which are physical assault, malnutrition or starvation, hygiene neglect, sexual battery, improper or non-existent medical care, psychological cruelty and, too often, murder.

Police say it is difficult to fathom the motivations behind child abuse, how adults can display such total disregard for the well-being of another human being, especially one they sired. Every day police must contend with a world of such cruelty. But, they readily admit, they never get used to physical or mental cruelty to small children and the elderly, both of whom are vulnerable and tend toward helplessness.

On occasion, fathers and stepfathers videotape sexual abuse of small children to trigger future sexual arousal. Mothers, police say, are also not without fault. Numerous cases are documented each year of mothers performing oral sex on their sons, barely out of infancy.

Police in Massachusetts have been assisted greatly by a law mandating that day care centers and other such care facilities notify police when evidence of physical child abuse is noted or sexual mistreatment suspected. One of the first signs of abuse or mistreatment, police say, is when a small girl is detected masturbating in class, believing that due to previous treatment by others this is an accepted practice for them. Telltale signs of sexual abuse are also detected by day care center workers when children display inappropriate behavior—for example, exposing, masturbating, or fondling themselves—or extreme nervousness. This, police say, is often a direct carry over from the child having been raped during the sexual abuse. Rape of small children, often as young as one year old, can be committed anally, orally, or vaginally and can also be carried out digitally (use of a finger), or by the insertion of a foreign object.

How common is the practice? "Much too common," police respond quickly. They estimated that hundreds of cases were investigated each year. The majority of child abuse cases that cross the desks of Juvenile Division or Detective Bureau investigators stem from reports made by child care facilities, medical personnel, or teachers. Part of this can be traced to an increase in the number of working mothers placing their small children in day or night care, and the more highly-trained workers staffing these centers. Also, police say, an increase in public awareness of the nationwide child abuse social problem brought about a sharp jump in the reporting of suspected abuses cases.

Police say child abuse cases generally fall into the following categories. Starvation of children is almost invariably related to low-intelligence adults or teenagers with no parenting skills. Neglect of child health and hygiene are common abuses for the same basic reasons, police say. Police case files indicate that empty refrigerators and uncaring mothers at home are responsible for the widespread sight of children scrounging around for food in the neighborhood.

"Whenever children are brought in for stealing food, we almost automatically know we will be investigating an abuse case," one police official stated.

Physical attack is perhaps the most common abuse of a minor. Beatings and assaults against children can, and do, come in almost any form, usually because the child is sickly, colicky, or crying and the immature parent, step-parent, or boyfriend of the child's mother is impatient or unable to control a temper.

Such a case was reported at a local supermarket. A female detective in uniform working an off-duty security job at a supermarket observed a mother become agitated at a fussy infant daughter. When the mother bent over and bit the child, the detective, fearing the baby was in future danger, immediately took the crying baby from the protesting mother and called Comprehensive Emergency Services, a subsidiary of the state Division of Social Services, for assistance. Within minutes, a social worker arrived and the child was taken into protective custody. Police were quick to praise CES workers and their dedication to child care.

DRUGS AND ALCOHOL, POLICE INVESTIGATIONS HAVE FOUND, ARE the major factors behind child abuse. "Generally, with abusers, we find that their lives evolve around drugs or booze, not their kids. The principal concern of abusers is their addiction, supporting their drug habits, or their alcoholism rather than the well-being of their children," one investigator explained.

Police files were filled with investigations into child abuse cases that escalated to the next level and resulted in murder. After autopsies were performed, causes were almost unlimited. Some infants were literally boiled alive in scalding water, or had lye or furniture polish poured down their throats. One was drowned in a toilet; others were repeatedly bounced off the floor. Some were held by the legs and slammed against walls until their small, battered skulls were fractured.

The most common cause of death in murdered children is the shaken baby syndrome, where the infant is violently shaken until their necks, spinal cords, or backs snap. Skull fracture deaths are almost common among babies whose only fault was crying or soiling a diaper.

Parents of low mentality, or mothers' boyfriends, and uncontrollable tempers accounted for many of the more severe abuse cases encountered by police. Too commonly, children's fingers are forcibly held over open flames to punish them or teach them a lesson. Another form of child abuse, one that is almost never reported by the media, is the forced incestuous relationship between fathers and daughters, mothers and sons, older brothers and younger sisters, older sisters and younger brothers, or grandfathers and granddaughters. Seldom do police become involved in these unnatural liaisons until such behavior is revealed by the victim during an investigation of an abuse-related crime. Police say that, in most cases, the mother of the victim ignores or even condones the criminal violence out of fear the husband or boyfriend will leave her if she interferes.

In most cases, counseling is only of minimal benefit to abusers, especially when it is offered to people of very limited intelligence. Police say that one remedy to child abuse would be to speed up the process of handling such cases and to remove the child from the cruel or unhealthy environment immediately. Police investigations could be expedited by making abuse cases high priority. When allegations prove founded, it should be standard procedure to make sure that the child is not returned to the abuser. Instead, the child should be quickly placed in a proper, safe, and healthy home or agency.

Police say the book is filled with laws pertaining to child abuse or cruelty in all forms. The most common criminal charges leveled against abusers are indecent assault and battery, assault and battery with a dangerous weapon, and rape of a minor child.

ONE CLASSIC EXAMPLE OF CHILD ABUSE THAT COMBINED PRACTICALLY all of the varied abuse categories—beatings, medical neglect, emotional cruelty, sexual mistreatment and starvation—was so cruel that veteran officers in the department talked about it for months.

Juvenile authorities told me that they had a child abuse case in which I might be interested. In police protective custody was a small, emaciated, pathetic looking boy, with floppy, ill-fitting clothes, happily chomping away on doughnuts, hamburgers, and milk being served to him by Police Officer Dorothy McCarthy. Each time he paused from shoveling food into his mouth with both hands, he joyously banged away at a new-found toy, an old, beat up manual typewriter.

"Rock, this is Michael," police said, introducing me to the waif. Seeing someone new in the room, the boy looked up at me and proudly announced, "Hi, I'm Michael. I'm eight."

In a whispered aside, I was told Michael appeared to be slightly retarded and that he had been kicked literally naked down a flight of stairs and out of his home into the bitter cold of a winter night. A route car officer had discovered the boy crying and grubbing for food in a rubbish barrel in an abandoned gas station. Protected by almost no clothes, the boy's body was covered with welts, bruises, and a skin rash.

"My mother kicked me out for two days because I asked to go to school. I'm afraid to go home," he said through tears running down his face. He said he had nothing to eat during those two days. His eighth birthday had been only twelve days before. Michael was not unknown to police. The night before, the boy had wandered into a precinct house looking for food. His shoes had no laces, he wore no hat, and his coat, soaked through by snow, was unbuttoned. On that occasion, he was driven home, where the boy's mother and stepfather said they did not want him. In Michael's bedroom, police found a mattress blanketed by a rubber sheet soiled with human waste and urine. The apartment was only a few degrees warmer than the temperature outside. The route officer lighted a fire, dressed Michael in some pajamas, and wrapped two tattered blankets around him. It was all he could do. When Michael was found the next night under even worse circumstances than the night before, he was taken directly to a local hospital for hot food and medical attention and then into police protective custody. There, Michael pleaded through rivulets of tears not to be taken back home. He was terrified of his mother and stepfather.

Investigators questioned neighbors, some of whom admitted they tried whenever possible to care for the tyke. They told of Michael being punched, beaten, and kicked repeatedly. One told of seeing Michael on a neighborhood front porch at four A.M. one winter morning and then watching his mother kick him down a flight of steps to the concrete sidewalk.

"He's a good kid," the neighbors told investigators, "until he sees his parents coming and then he runs in terror."

Neighbors told police that Michael's mother had a history of mental disorders. Some neighbors volunteered horror stories of the abuse to which Michael had been subjected. When investigators confronted Michael's mother, she screamed, "Put him away. I don't want him. He doesn't behave."

When I first met Michael, he was gleefully playing out his star role at headquarters. He was warm at last, had new clothes purchased by the Juvenile Division from a nearby department store, was no longer hungry, and was the center of everyone's attention. He delighted in posing for pictures, playing with handcuffs, and pounding away on typewriters. Much to the amazement of the officers who were now coddling him with love and attention, Michael correctly typed his name and the date. As soon as he relaxed in his new surroundings, he talked a blue streak to anyone who would listen.

A trust fund of police donations was set up by juvenile authorities to be held until the boy was of age. A Juvenile Court judge remanded him to the custody of the Division of Youth Service (DYS) for eventual placement in a foster home. It was a whole new threshold, leading to a new life for the boy. Several days later, I looked up Michael and talked to him again.

"I like it here (DYS holding facility). They gave me a big piece of cake. It was good. I'd like to stay here. There are lots of kids my size to play with," he said, holding up three fingers. DYS psychologists determined that Michael was emotionally disturbed, not retarded as originally thought. Police did not press charges against the mother but recommended that she be committed for psychiatric treatment.

I pulled out all the stops when I wrote Michael's story, tugging at the readers' emotions and proved that truth, no matter how upsetting, how tragic it might be, was the best portrayal of the reality of life, especially in the police world. After the story was published, offers to adopt Michael came from families in nearly a dozen cities and towns in eastern Massachusetts. Letters of appreciation poured into the newspaper from the Associated Press and other newspapers around the country, each of which had given the story a prominent display under my byline. Three months later, I was notified that I had won the United Press International annual news writing competition.

But the story was not over yet. Eighteen years later, in July 1985, a strapping twenty-six-year-old walked into my pressroom at the new headquarters building and hesitantly asked, "Are you Mr. Blunt? I'm Michael." As we sat and talked, the grown-up Michael said, "There surely is a God, for he gave me you and the police officers who saved my life."

Then he related stories of two decades of mistreatment and psychiatric counseling in various foster homes and orphanages in Massachusetts and Rhode Island. He told me of living alone afterwards and the long uphill battle to escape the throes of neglect, more physical abuse, and a seemingly uncaring society. Michael filled me in on more sordid details of his childhood life and treatment that had not been included in the original abuse and referral reports written years before by police.

"I was bounced off walls by my stepfather almost every day, once because I got wet paint on my clothes. Most of the time to stay out of the rain or snow, I slept under cars or in barrels when I could find them near railroad tracks," he said. When he wanted food, he begged for handouts or stole it. "My mother, when she washed me, heated the water in a roasting pan and tried to scald me in the summer time. Sometimes she would put me in a tub filled with ice cubes in the cold water and leave me sitting there in the winter. Other times she rubbed my head with kerosene."

The expression on Michael's face turned grim when he told of repeatedly being sexually molested by his stepfather and an uncle who used to tie him to a bed and play with my "you-know-what." One time when he was hurled from a second-floor window by his mother, he landed on a discarded mattress in the back yard.

"I got hurt that time and now I'm blind in one eye," he said. "But I'm grown up now and I'm getting along OK. I have a girl who I think likes me," Michael stated, beaming all over. He told me he was working for a local wholesale food company. "I was never arrested, not even once after I got out of the homes and orphanages," he boasted as he told me more about his emotionally troubled younger life. Depths of despair were brought on when psychiatrists warned him he would become a hermit as he grew older or become sexually disturbed because of his past abuse and that he could, in turn, abuse other children. "I showed them that they were all wrong. I'm not violent. I'll never do to anyone what was done to me," he promised. As he spoke, his eyes often drifted away into the not-so-distant past, recalling the cruelty and indignities to which he had been subjected as a frail, often sickly boy. They were somber, troubled recollections, difficult for one to comprehend, but all verified by police.

When Michael said he had returned to thank McCarthy, by that time the head of the police Missing Persons Bureau, I called her and blurted out, "I have a big surprise for you. Little Michael is now big

Michael and he's sitting in my office. He wants to thank you for what you did for him," I said. The reunion was a happy one. We all hugged and then McCarthy reached into her desk drawer and handed a sheath of pictures to Michael. "These are yours now," she told him, slightly misty-eyed.

"I can laugh now. The terror is over. But I have a lot of time to make up," he smiled. I asked him if he had contacted his mother. "Yes, I found her in a nursing home. All she did was scream at me when she saw me. I had to leave," he answered, turning away suddenly.

With that, Michael was gone again. "There goes a perfect example of what this job is all about," McCarthy said. I eagerly wrote the story, but the copy of the return of Michael was given only a minimal spread by a new generation of editors.

A FEW MONTHS LATER, IN EARLY SEPTEMBER 1969, JUVENILE authorities again laid open a file for me to read.

Frank, was fifteen and a twice-convicted car thief. Since the day he was born, his had been a struggle for respectability. When I read his case history, it was obvious that Frank was losing the fight. When I first met him, he merely sat and brooded, rarely smiling. With eyes riveted to the floor, he offered single-syllable answers to questions in a low monotone.

Frank was born in Worcester State Hospital, an institution for the insane. As an infant, he was committed to a foster home, his file said. Soon afterward, the foster mother died and Frank was again a ward of the courts. An elderly grandmother tried to raise him but had to split her time between the infant boy and his mentally deranged mother. Frank never knew his father. For the first few months of his life, his grandmother was able to cope with him. But as he grew, his adolescent problems became too much for her.

Repeatedly, he became a truant from school, hanging out downtown where he fell in with a new element of delinquents. During a stolen car episode, he and an acquaintance rammed a barn in a near-by suburban town, resulting in an eight-day hospital stay for multiple injuries.

Upon his release, he was remanded in Juvenile Court to a state correctional institution near Boston, and eventually transferred to a similar facility nearer to Worcester. The courts gave him back to his grandmother.

Ashamed of his ragged clothes, all that the grandmother was able to provide, Frank started skipping school again, running away, living in sheds and garages, begging money for grape tonic, potato chips, and occasional cupcakes. Soon he was hanging around street corners seeking out cars to steal. Recommitted to a "reform school," older inmates picked on him. In desperation, he and two other youths jumped out a window, fleeing through woods and swamps before going underground begging again for food, never remaining in one location for more than three days.

When he was eventually apprehended by police, the first thing juvenile authorities did was to feed the youth a full meal. Twice, the boy almost made it back to respectability. He badly wanted to become an automotive mechanic. Police got him into a trade school, but his background again overwhelmed him. He flunked out of school, a victim of circumstances. Not long afterwards, Frank disappeared, another victim falling through the cracks of society. He was never heard of again.

ALL THE STORIES RELATED BY ABUSE VICTIMS HAD A COMMON thread running through them: violence, fear, attempts to escape from it, and desperation.

After being alerted by police to another possible feature of reader interest, I interviewed Joanne, fifteen, frail, scared, and suffering psychologically from hopeless bitterness. "My mother held me while my stepfather beat me with his belt across my face and head. Every Thursday night he would get drunk and come home and work me over. Then my mother kept me home from school so nobody would see the marks on my face."

When does an abused child's emotional breaking point come? "I gave up on New Year's Day when my mother hit me with a mop because I wasn't doing a good enough job washing the floor. She gave me a black eye and a split lip. I couldn't take it any more. I ran."

Joanne, like most other victimized children, stared at the floor without emotion as she spoke in an expressionless voice. Joanne had a runaway partner, fourteen-year-old abused Susan, soft-spoken and nervous, twitching back and forth constantly in her chair as she answered my questions. Both girls had wandered to Worcester from a New Hampshire city in jeans, cotton blouses, and waist-length, imitation suede jackets. Their summer-weight clothes were old, dirty, and filled with holes. The two friends were fleeing from a life they could no longer endure.

Susan: "When I was seven, my mother and father split. My father put me in an orphanage and I stayed there until I was twelve. He came to visit me twice. My mother came more often and tried to support me. At least the orphanage was better than being at home. Once in a while we got some ribbon candy. After they put me away, my mother's boyfriend moved in with her. They got welfare."

Two years later, Susan's mother won custody of her and she moved back home, joining two brothers and a sister, and her mother's common-law husband's three children from a previous marriage. "He gave my mother two more kids. There were nine of us living together. We used to fight. He favored his kids and ignored us," Susan related. The fights became more frequent and more violent.

"I knew what my mother was doing was wrong and I wanted to sit down with her and discuss it. She never would. I had problems and she wouldn't talk with me about them. All I ever got was a whack on the side of the head. Scream, scream, scream. That's all she ever did. I couldn't do anything right. I took off."

Susan told me she was on the verge of a nervous breakdown. "My stepsister had one. My mother had three. She was put away once that I know of. I ran away about ten times in the past two years. Once, I even went to Vermont. I never had any money but I usually stayed away about five days before going home to see if anything had changed. It never had." Susan moved into three different homes in two years. "Finally, I wanted to get some things off my chest to my social worker," she said. Her mother forbade her to leave. She went anyway. Joanne, her friend, also had problems with which she eventually could not cope.

Joanne: "My mother has been married five times. My father was the fourth. He died when I was twelve. He was seventy-two when he died. My grandmother divorced my grandfather and she remarried. When she died, her husband married my mother. He was my grandfather and my stepfather at the same time. He was sixty-six and my mother forty-four. He was a wanderer. Every so often, for a month or so he went back to one of his first wives. He had an awful temper. Every Thursday night he would come home drunk and knock me around for no reason. My mother never tried to stop him. She even held me or sat on me so he could finish beating me. If he didn't use the belt he would grab the closest thing, even a chair. When they left me alone on New Year's I told them I was leaving. They laughed and told me not to bother coming back. They favored my thirteen-year-old brother. He had been arrested three times for setting fires in a warehouse and a gas station."

Susan and Joanne decided to run away together. They said they spent the first two nights with a man they called "Satan," because of the way he looked. A friend drove them to another New Hampshire city where they spent the third night sleeping in a hotel restroom—one of them on the floor, the other in a bathtub. "It was bitter cold," Joanne said.

"Mike the Greek," came along and took them to a doughnut shop where they met Doug, who sympathized with their dilemma and agreed to drive them to Massachusetts. He fed them at a Worcester diner before dropping them off "frozen, scared, and tired." A gas station attendant allowed them to sleep in his car until daylight when he turned them over to a Worcester man who gave them food and shelter before calling his parents for advice. The parents took the two girls into their home, bought them warm clothes, and then contacted Worcester police. Welfare authorities in New Hampshire were notified and they promised new homes for both girls. When my interviews were completed, Susan and Joanne were returned to New Hampshire, dressed in warm new clothing, but with deep-seated apprehensions about their futures.

ABOUT A YEAR LATER, POLICE WERE CALLED TO A DOWNTOWN office building and here they were told that a teenager was on the roof threatening to jump.

"What's your name, son?" one officer asked.

"Tom," he answered, leaning further over the narrow ledge, all that separated him from oblivion.

"How old are you?"

"Fourteen."

"Where do you live?"

"North End."

"You know, don't you son, that this isn't the answer to anything. Killing yourself doesn't solve anything."

"Yes it does. They won't be able to beat me any more."

"We won't let anyone beat you. I promise. I really promise."

"You guys said that before, when you arrested me when I was hungry and stole some food when I was running away from the whippings. They've been hitting me since I was a little kid. Life ain't worth it. I'm not going back there," he said, ending the conversation by turning and preparing to jump.

While the officer talked to the crying boy, trying to calm and, at the same time, distract him, another officer continued to inch his way toward the trembling teenager, a foot at a time, until he was at a point

154 ROSCOE C. BLUNT, JR.

close enough to pounce forward, encircle the youth in a bear hug and yank him backwards to safety.

My story read that the two officers had done their job, had saved a life. What the story did not say was that the rescue saved a life only in one respect. The rescuers were forced to turn the boy over to the only social agency available to them at the time. It was the same agency that previously had remanded an abused boy named Tom to the foster home! This futile aberration of justice was something one had to get used to on a police beat—not ever accept, but get used to.

SEVERAL CRUISERS WITH SIRENS MUTED STEALTHILY RESPONDED TO a break-in-progress call. With military precision and revolvers drawn, several officers surrounded the three-decker and, on a given signal, closed in. With ear pressed against a rear hallway door, one officer could hear faint rattling noises inside the apartment. He turned to other backup officers, nodded silently once and then burst through the door. The burglar was quickly overpowered. He offered no resistance. He was a hungry five-year-old boy looking for cookies. He said he had not eaten all that day. By law, the tot could not be charged with a crime for he was not yet seven, the age of reason when he could distinguish right from wrong.

When the officers returned him to his home, they found three other unattended children, ages four, twelve and fourteen, in a sparsely-furnished apartment with a foodless refrigerator. One of the older girls had been delegated by the mother to be a baby sitter for the day while she went out drinking. The five-year-old had been sent out to forage for food. The apartment, the police report read later, was considered unfit for human habitation from a health standpoint. The cop also wrote that in his estimation the woman, eventually located in a neighborhood barroom, was an unfit mother. The children, upon police recommendation, were placed in the custody of the Department of Social Services (DSS).

ABANDONMENT, POLICE SAY, IS ANOTHER FORM OF CHILD ABUSE. While there are cases of children being abandoned when they are of considerable age, most cases I covered during my tenure involved new born babies. Often, the mothers were teenage girls trying to conceal their pregnancies from their parents. Two years before my retirement, a phone tip from a route car officer told me that a one-day-old baby boy was found abandoned on the doorstep of a home on his route. The infant had been wrapped in a blanket, placed in a wicker basket, and was found in good health. At a local hospital, the infant was quickly named Baby Michael by an adoring nursing staff.

Without hesitation, the family told police they wanted to adopt the baby, but until all the legalities could be worked out, the courts remanded the baby boy to the temporary custody of the state DSS.

Police, baffled at first by the abandonment, researched recent birth records at all area hospitals, standard procedure in such cases. Little by little, pieces of the puzzle fell into place. A grossly overweight young woman had checked herself into a local hospital previously and had given birth to a boy. Later, the woman wrapped him in a blanket during a feeding period and quietly slipped out of the hospital.

Witnesses told police they had seen a woman fitting the new mother's description getting into a taxi and being driven away. Hospital authorities turned over to police a note they found in the woman's maternity room after she disappeared. It read: "Thank you for all you [sic] help with everything. Me & the baby cann't [sic] stay becauce [sic] a problem at home we have. We are both doing fine and I know how to take care of him. I'm gonna give one of the pediatricians at UMass a call to take care of the baby, as I believe this is my decision to leave so their [sic] shouldn't be any problems."

Police said the woman gave the hospital a false name, age, and address when admitted.

Twenty-nine hours after the woman drove away in the taxi, her new-born son was found on the doorstep. With the infant, police found a crudely-written note meant for the family to whom the baby had been consigned. It read: "Bring my baby up like your to [sic] ball players. To [sic] much trash and drugs where I come from. Thank you. His Daddy."

Anxiously, Juvenile Division officers dug into the case to reunite the baby with its natural mother and to help her work out her problems. I published appeals daily to the mother to contact police. Eight days later, the mother called Juvenile Division investigators and agreed to discuss her problems and her reason for abandoning her son. She said she had been agonizing painfully over her decision since reading my stories.

Police contacted the DSS to determine what options were open to the mother. During her initial meeting with police, the woman said she was afraid of her father's reaction to her out-of-wedlock baby. Baby Michael was placed in a temporary foster home. A week later, the mother reappeared at Police Headquarters to reclaim her son. I convinced her that due to the tremendous human interest and concern the case had generated in the city, she should share Baby Michael with the world by allowing me to run a picture of him. She agreed and the whole city smiled that night. Before Michael and his unwed mother bowed out of the public limelight, she told me she planned to keep the name her baby had been given by hospital nurses. Michael it would be.

Child abuse, because it strikes so close to the emotions of most police officers, is a commonly discussed subject over the cups of coffee on which cops practically survive. But, the discussions often are filled with the helplessness confronting police who readily admit that nothing they do will produce a solution to the child abuse problem. There is no perfect world, they conceded. Being realists, police know that intelligence, maturity, and parental good judgment cannot be legislated. They say all they can hope for is that their prompt intervention, in each case, will keep the child involved from more serious physical and emotional trauma, or even death.

rivalries: municipal, county, state, and federal egos

POLICE ARE HIGHLY COMPETITIVE. ONE-UPMANSHIP IS THE NAME of the game. Cops compete with the public, with other law enforcement agencies, and, if they cannot find anyone else with whom to contend, they even vie among themselves. On a police beat, a reporter constantly is confronted by police officers wearing what they refer to as "a heavy badge," usually worn by new officers who have not yet been tempered by time on the job and the realities of the street. Older officers seldom correct the methods of over-zealous rookies. They let society do that.

The best recourse a police reporter has when facing down heavy-handed new cops is to ignore them, to make them think that until they pay their dues, they are not worth acknowledging. With the monumental egos that are sometimes issued at swearing-in ceremonies with the uniform, badge, and sidearm, these officers can seldom handle rejection. Fortunately for police reporters and society, the vast majority of police officers do not fall into this category. But unfortunately, too many do.

There is considerable psychology involved in police reporting. Egos have to be massaged constantly, and the personality shortcomings of those with whom you are often in conflict have to be recognized and dealt with, often by circumvention. A police reporter, when demeaned by a police officer, must learn to react swiftly in self-defense, based on the offending officer's personality, and position in the department. Operating in a police environment is a perpetual battle of wits, adapting to and constantly coping with varying situations. When facing off against a confrontational officer, the reporter must not budge an inch, nor blink first.

Police officers are street fighters. Reporters, on the other hand, often sheltered by the confines of the Fourth Estate, must learn to live and let live, if they are to survive the rigors of coexistence in the cops' world. Too often, police officers and reporters become natural adversaries. Only through years of acclimation and a stronger understanding of each other can this be diminished—never eliminated, just diminished. Many officers are almost paranoid about what the world is doing to them, but seldom are they concerned about what they, in turn, are doing to that same world.

Police reporters must learn to accept, or at least live and work with certain peculiarities within the "police mentality"—one of which is the impossibility to satisfy a cop. I found, through the years, that with many officers, no matter how much was done for them, no matter how many favors were granted, or "freebies" offered, there was never enough. The secret was to turn that almost inherent greed to the advantage of the reporter.

As the months on the beat extended into years, I settled into a routine of observing, listening, learning what to see and what not to see, what to hear and what not to hear, what to report and what to walk away from. To survive working inside a police station, and that is the name of the game for both reporters and cops, I had to polish a writing style and technique that allowed for certain small degrees of discrimination when writing a story, without compromising the journalistic ethics to which I so staunchly strived to adhere.

To win over those with attitude problems, I used as leverage the similarities between the two jobs. Investigators search for truth while reporters try to determine fact, I reminded them. Reporters and police investigators both spend much of their time talking to people reluctant to talk to them. And lastly, I argued that neither police nor reporters are particularly popular in most communities.

Regardless of the similarities, there always existed an unspoken confrontational feeling between the two sides, and there probably always will. Both parties engaged in the confrontation are suspicious by nature simply because their careers make them so. In only a very few instances did these Mexican stand-off situations erupt into direct threats and counter-threats of reprisal. When almost everything else failed, I resorted to the tactic that a strong offense is a good defense. There came a time when my patience with childish, vindictive officers came to an end. When that happened, I pulled out the ultimate weapon: ignoring their deeds while glorifying those of others. I kicked off an all out campaign of writing about the State Police, the Registry of Motor Vehicles, the FBI, Bureau of Alcohol, Tobacco and Firearms (ATF), and even suburban police departments where the chiefs, in my earlier days on the beat in their districts, had become long time contacts. Most of them were only too happy to have their departments recognized at long last.

Whenever other law enforcement agencies sneezed, it rated a glowing feature. Federal agencies, whom many in the public had never even heard of, were now making headlines over my byline. I gave full-page coverage to the FBI's on-going fight against organized crime and booking operations in the city. I wrote of ATF arrests and investigations into bombings and illegal possession of weapons. I parlayed into lengthy feature stories rides throughout the night with State Police troopers, telling of how troopers rid the highways of drunk drivers and enforce Chapter 90 highway laws.

Then a strange phenomenon developed. I started getting calls from many law enforcement sources who had largely ignored me in the past. State Police seldom, if ever, called me for anything. Now they were. So was the FBI and other small town police departments. The wave was surging. I wrote features about anyone and everyone: except Worcester Police.

The same tactic worked effectively within the department where inter-divisional jealousies were always rampant. The "slight them all" campaign worked, if and when I wrote about the department at all. When detectives insulted me, swore at me, or in any other manner demeaned me, I wrote about every other division in the department, even the garage mechanics, but never once about the Detective Bureau. Inter-service rivalry, in many instances, was so acute that the commander of one work relief (midnight to 8 A.M.) vehemently accused me of ignoring his men while writing too much about the accomplishments of other reliefs.

If there is anything that sticks in the craw of the average police officer it is when some other agency gets, or unjustly steals credit for solving a major crime case. Through the years, it was almost comedic to stand on the sidelines observing the indignant outrage of investigators and commanders, when other individuals or agencies jockeyed for position to obtain an undeserved headline. One of the prime offenders was the district attorney's office, always finely tuned to a credit headline when other agencies more often than not did all the digging and footwork. To give my tormentors a dose of their own medicine this was the Achilles heel of the unabashed police ego that I often used to my own advantage.

Intense rivalry between local, state, and federal agencies was a constant in law enforcement. Headline grabbing was a skillful art practiced by many who wore badges. To leave another law enforcement agency out in the cold when a story was given out was standard practice for many individuals or agencies. Police generally spoke in superlatives. If local police did something, State Police often claimed something bigger, faster, or better. On occasion, the feds chimed in with more boastful claims. This professional pettiness was further compounded by a publicity-seeking, self-glorifying district attorney claiming he had done something bigger and better than anyone would ever be able to repeat again in the future.

It became a circus of one agency vying against another for media attention, a circus that, sitting back I often laughed at, all the while skillfully working to best advantage one side against the other. One-upmanship was the name of the game: and I was always the referee. A steady stream of "puff" stories extolling other department's accomplishments irked the city's finest, many of whom considered themselves the most overworked, underpaid, least appreciated, and most put upon of all peoples on the earth. For more than a month, I turned my back on those who had perpetually ground me under their collective heels.

The first leak in the dike that developed between me and some in the department came when a few divisional commanders, ethically unable to volunteer stories to the media themselves, sent clandestine messengers to the pressroom to disclose sketchy details of a story. One of the purposes behind this trend, one that was never spoken aloud, was the hope that I, in return, would come running to those commanders for all the gory information. This, many of them thought, would open up the opportunity for their names to be prominently mentioned in my stories. I didn't bite.

Begrudgingly to be sure, but steadily, the invisible barrier that separated me from many in the department was gradually being dismantled. It was only a matter of time before those who had been the most vindictive in my regard would be sucking around again trying to curry favor. But, I had a long memory, and never fully forgave most of them, even after they retired.

One of the first lessons I learned on the beat, a lesson that helped shape my approach to news coverage, was that there are two types of police officers: those who itch to get their names in the paper and those who fight hard to keep it out. I learned quickly which were which and played them accordingly. "Hero today, bum tomorrow," was a common police response thrown at me when I attempted to do "pat-on-the-back" features about some officers. The road to respectability was indeed long for many officers. If there is an eternal verity in police work, it is the defensive attitude of many officers, bordering on paranoia in some, about what society does to them.

Grabbing headlines from fellow officers was the accepted practice among detectives. A uniformed officer tracks down, apprehends, and holds at gunpoint a blood covered murder suspect. When he radios for assistance, detectives gallop in. In the case of the strangling murder of a news vendor, a foot beat officer develops the information that leads to an arrest. In neither case do the names of the officers appear in Detective Bureau journals.

A Worcester detective, through street information, learned the out-of-city whereabouts of three much sought after, heavily armed bank robbers. Together with the police in the other city, the Worcester detective apprehended the trio without incident. His mistake in the whole caper was, however, making a courtesy call to the district attorney's office notifying them of the impending raid. The DA's men arrived after the arrests were effected and the danger over, but they felt compelled to conduct a large scale press conference during which the Worcester detective was not mentioned, even in the fine print.

Tired of the abrasive arrogance of politically assigned detectives, I, in retaliation, devised a devious scheme for their crass treatment. Every plain clothes investigator I interviewed or quoted in the Juvenile Division or Vice Squad, I promoted to "detective" in print. Uniformed officers who went out of their way to make my job easier, slipping confidential reports under my pressroom door before I arrived for work, or remaining at the station on their own time after their work relief was completed to fill me in on an incident, became "investigator" so-and-so. Some, received full-blown titles. The more help that was given, the longer and more impressive the titles became. Soon, cops everywhere were vying for one of Blunt's classic, always different, personalized titles for their family scrapbooks.

Resentment from the "defective bureau" was instantaneous. Those who had been stripped of their vaunted titles in my news stories resorted to the oldest police punishment: shunning. This punishment had little or no effect on my news coverage capabilities, for the bulk of the police work is traditionally performed by uniformed divisions. I was usually able to develop full detail news stories during that period from my other "Detectives," "Investigators," and "Deputy Commissioners in Charge of Investigative Procedures" and "Crime Analysis Supervisor of Detailed Operations and Advanced Tactics."

For thirty years I tiptoed the fine line straddling the egos, arrogance, vindictiveness, and ignorance of many. But, at the same I also walked in the glow of many staunch friendships. Before it all ended, I had surely earned an advanced degree in the practice of amateur psychology.

homicide

PRACTICALLY NO CRIME TRIGGERS MORE SORROW, MORE OUTRAGE, and intensive, sustained, all-out police effort, in a community, than murder. No other crime is more final, tears more viciously into the moral fiber of a community, or is more unacceptable in a civilized society. Murder comes in every imaginable form possible, is committed for any conceivable motive, and, according to police, is the least preventable. And, above all, for police, it is often one of the most intricate of all crimes to solve.

Some homicides are solvable almost instantly. All the pieces of the pie—the murder weapon, the motive, eye-witnesses, material witnesses, physical evidence, even a confessed killer—are waiting for police when they arrive at the crime scene. These are the few easy ones that are neatly wrapped up and packaged in a matter of days.

But more often, homicide solutions are not handed on a platter to police. They require weeks, months, even years of leg work to interview hundreds of people, to search meticulously for evidence or weapons, or to painstakingly track down suspects who have fled the country. In some cases, the element of luck makes the difference.

When everything possible has been done fruitlessly to determine a culprit, police sometimes are destined to wait patiently, with eyes open and ears to the ground, for someone's memory or conscience to kick into gear. Even a deathbed confession will do. It is a maxim in police work that a homicide case is never closed; until it is solved, it is merely reclassified as inactive.

Homicide, rape, and highway fatalities are three areas of law enforcement that are largely unenforceable. Murder, statistics show, is usually committed without premeditation, and is apt to be a spur of the moment crime of passion, of uncontrolled rage, or the result of a robbery or barroom brawl. More than half of those killed on the highway are the result of alcohol consumption, again outside of police intervention. Rape, like murder, can result from a variety of circumstances ranging from commission during a burglary, to loss of reason because of intoxication, to date rape, to chance encounters. Police describe rape as a murder in which the victim survives.

The resolution factor in homicide fluctuates greatly. During my thirty-year tenure at Worcester Police Headquarters I and II, I reported about 400 homicides. Some years, the percentage of the cases solved was low. Other years, police sported an almost perfect solution ratio. For example, in the year 1988, eleven of the city's twelve homicide cases—better than ninety-one percent—were closed with arrests and convictions or state hospital commitments. Lieutenant John McKiernan, Chief of Detectives, and one of the department's top investigators, points to a massive file of solved homicides and says, "During the twelve years I have been in the Detective Bureau (1980 to 1992) we have solved ninety-two per cent of the murders. Sounds pretty good, doesn't it? Only ten unsolved out of every 120. That is not good enough. If you project that solution percentage over thirty-six years, there remain thirty unsolved homicides. That is far from satisfactory, in fact, not acceptable at all."

Time is the major stumbling block hampering police investigations into homicides, veteran investigators say. In most instances, if the murder investigation is not completed and the case solved within forty-eight hours, while the memories of witnesses are fresh, before evidence is lost or destroyed, and before suspects can flee beyond the case jurisdiction, the chances of a solution decrease rapidly. Police maintain that it is imperative that the case be cracked while all the elements involved are still hot. With each passing hour the chances of solving a murder case diminish. In the old black and white gumshoe movies of yesteryear, the dialogue usually was "the trail is still hot," or "we're following a cold trail."

What was true then remains true today. Every case remains open, no matter how long, until it is closed with a solution. But, police admit, many unsolved cases reach the point where sheer luck will be the determining factor. "There's always hope," investigators say. "We always have to believe that new evidence will eventually turn up or that someone will come forward with the missing piece of testimony needed to button up a case. It happens," they maintain. In police circles, being a good detective also means being an optimist.

Detectives commit themselves to a hectic life of constant phone calls, even in the middle of the night; interrupted vacations; case progress conferences; analyzing evidence; attending gruesome autopsies; pounding pavements searching for witnesses; and pressure from the media. There is no clock in a detective's life when a homicide investigation is under way. He or she, for example, is on twenty-four-hour call, every day of the year, and his bedside phone tattoos his eardrums regularly. When a murder is committed in the city, fourteen to sixteen detectives—seven or eight teams—are assigned to the case. This almost instantaneous massive involvement in the investigation is the best defense against the detectives' primary adversary: time. An all out investigative effort is imperative at the outset to blanket all aspects of the case as soon as possible.

One team secures and meticulously searches the crime scene. A weapons search is conducted over wide areas if need be. Sewers are emptied; metal detectors sweep tall grass and wooded areas; buildings, vehicles, and dumpsters are searched; lakes are scoured by scuba teams. No avenue of exploration is overlooked.

A second team moves in, dusts the crime scene for fingerprints, photographs the victim and every object that may be related in any way to the crime. This must be methodically done, for in many cases the photographs and any dusted prints found will play an integral part in future court presentations.

A third team tries to identify the victim through the files of the police Bureau of Criminal Identification, distinguishing marks on the body, dental charts, clothing, morgue IDs by friends or family. If all else fails, news media are enlisted to publish a description of the victim or an appeal to the public for information. Coordination of these investigative actions usually produces an ID, so that family notifications can be made.

When victim identification is established, a fourth team of detectives notifies the family of the victim or victims. With this done, the team maintains open informational channels with the victim's family, updating them periodically on the progress of the investigation.

A fifth team of investigators is assigned to locate and interview eye witnesses, possible material witnesses, and anyone else who may contribute information relative to the case. This, police say, is one of the most vital of all investigative avenues. If the investigation drags on or bogs down, this team may interview upwards of several hundred people. Relatives, business associates, social acquaintances—practically anyone who came in contact with the victim when he or she was living—have to be questioned. Often, these interviews are conducted repeatedly as new leads are developed. This is followed by the painstaking, slow process of correlating hundreds of pages of testimony to weed out duplication and establish a central focus to the investigation.

Still another team knocks on doors, canvassing neighborhoods, housing developments, business establishments, recreational areas and shopping malls. Possible eye witnesses are sought in even the most remote locations, those not believed at the outset to be related to the crime. The intensive leg work continues for as long as it takes to open a crack in the mystery surrounding the killing. If the investigation eventually starts to point in one direction, and the number of possible suspects is successfully narrowed down, another team of detectives hits the streets to dig out of hiding those possibly involved. If the investigation suddenly focuses on one or several suspects, more teams are assigned to the search.

Physical evidence found, including weapons, is analyzed in State Police crime laboratories in Boston or at FBI laboratories in Washington, D.C. Because these agencies are overwhelmed by the preponderance of evidence sent to them each year, they are often agonizingly slow returning test results to the investigating department. If urgency warrants it, requests for psychological profiles of a suspect, and samples for blood analysis, chromosome and DNA [a genetic molecule that, because it does not vary from cell to cell, is used to determine whether semen, hair, or blood at a crime scene matches that of a suspect] tests, are hand-delivered to the FBI to hasten the process.

It is imperative that the initial step in a homicide investigation—securing and searching the crime scene—is done correctly and thoroughly the first time. "You only get to do it once. After that, rain, snow, wind, or people walking over the crime scene obliterate overlooked evidence," veteran investigators say.

From the outset of the investigation, police try hour-by-hour, minute-by-minute to trace the activities, whereabouts, and last known companions of the victim. The closer police can come to the time of the actual crime, the more enhanced the chances of a solution become.

As soon as is feasible after a murder has been committed, police notify the district attorney responsible for prosecuting the case in court. Thereafter, police touch base with the assistant DA assigned to the case, offering daily updated reports. Conversely, the systemic inquiry is strengthened with legal advice and counseling to investigators and their superiors. This ensures that the search remains on firm legal footing as it progresses. A case in point involved the bludgeoning death of a seventeen-year-old high school student near her home, in 1984. It remains open and still unsolved, but not for lack of effort. Nearly 400 interviews were conducted over the years.

When police feel they have amassed enough evidence or witness testimony to bring the case to court, they huddle again with the district attorney. If they agree that they have an "iron clad" case, arrest warrants are issued. If a suspect out of the local jurisdiction is taken into custody, rendition or extradition proceedings are instituted. If, on the other hand, the suspect for whom an arrest warrant has been issued is located locally or within the state, as many as thirty detectives and uniformed officers may be used to make the arrest, especially if the suspect is believed to be armed and unwilling to surrender without force. A battle plan is formulated. Every officer has a specific assignment and is responsible for carrying it out effectively. The building where the suspect is holed up is stealthily surrounded with teams of officers at every door and window. Entry is battered into the building as suddenly as possible to assure an element of surprise.

A major stumbling block in solving many homicides, police say, is the lack of eye witnesses to the crime and lack of physical evidence. Every year, in Worcester, the majority of those murdered were prostitutes or street derelicts with little or no ties to the community. Witnesses to these crimes are usually other derelicts, their brains and memories so sodden by booze that they seldom have any recollection of where they were, much less what they saw during the commission of a crime. The majority of those murdered each year are apt to be what police call "low life" residents in areas frequented by hookers, drug traffickers and addicts, teenage gangs, or alcoholics drawn like magnets from throughout the city to inebriation shelters.

The solution of murder cases often is a "lucky roll of the dice," the fate that hands police the components of a mystery on a platter in one instance, or yanks them away just as inexplicably in the next. Someone witnessed the crime, or no one did. Fate. Tell-tale physical evidence was left at the scene or it was not. Fate. Someone comes forward to offer vital information, or everyone hides in the shadows. Again, fate.

No two murders are identical, nor are the motives behind them. No two witnesses see things the same way. No two means of killing are the same. They may be pistols, knives, baseball bats, shotguns, machetes, lumber, clubs, flashlights, fists, shod feet, fire, daggers, kitchen knives, switch blades, concrete blocks and rocks, pillows, ropes, and hands, or eyes burned out with cigarettes, genitals sliced off, or breasts carved off. Only the degree of viciousness varies. But in homicide it is a truism that there is absolutely no limit whatsoever to the violence or methods used by one person to inflict death on another. Often, the degree of barbarism is limited only by the imagination or anger of the killer.

MY FIRST MAJOR MURDER STORY STARTED ME OFF WITH A BANG soon after I was assigned to the police beat. A thirty-five-year-old man, living in a suburban area, was apprehended by two Worcester police officers after he went on a rampage, stabbing his wife and two small children in a nearby town; then murdering his former wife in another town, a few miles away. He effectively wiped out almost his entire past domestic life in one fit of demented rage.

According to police accounts, the man stabbed his eight-month pregnant wife who managed to grab her two-year-old son and nine-year-old daughter and stagger from her home before collapsing a few feet away. The accused killer, waving the knife wildly, ran after her before repeatedly stabbing her and her children with an eleven inch kitchen knife as they lay terrified and screaming on the ground. With her last breaths of life, the wife continued to fight off her attacker to protect her children. But the butcher knife, wielded over and over by her almost maniacal husband, won the battle. The blood of the three victims soaked the earth beside the family station wagon where the woman had sought to escape from her attacker before she bled to death.

A third child, age fourteen, ran screaming hysterically to a neighbor for help. When police and neighbors arrived, they found the dead woman's two small children moaning and whimpering softly, and bleeding profusely beside their mother's blood-covered body. Both died before medical assistance could be administered.

The killer then drove a few miles away, where his thirty-five-year-old former wife lived with their four small children. Police said the killer entered the family kitchen and calmly kissed his children before he viciously attacked their mother, stabbing her repeatedly until she too was dead. As soon as the frightening news spread throughout the two normally serene towns, a Worcester County all points police bulletin was issued identifying the killer and describing the pickup truck he was last seen driving. A short time later, two Worcester police officers spotted the truck, blockaded it with their vehicles, and took the killer into custody without resistance. Arraigned in court the next day, he was remanded to a state psychiatric hospital for an indefinite term.

ONE OF THE MORE COLD-BLOODED MURDERS IN THE CITY OCCURRED the next week when a thirty-year-old branch bank manager, the brother of a Worcester police officer, was shot in the head as he lay on the floor during an armed robbery by four masked men. It was a senseless crime, one that outraged the community. As the four nylon-masked gunmen fled from the bank with $7,477 in cloth bags, one of the men, a long-time hoodlum noted for his violence, leaned over the teller counter and calmly fired a large caliber round into the back of the manager's head. The manager was one of three tellers and five customers forced to lie face down on the floor by the gunmen during the robbery. Despite emergency surgery, the manager died a few hours later.

In a desperate escape attempt, the robbers careened wildly away from the bank at high speed, in a stolen car, doubling back and forth over several North End side streets to throw off possible pursuers before heading back toward the downtown business district. The car swerved from side to side out of control before crashing into a tree. Three stunned bandits staggered from the wreckage, and limped away in separate directions through back yards and wooded areas. The fourth gunman, the shooter during the stick-up, managed to leap from the speeding vehicle before it rammed the tree.

Police responding to the bank robbery call quickly diverted their strength to the car crash scene when residents were flooding head-quarters with calls about suspicious looking men, with guns in their hands, running through their yards. Within minutes, cruisers fanned out, covering the residential neighborhood from four sides. As one officer climbed over a fence in pursuit of one bandit, a shot was fired at him. The officer managed to get off one round as he dove for the ground. At that moment, a second bandit, not realizing it was a cop lying on the ground, ran past him. More shots were fired.

Four residents of the area, hearing the car crash and gunfire outside their home, rushed vigilante-style to assist police. More shots were fired. In the confusion, police and assisting civilians were not sure who was shooting, the bandits or police. Moments later, one of the gunmen was tackled by a former prep school football player and held for police.

A bloodied bandit smashed his way into a nearby clergyman's home and demanded help. When a member of the family phoned for the police ambulance, the gunman lurched back outside and fell into the arms of police with drawn revolvers already closing in on the minister's home.

A month later, after one of the more intense manhunts I ever covered, "Joe the Pollock," the fourth bank robbery suspect, was apprehended by FBI agents in Kansas City, Missouri. At their trial in Worcester Superior Court, the four suspects were led into court heavily manacled, each with multiple jail guards, State Police, and Worcester police surrounding them, almost completely shielding them from the view of court spectators and reporters in the press row.

During the trial, the defendant accused of being the shooter stood up in the prisoners' dock, screamed hysterically, and tried to smash a heavy court chair over the head of one of his co-conspirators, in an apparent murder attempt. When guards and court officers wrestled him into submission and order was restored, the judge peered down at me and motioned me to the bench. As I leaned forward to hear him, he whispered, "I don't want to read about that in the newspaper. Do you understand me?" I nodded obediently and returned to my seat while the four bank robbers kept their eyes sullenly riveted on my every move.

When the trial was recessed for lunch toward the end of the deliberations, the trigger man's defense lawyer offered to buy me lunch at a nearby restaurant. Sensing a subtle bribery attempt, I declined. Later in the trial, the trigger man made an impassioned plea to the jury about his unhappy childhood and his many years spent in prison. After a brief jury deliberation, the four were found guilty of bank robbery, murder, and numerous other charges. All were sentenced to life imprisonment.

A FEW MONTHS LATER, THE POLICE RADIO IN THE PRESSROOM crackled that a car had tried to climb a utility pole near a troubled, low-income housing project, in the city's North End. Routine motor vehicle accident. I figured I had plenty of time to get the report later, when it was filed in the Bureau of Records by the investigating officer at the station, and still make deadline. Then the radio dispatcher casually mentioned, over the air, that the accident was a possible homicide. I sprung into action.

When police first arrived, the car was standing on its tail, its front end dangling from a guy wire supporting the pole. As EMTs (Emergency Medical Technicians) lifted the driver from the car's blood-soaked front seat, he repeatedly moaned," I've been shot. Get my lawyer." He died a few hours later while undergoing surgery. An autopsy revealed he had been shot ten times in the neck, chest, arm, and shoulder. Police determined that the driver, a small-time hood, had been shot elsewhere and was driving himself to the hospital when he fainted at the wheel from loss of blood.

Four months later, a man holding a handkerchief over his face calmly walked into a rug store in the city's Summit section and pumped four slugs into the store owner's chest and leg. One bullet fired during the fusillade wounded a musician who having fallen on hard times, was working as a store clerk. When questioned about the shooting, he turned into a clam. Four weeks later, the partially decomposed, bullet-riddled corpse of a man well known to police was dumped in woods on the outskirts of the city, four bullets in the back of his head—a gangland execution. Police confirmed that the paths of both victims had crossed and theorized that the violent deaths had underworld connections. No motive was ever established in the three cases and the investigations into each soon petered out.

THE CITY WAS SHOCKED IN EARLY JULY 1967, WHEN I REPORTED that an eighty-five-year-old woman was harassed and taunted to death in her home by a gang of neighborhood teenagers "just having some fun," on their way home from a church youth group meeting. Terrified, the woman called police for help. As she talked to the police Communications Division, she suddenly collapsed and died of a fright-induced heart attack. Within hours, Juvenile Division investigators had six of the gang rounded up and charged with harassment. Showing little remorse, they claimed the harassment was only a spur of the moment prank. They did not know the woman and had chosen her house at random.

Almost immediately, investigators voiced skepticism about the outcome of the case. One officer confided in me that all of the youths, both boys and girls, were from affluent families and he did not expect much, if any, punishment to be meted out, or even a disposition to be rendered in the case. Juvenile Court proceedings were kept unusually secretive and no dispositions were ever divulged. Police saw it as another form of homicide.

Throughout my career on the police beat, I became increasingly disturbed by what seemed to be two standards of justice in society, one for the affluent, another for the poor. It was just a feeling, spawned by too many closed door court hearings, too frequent plea bargaining, too many courthouse quashed charges, and punishment too lenient for those who police maintained were "connected."

IN MID-OCTOBER 1967, A BARROOM OWNER WAS FOUND WITH HIS head reduced to a pulp by a twelve pound sledgehammer that the victim kept in the kitchen of the café. The injuries were so severe, the skull so fragmented, it was almost impossible to determine how many times he had been bludgeoned. In a strange twist, the attacker placed a towel underneath the victim's head, apparently to prevent the massive bleeding from staining the barroom floor. An autopsy revealed that the killer, to make sure his victim was dead, pumped a "coup de grace" .22 caliber bullet between what had once been the victim's eyes. Detectives milling about the bloody corpse and lake of blood on the barroom floor and on chairs, tables and walls, caught a glimpse out of the corner of their eye of a drifter and part time sweeper at the café. He was casually rifling the cash register and stuffing money in his pocket, while with their backs turned, they examined the corpse. He was charged with larceny of forty dollars.

Catch basins in a one mile radius from the beer joint were emptied searching for a gun and the victim's wallet. Nothing was ever found. Investigators questioned employees, the victim's wife, and neighbors about possible robbery motives: drunken fight, sexual encounters, domestic difficulties, or jealousy. More than thirty years later, the case remains unsolved.

THE NUDE, FROZEN BODY OF A TWENTY-ONE-YEAR-OLD CLARK University student was discovered, covered by cardboard, in a shallow roadside ditch, two months later. She had been strangled. Several days later, her clothing was found in a suburban town five miles away. On Easter Sunday in April 1968, a seventeen-year-old Blackstone Valley girl was found floating face down in a quarry-like pond adjacent to a junior high school. She had been stabbed fatally in the abdomen with a two-pronged dandelion remover. Investigators traced her whereabouts covering the several days before she was murdered, but, as often happened, they were unable to connect the last few hours of her life. The killers were never found and both cases remain open.

SOME MONTHS LATER, A TRIPLE MURDER WAS SOLVED, ALMOST before the eyes of the investigators. Three people had been shot to death and a fourth person critically wounded in what police deemed to be a triple homicide and an attempted suicide. It was the case of an estranged husband wanting to kill his wife and everyone who happened to be around her at the time. The killer, during his rampage, turned two rubbish-strewn apartments into shooting galleries. When police battered the door at the second apartment, the killer turned the gun on himself. Investigators poked through the blood-spattered areas, digging bullet slugs out of walls and furniture for evidence.

IN MID-JUNE 1970, IN WHAT POLICE CALLED A RACIAL ATTACK, THE stabbing death of a nineteen-year-old Polish immigrant in the city's Island District, again inflamed the emotions of city residents. The murder victim had been in the United States only seven years. The stabbing was cold blooded and unprovoked. It took place near the youth's home shortly after police dispersed an out of control rock concert, at a nearby park. The concert was shut down by police after roving gangs of teenagers started attacking one another in the park and on nearby streets during the concert. Witnesses told police that a group of black youths swarmed over the victim and his brother. Shouts of "Hey, Whitey. Get 'em. Get 'em. Hold 'em. Kill 'em," rang out in the darkened street. Mortally wounded, the victim stumbled toward his home. His brother was also assaulted by the gang but managed to run away. As quickly as the viciousness started, it was over. Laughing gang members scattered through back yards and were swallowed up by the night. An autopsy revealed that a long bladed knife was plunged once into the youth's back, puncturing a lung. Police said the attack was racially motivated. Conclusion: The case of a youth being in the wrong place at the wrong time.

Twenty-nine detectives were assigned to the case. A year later, they were still digging. There were volumes of hearsay evidence and contradictions. Lots of third-hand eye witness accounts such as "I know a kid at school who knows someone who says he knows everything and was actually there," were checked out and eventually discarded. In the end, the finger of suspicion was narrowed down to one youth, another teenager. But again, justice was denied: again and again, the suspect's mother refused to allow police near her son. The mother staunchly reminded detectives that he had constitutional rights against incriminating himself. Months later, I received a letter at the newspaper naming the alleged killer. I turned the letter over to police. The suspect named in the letter was the same teenager originally zeroed in by the investigators. The identification I gave them was ground that police had already covered multiple times. The case file remains open.

THREE MONTHS LATER ON A LOVELY AUTUMN MORNING, I ARRIVED at work and was greeted by a uniformed officer climbing into his cruiser, "You are going to be busy today, Rock." The night log in the Dispatch Room clarified the cop's comment to me. A popular sixty-seven-year-old North End church priest had been stabbed to death and robbed of seventy-five dollars in his rectory by a State Hospital mental patient escapee. Investigators said another priest in the rectory heard the murdered pastor's car being stolen and when he went to the victim's quarters to tell him, he found the priest's mutilated body in the rectory office, his head propped against a chair in which he had been either reading or watching television. An autopsy revealed the priest was repeatedly stabbed in the chest and neck. A bloody jack-knife was recovered.

Worcester police arrived at the church rectory within minutes and broadcast a description of the dead priest's car over the regional police radio network. Eighty-five minutes after the murder was discovered, a suburban town police officer on routine patrol, with the help of two backup officers, apprehended the suspect.

Without even pausing to catch his breath, the patient's defense attorney announced publicly he would cop an insanity plea after his client completed a psychiatric examination. At the time of the murder, the suspect was free on continuances granted by the court six days before, on charges of assault and battery with a dangerous weapon (a pipe), breaking, entering, and larceny, malicious mischief, and drunkenness.

FROM MY VANTAGE POINT AT HEADQUARTERS, ON A NUMBER OF occasions, I reported homicides in suburban towns and elsewhere. However, the most prominent case involved the shooting murder of a Boston cop during a bank robbery, and the massive man hunt throughout the eastern seaboard for his killer. Only days after the stabbing murder of a city priest, I sat in my easy chair munching on a sandwich and reading the paper, relaxed in the knowledge that I had gotten past another deadline without major incident. I was only sub-consciously listening to the squawk box over my desk. For all practical purposes, my work day was over. The monitor droned about a state trooper following a car headed toward the city from the Massachusetts Turnpike. Nothing unusual, or even of interest. When suburban police called Worcester police to alert them, I continued eating. The calls were routine, nothing about which to be concerned.

Then the dispatcher's voice boomed louder over the air, "Attention all units. Attention all units. A car containing William Gilday, wanted for the murder of a Boston police officer, is heading into the city. The car is being followed by an off-duty trooper in an unmarked car. Gilday is armed and considered extremely dangerous. Use all caution. What units are responding?"

Suddenly, the name Gilday cut through my subconscious. He, with three others, was being sought during a week long, six state manhunt, in connection with the murder of Boston Patrolman Walter Schroeder during a bank robbery. Almost hourly during that time, all points bulletins had been issued throughout a nine state region for him. Without taking the time even to find a pencil or paper, I bounded up three flights of stairs to the Detective Bureau. The chief was already there, and several detectives were milling around preparing for the accused cop-killer's capture. As I barreled through the DB door, the chief greeted me. "My men have got him, Rock, and are on the way in with him."

With that, he locked the door behind me, adding, "It's OK to stay here but if you leave, I won't be able to let you back in." I snatched a discarded envelope from a wastebasket and a pencil off a detective's desk. I was ready. Minutes later, "Lefty" Gilday and two alleged hostages were shoved into the room, surrounded by a phalanx of state troopers adorned with bandoleers of rifle ammunition criss-crossing their chests like Pancho Villa's banditos. It was a kaleidoscope of motion and sound, everything moving fast in a surrealistic drama. An impromptu mob of city cops burst into the room. When the outer door was again closed and locked for the final time, there was scant room to move around.

Furiously, I started to transcribe everything I observed. Nearby, Detective Sergeant Ted Peterson smiled and said jokingly, "Good day for reporters, huh?" Knowing how important and newsworthy the apprehension was to me, the chief motioned me closer to where the accused killer was seated. He told me that one of his officers, had swerved his cruiser in front of the wanted vehicle, blocking it from entering a street rotary. When the car abruptly tried to outmaneuver the cruiser roadblock by careening the wrong way around the rotary, it ran into another roadblock of three motorcycles, forcing it to stop. As it did so, the state trooper overpowered one of the alleged hostages who tried to flee out of the passenger side with a revolver in his hand. A city motorcycle officer wrenched the driver's door and wrestled Gilday out of the vehicle and into cuffs before he could reach beneath the front seat of the car for a loaded, large caliber revolver.

A caravan of six State Police cruisers, four others from Worcester Police, three motorcycles, and a police helicopter escorted Gilday and his two reported hostages to police headquarters. "Let me know what you need and I'll get it for you," the chief offered. Frantically, I wrote my impressions and asked questions as the hubbub started to simmer down.

I glanced at my watch: 12:45 P.M. and almost two hours past deadline. Without raising anyone's attention, I eased my way to the nearest telephone and called the City Desk, where an agitated managing editor started a torrent of sputtering questions. "I've got the whole story already!" I yelled at him, sounding as dramatic as I could. "I'll dictate it! I'll call you right back!" I slammed the phone down quickly before more questions could be asked or any orders issued. I had just bought myself a few more minutes of time. I was determined to play this one out my way. The paper could not call me back. They did not know where I was, and operators at headquarters were under strict orders from the chief not to transfer outside calls to the DB.

The chief, always willing to help me for he was a long-time proud navy veteran who knew that one of my sons was headed for the U.S. Naval Academy at Annapolis, tore himself away from the core of activity and instantly, accurately, and patiently answered my eager questions. Then he prevailed upon state police to give me what they had.

Within minutes, I was back on the phone rapidly dictating the complete capture story. I knew I had a nationwide exclusive, and the adrenaline was pumping. I happened to glance out a window and on the street below was a group of more than a dozen print and television reporters and cameramen, jumping up and down, waving their arms in frustration. They were locked out and no spokesman had been assigned to brief them on the arrest. I thanked the chief profusely and then collapsed in a corner to catch my breath. I glanced at my watch again. It was a few minutes after one P.M., two hours past normal deadline, but still in time to get most of Page One under my by-line.

A few days later, the chief phoned the brass at the newspaper telling them that he and all of the other police agencies involved in the Gilday capture agreed that my story was the most accurate of those published, and that I had covered it in a "cool, efficient, and courteous manner under very difficult circumstances." The managing editor did manage to drop me an inter-office note saying my beat coverage was one of the "strong points of the *Gazette* and my coverage of the Gilday capture was a time of excellence and I more than rose to the occasion." Glowing praise from those who seldom gave it.

Nine months later, United Press International announced that four *Gazette* reporters had been awarded a prize for spot news coverage of the Gilday caper. Nowhere during the capture were any of the other reporters seen by anyone. They surely were not reporting the story from Gilday's side inside the station. But, as often was the case, I had the last laugh. Sometime afterwards, ten officers were honored by the Worcester Lodge of Elks for capturing the, by then convicted, cop killer. I was included in the ceremony, and was presented a Governor's Council proclamation and an award for my work. Of the ten officers cited, only six actually took part in the roadblock apprehension. The four others were detectives who, as usual, appeared when there were backs to be patted after the danger was past, and only the glory remained. I noted the strange similarity between how the newspaper and the police department divvied up credits.

ONE MORNING AS I SCANNED THROUGH THE NIGHT LOG THE DAY dispatcher advised me "Rock, you had better get up to the DB. There's a homicide that might interest you. I think your folks knew this woman."

"Female homicide victim transported to City Hospital morgue," it stated simply.

I ran up the stairs to the Detective Bureau where night-relief investigators filled me in. An eighty-three-year-old woman had been beaten to death during a burglary as she slept. As a small child, I had spent many evenings in her home in "the Flats," the section between the Swedish neighborhood and a suburban town line. Numerous times, I had fallen asleep on her bed and had been carried home on my father's shoulder.

Investigators always seemed to dig harder and longer on murders of children, the elderly, and the prominent. A suspect was brought in and a screwdriver taken from him that matched perfectly the pry marks on the dead woman's bedroom window sill. Police already knew the suspect had committed a particularly vicious rape and assault a short distance from the murder victim's home, at about the same time she was beaten to death. Detectives told me they were certain the rapist had also committed the elderly woman's murder, but they were unable to put together enough solid evidence to bring the case to court. The prime suspect was convicted of several other crimes and sentenced to a lengthy prison term. With that, the woman's murder was relegated to the unofficially closed, inactive file.

IN EARLY SEPTEMBER 1973, THE PARTIALLY NAKED, MUTILATED body of a middle-aged alcoholic, his head crushed beyond recognition by a concrete block, his genitals slashed off and stuffed in what was left of his mouth, was found in a roadside gully three blocks from City Hall. His pants were found thrown over a concrete barrier that shielded the body from earlier discovery. A blood-stained block covered with particles of flesh and tissue, a wine bottle, and a broken beer bottle were found near the body. Investigators said the murder had homosexual overtones. The man, a former textile worker, had been arrested for public drunkenness twelve hours before his body was found, and had slept it off in a police jail cell. After an investigation, the search for a killer was narrowed down to a female teenager, but her involvement in the crime never was firmly established and the case was never closed.

AN EIGHTEEN-YEAR-OLD YOUTH WAS FOUND BEATEN AND STABBED to death on a sidewalk next to an elementary school near his home. When anyone in the city was murdered, it was standard procedure at the paper to interview the victim's family. After an emotion charged interview with the teenager's mother, during which her near hysteria made it almost impossible for her to answer questions, I drew a profile of the youth, his interests, his activities, and his friends.

My story ran with a snapshot of the boy borrowed from a family photo album. Any police officer will readily admit he dreads making death notifications, saying it is the toughest duty he has to perform.

For a police reporter to conduct interviews with a murder victim's loved ones has to be the journalistic equivalent of making death notifications. I did many of them, starting with my cub reporter days in a county town, and I abhorred each one of them. I can never forget the anguish I felt each time and the pain I caused the families of the victims. My story told of a boy who had everything for which to live, a youth who was the hope of a family's future. I described his family's love and their shattered dreams. I called upon possible witnesses to come forward and help police crack the case. A few anonymous tips, a letter or two, and then nothing. At one point, investigators thought they had a motive and possible prime suspect, but both eventually fizzled out. During the ensuing weeks, I phoned the mother several times to offer emotional support. Each time I propped her up by telling her how hard police were pressing the investigation, but eventually I had to tell her the truth: police had nothing to go on and were up against a blank wall.

THE LAST DAY OF MARCH 1972, THE CITY'S CONSCIENCE WAS rocked by violence when a young Worcester cop, depressed over a failed marriage, went berserk, killing his estranged wife's baby-sitter, shooting his police partner, and then committing suicide. Since his teenage years, the distraught officer had wanted badly to be a policeman. He studied law and fire science and was eager to please people. He looked young for his age and was modestly handsome in a boyish way. At the police training academy, he was an average student, quiet, reserved, and normally did not mix well socially with other trainees. At the end of his nine-month probationary period, his performance was rated as excellent.

But soon afterward, his career became more turbulent as his marriage deteriorated. When his wife left him taking their two-year-old son to live with her parents, the young officer claimed she had deserted him. While he tried to work out his domestic problems, his youthful countenance gained him an assignment in the Vice Squad, working the districts where prostitution was most rampant. A man in a car tried to run him down one night and the officer retaliated by firing a shot through the driver's rear window. Other officers said his marital separation tore him apart emotionally and physically. Soon, the familial problems affected his work performance. He began to drink and took off unexpectedly for Florida. There, a doctor, finding the officer despondent and on the ragged edge, recommended he be given ninety days off for therapy and treatment. Back in Worcester, he was re-examined and granted a month off, after which another evaluation found no anxiety or depression. The troubled officer was judged fit to return to duty. A month later, he broke.

In a highly agitated state, he drove to the home of his wife's parents with the intent of grabbing his son and running away with a girlfriend. When he arrived at the home where his wife and son were living, she was not there, only her seventeen-year-old sister who was baby sitting the officer's small son was in the house. In an apparent dispute over the child, the officer shot and killed his sister-in-law before abducting the child and returning to Worcester. Back at his girlfriend's home, he told her what he had done. Becoming alarmed, she called police. When the first officers arrived, a standoff developed: the officer with gun in hand challenged by fellow officers, also armed. A brief exchange of gunfire broke out. The officer's off duty partner was called to the scene to talk down the almost incoherent officer. He failed. The partner was shot in the neck, inflicting a superficial wound. Then, as horrified officers watched helplessly, the now crying officer placed his service revolver behind his left ear and pulled the trigger. With a single bullet, the young cop whose ambition had been to study law and please people ended his emotional roller coaster.

IN EARLY APRIL 1981, A CAB DRIVER WAS SHOT TO DEATH BY THREE fares during a robbery, three blocks west of City Hall, in the city's "Congress Alley," the motorcycle gang conclave. In the last moments of his life, the cabby had lost control of his vehicle as it veered off the street, struck three cars, and slammed into a house before rolling onto its side. After shooting him once in the back, the three fares rifled the cabby's pockets, stole his money and climbed out windows to escape. Witnesses told police they heard a gunshot and screams before seeing three youths run from the smoking vehicle.

After an intensive search, the three fares were located, arrested, convicted of complicity to robbery and murder, and sentenced to long prison terms. The cab driver was the father of several children. The area was noted in the city for outlaw motorcycle clubs, drug addicts, hookers, and pseudo-avant-garde fringe elements. The once proud

center for much of the city's gentry, had by the seventies become sort
of a no man's land.

IN MID-JUNE 1983, A PROMINENT WORCESTER BUSINESSMAN WAS
found stabbed to death in his affluent west side home, in what police
called an "unusually vicious, brutal killing." The victim had been
mutilated and stabbed forty-five times in the upper chest and extremities. Immediately, police clamped a tight lid of secrecy over the case.
This was almost standard procedure when prominent people were
killed, robbed, or arrested. I never understood why the privileged few
were afforded the luxury of a shield of anonymity and privacy while
others in the community were not.

The Detective Bureau released only sketchy information on autopsy results, possible weapon used, motives behind the killing, suspects,
crime scene description, or case direction—the basic ingredients of
homicide news coverage. In a empty corridor away from his office and
superiors, I asked a trusted news source, "Off the record, what do we
have?"

"Fag fight," he said, looking around furtively to make certain that
his answer had not been overheard by superior officers. "They really
tore up the place, blood all over."

When police were called to the murder scene to check on the victim's welfare after friends became concerned about his safety, they
found the house locked with a dead bolt. Police were forced to smash
a window to gain entry. The victim's badly slashed and stabbed corpse
was found lying on a bed in a second floor master bedroom. One
detective later told me the bedroom resembled a battlefield.

Checking the "morgue" (newspaper clipping and picture library), I
found that three years earlier, three men had been charged with
extorting $20,000 from the victim after threatening to accuse him of
a crime or offense. Police refused to tell me what the alleged crime or
offense was. Again, resorting to a mens' room informant, I was told

the murder victim was being blackmailed with the threat that his homosexuality would be exposed. Several days later, a southeastern Massachusetts factory worker was arrested and charged with the crime. Superior Court testimony during the murder trial indicated the killing was a falling out of two homosexual lovers. The suspect had been paroled from state prison three years earlier in connection with the stabbing death of a Worcester woman, whose body had been dumped in a secluded section of a city cemetery ten years earlier.

LATE IN JULY 1983, TWO TEENAGE GIRLS, ONE THE MOTHER OF AN infant daughter and pregnant with another child, were picked up while hitchhiking on the Worcester Expressway. Instead of taking them in the direction they wanted to go, the car took them almost to the New Hampshire state line. Faced with unfamiliar landscape, the teenagers had no idea where they were.

The two hitchhikers desperately tried to open the passenger side door and jump out as they struggled with the driver. The car swerved violently all over the narrow country road as the driver fought to maintain control of the vehicle. Suddenly, the car skidded to a stop at a school bus turnaround. Wildly, the driver groped at the two girls, attempting to rip off their blouses and other clothing. Both fought back, screaming and clawing at the driver's face when he started attacking them sexually.

One of the teenagers was finally able to break away from the driver by squeezing through a side window of the car and dropping to the ground. Blindly, she ran stumbling away and disappeared into dense underbrush beside the road, trying to escape from her attacker. She had to find help for her friend, still back in the car being viciously attacked. As she lunged with arms flailing through the woods, the screams of her pregnant girlfriend echoed behind her.

With her blouse and bra ripped off, the hysterical girl ran through a half mile of thick underbrush to a junk yard where she screamed out to workers there details of what was being done to her friend. Employees quickly called police and covered the half exposed teenager with a blanket. Unfamiliar with the area, the girl was unable to tell the responding officer immediately where precisely the attacker's car was. After she blurted out what details she could remember of the area where she had been attacked, searchers headed for the bus turnaround. They found no car there and no immediate signs of trouble.

But, within several minutes, as the searchers probed through brush along the roadside, they found the body of the seventeen-year-old pregnant girl, her throat slashed savagely with a knife or razor, her head nearly decapitated. The corpse had been dragged off the road and into the woods, where it was partially concealed by being rolled down a six-foot embankment seventy-five feet from the road. Blood stained trees and broken branches lining the path the killer used to drag his victim to the gully offered stark testimony to the savagery of the slaying.

Sobbing uncontrollably at the gruesome discovery, the surviving teenager supplied police with a description of the murderer. After police calmed the girl, she described the interior of the killer's blue compact car. The descriptions of the murderer and his car were burned into her memory. When my story hit the street, more than 200 calls from an indignant public poured into area police departments. The aid of departments throughout Worcester County was enlisted to perform the leg work needed to track down tips received from hundreds of callers. The outpouring of public assistance became a stimulus to the investigation.

Three days later, a twenty-three-year-old north county man was charged with the teenage mother's death. He was an apprentice baker at a Worcester bakery. I interviewed the bakery owner and some of the suspect's co-workers. They said he had been a prisoner at Franklin County House of Correction, charged with kidnaping, assault with intent to rape, and assault with a dangerous weapon (a gun). The chief instructor at the prison offered the bakery owner a letter of recommendation testifying that the now accused murderer possessed "out-standing ability, initiative, and cooperation" in his work at the prison. The convict was paroled after the bakery owner offered him a job as an apprentice baker, replacing striking union bakers.

Twelve days after this fateful decision, a teenage mother was dead. Ironically, the Worcester hitchhiker's murder was committed on the killer's twenty-third birthday. Digging further into the killer's background, I uncovered his high school graduation yearbook. Almost as an epitaph, the year book said of him, "Go now, I think you are ready."

THE PRESIDENT OF ONE OF THE AREA'S LEADING SUPERMARKET chains arrived at his affluent suburban home to find the body of his wife, on the kitchen floor, her head caved in with a large pipe wrench. In total shock, he failed for several minutes to hear a car with its engine running in an attached garage. When he did, he ran to the garage and discovered the couple's eighteen-year-old son slumped over the front seat of his sport car, a vacuum cleaner hose stretched from the car's tail pipe to the passenger front window. Autopsies revealed the mother died of massive head trauma, the son of carbon monoxide asphyxiation, a suicide.

When police at the scene refused to talk to staff suburban reporters by phone, the City Desk hurriedly enlisted my assistance. I was told the wrench, believed to be the murder weapon, had been recovered on a kitchen table beside the murdered woman's bloody corpse. The chief filled me in on other pertinent details of the investigation as they developed. Searching for a motive, police delved into their files. The son, they found, had been arrested four months earlier for operating under the influence of liquor and leaving the scene of a property damage accident. He was scheduled to appear in court two weeks after the murder-suicide occurred. Police would not speculate whether this was a motive for the double deaths. There were no culprits in the case, only two victims.

NOT LONG AFTERWARD, A SIMPLE-MINDED STREET CHARACTER, A familiar figure in the Green Island section of the city, was found murdered, his head crushed by a large rock in an abandoned car he called his home, three blocks from City Hall. The man, police said, had existed by running errands in return for food, or performing odd jobs for area barroom proprietors, and car dealership salesmen for spare change. Operating usually within the confines of the Green Street section where he felt familiar and comfortable, the victim was a simple, quiet, friendly man liked by everyone. Because of this, investigators were baffled why anyone would harm him. He had no money, was not a known drinker, nor was he a troublemaker. Police determined he had no known enemies and was not a homosexual. Most people in the area did not even know the victim's last name. He was just "Lenny."

When I examined the scene, detectives and technicians from the Bureau of Criminal Identification (BCI) were already going over the victim's four wheeled, rusted home dusting for prints, and microscopically searching for fibers, hair, lint, anything that could be considered evidence. Blankets, canned goods, rumpled clothing, and bags of partially eaten food filled the front and back seats of the car. Where his body over a long period of time had cradled out a bed in the back seat, blood soaked everything: seats, windows, floors and headlining. As I studied the interior closer, leaning over and peering in while not touching anything, chunks of bloodied flesh were spattered everywhere by the viciousness of the attack, turning the car interior to a crimson brown. A bloodied rock the size of a grapefruit, strands of dried hair still stuck to it, was lodged on the floor beneath the car steering wheel.

The gory interior of the car caused no revulsion. I had seen it too many times before. It was just another homicide scene and people bleed when their lives end so violently.

Because Lenny was such a popular, seemingly innocent character in the city, police dug into the case long and hard. It became a case of everyone wanting to champion the cause of an underdog. Lenny was certainly that. From his younger years, he had asked for very little in life, had required and desired practically nothing, and even in the pinnacle of his existence, he had been a nobody—just a face in the crowd as those who knew him best described him. I published a composite sketch of a man wanted for questioning as a material witness, a man known to be in the area about the time the murder happened. The prospective witness, probably reluctant to become involved with police, never volunteered himself. Despite all the effort, no motive was ever established and the case was never solved.

IT SEEMED THAT ONE AFTER ANOTHER, THE HOMICIDES KEPT COMING. A South End man was beaten to death in his apartment, during a violent argument, by a later convicted Worcester State Hospital escapee. The man's life might have been spared if the police had picked up the hospital patient before he committed murder and returned him to the hospital, an almost daily procedure for police route cars. But they were not even looking for him.

Due to a typing error at the hospital, the spelling of the man's surname had been reported incorrectly to police on the missing-patient bulletin. As a result, police were unaware that the patient was off campus. Searching through the files of the police Bureau of Records, I discovered the discrepancy in the spelling of the murderer's name. I pointed out in a subsequent news story that a man's life had been snuffed out because of a simple clerical error that no one had identified. These misfortunes occurred in police work. They are difficult to accept, but pragmatism is the by-word in the environs of law enforcement. Some things in the world just cannot be altered, no matter how much one might demand it.

IN ONE SUCH INSTANCE, A MOTORCYCLIST BELIEVED TO BE ON A stolen bike was chased by Worcester police into an adjoining town, where he lost control, rammed a tree, and was killed. The motorcycle had been reported stolen some months before but had been recovered and returned to the owner. This fact was not updated in stolen vehicle computer files at the Registry of Motor Vehicles. When the Worcester cop tried to stop the cyclist for a moving violation downtown, the operator took off for no apparent reason. During the chase, the pursuing officer radioed headquarters requested a status report on the bike. It came back as a stolen vehicle.

The chase revved up as the motorcyclist headed north trying to escape the Worcester cruiser. Minutes later, the chase ended violently. It was only sometime later when the city cop made out his highway fatality report that a Registry correction was sent through—a few hours too late.

Who was responsible for the death? A Registry computer clerk overwhelmed with paperwork report? A motorcycle owner who took off instead of stopping when the cop signaled him over? The cop for chasing him? A society burgeoning with paperwork and red tape? Responsibility is seldom cut and dried. Ask any cop.

IN THE WANING DAYS OF OCTOBER 1984, THE CITY WAS SHOCKED when the nude, battered, and possibly molested body of a popular high school student was found in a factory window well two blocks from her home. The body was covered with cardboard and discarded lumber in a crude attempt by the killer to camouflage it. A subsequent autopsy revealed the girl died of massive head trauma—weapon unknown.

The corpse was found when a group of friends and relatives, concerned that the girl had not returned home from visiting with her boyfriend, started a search of the neighborhood. When some of her personal belongings and a blood-stained jacket were found, the searchers called police. Investigators refused to say whether the girl had been sexually assaulted or raped, but the condition of the body, and the fact that she had been murdered to conceal the identity of a possibly known attacker allowed some conclusions to be drawn. Witnesses reported seeing the girl get off a bus in a heavy rain near a city university shortly before midnight. Police pieced together testimony that the victim was intercepted while walking toward her home. Investigators theorized she took an alley shortcut behind an abandoned factory complex. She was probably hurrying because of the rain, even though she carried an umbrella. That was the last time anyone saw her alive.

A factory loading platform near where the girl's body was found was a favorite hangout for teenage drinkers, police revealed. As police detectives and Bureau of Criminal Identification teams combed the crime scene, neighbors and friends of the girl stood nearby and wept in shock and sorrow.

Fourteen detectives assigned to the case followed up on dozens of phone tips during the initial days of the investigation. Uniformed patrol officers pitched in with information assimilated on the street. The FBI was enlisted to analyze more than eighty items of the dead girl's clothing and other personal possessions. More than 100 people were interviewed during the seven days after the victim's body was discovered. Police steadfastly refused to identify the weapon used to kill the girl. Months later, other police sources told me the FBI labs had failed to identify any weapon for certain. Strewn near the body when it was discovered were several pieces of lumber, the girl's purse, umbrella, and some items of clothing. A heavy rain when the crime was committed probably washed away valuable physical evidence that could have aided the investigation, police said.

The educators at the murdered girl's high school described the victim as an A and B student, popular, involved, and outgoing. She reportedly was excited about enrolling in a California college the following year, and worked part time in a suburban fast food store to finance her planned college education.

Six months later, police revealed that they believed the murder victim knew her assailant and that the killer was from the girl's neigh-

borhood. It was a case that the newspaper would not abandon: six
years later, the *Evening Gazette* was still running anniversary stories of
the teenager's death. Appeal after appeal was published, hoping that
each would jog someone's memory. Investigators claim the case is still
open. Tenacious investigation traced the girl's activities and whereabouts up to about an hour prior to the fatal attack. But private investigators could not account for the final, extremely vital few minutes of
her life.

It was the lengthiest, most intensive murder investigation I covered
during my tenure at the newspaper. There are times in life, every cop
knows, when everything possible is not enough.

MY QUIET LUNCH IN THE PRESS ROOM WAS ABRUPTLY DISTURBED
when the police scanner announced a double shooting inside a hospital, two blocks from headquarters. It was another instance of being able
to sprint to the scene faster than I could drive and try to park. My
arrival at the hospital coincided with that of a small army of police officers responding to the call. Mingling among them, I breezed unnoticed past hospital security and knots of doctors and nurses congregat-
ing around the hospital's Intensive Care Unit, where the shooting had
shattered the serenity of the hospital. An elderly woman had been shot
to death by her seventy-nine-year-old distraught husband, who then
turned the .38-caliber pistol on himself. The hospital ward was in total
confusion as doctors and nurses frantically tried to tend to the husband's massive head wound. Within minutes of the shooting, he was
rushed to an operating room where doctors fought to save his life.

Cops everywhere, notebooks in hand, fanned out to interview in
hushed tones everyone they could find. I tried to blend into the woodwork so I would not be noticed and thrown out. Quietly, I watched
and listened, committing to memory most of what I saw and heard. I
did not want to attract undue attention with a reporter's notebook in
my hand. Doctors had quickly disarmed the badly bleeding husband

as he slumped to the floor, mortally wounded. The gun was given to the first cop who came through the ward door.

A hospital spokesman told me that the murdered woman, was recovering from surgery for peritonitis, but was not considered a terminal case. Her bed was enclosed behind a cloth curtain that shielded the husband's actions from hospital personnel until the fatal shot resounded throughout the hospital. Police ruled the shooting a mercy killing and suicide attempt. The medical teams in Memorial Hospital's ICU were in such shock from the unexpected violence that they allowed me to walk everywhere unchallenged as the police completed the initial investigation. I remained at the hospital long enough to collect and confirm the information needed for my story, and then ran at full tilt back to the pressroom. The husband did not recover. Police changed the case classification to a murder-suicide.

PERUSING MY HOMICIDE FILES ON A MORNING, IN JUNE 1986, I noticed that the city had been without a murder for nine months. This, I knew from experience, was an unusually long span of time. I dug deeper into the files. When I found that this was the longest murder free period, in the city, in about four decades, I knew I had the basis of a good news story, especially since the city normally averaged ten to twelve homicides annually. One possible reason for the homicide hiatus was credited by veteran detectives to increased public involvement in investigations. But no one was boasting, not just yet. We all knew that murders often come in bunches, well in accordance with the syndrome that "it never rains but it pours." To flesh out my story, I rehashed the previous seven homicides, what the police solution percentage had been (six out of seven), and the weapons used in each case: three by guns, two by strangulation, one stabbing, and one arson fire.

The belief that murders often were clustered together again proved valid when five killings took place during the next nine months, three by gunfire, one, a multiple stabbing by three men, and the other, a pillow suffocation of an elderly woman. Arrests were made in four cases. The following year, there were twelve homicides in the city, eleven of them solved with arrests.

LESS THAN THREE WEEKS BEFORE MY RETIREMENT, AND OLD WAR horses being what they are, I wrote my final homicide story. Tragically, it was the brutal strangulation of a seventeen-year-old high school student, whose body was found in a park overlooking the city, six blocks from headquarters. She was murdered, police said, the day before her scheduled high school graduation. The weapon used to choke the life out of her was apparently the leather carrying strap on her pocketbook.

The park where she was found was known as a lovers' lane and was also a favorite spot for car thieves wanting to burn stolen vehicles. Her purse was found by a resident of the area walking through the park, and turned over to police about 7:30 P.M. Meanwhile, relatives filed a missing person's report on the girl about thirty minutes later. The missing person and recovered property reports crossed paths in the Missing Persons Bureau. The next morning, when a possible link between the two reports was suspected, two Juvenile Division detectives were dispatched to search the area where the purse was found. But, because the initial report by the man turning in the pocketbook was not specific as to the location where it was found, the police officers searched the wrong area and came up empty handed.

Later that day, the girl's family was notified by police that the handbag had been found and was at headquarters. Concerned when the girl failed to come home to prepare for her graduation, relatives and friends started a search of the area. They found her fully clothed body partially concealed by leaves in a remote, hilly section of the park. Matted-down grass where the body was found clearly indicated she had curled herself into the fetal position in an apparent defense against her attacker as the last terrifying moments of her life ebbed away. Immediately, police started tracking down her whereabouts prior to her death. Dozens of people were interviewed: fellow students, a boyfriend, family members, neighbors where she lived, residents of the area where she was found, her employer, her school chums. No one could provide the one missing link that would identify her killer. The case, now more than a decade old, reposes, as far as I know, in the inactive, but still open detective files.

Homicides were the most intricate, frustrating crimes I had to report through the years, primarily because police, trying to protect the feelings and privacy of crime victims and their loved ones, seldom revealed investigation details. In murder after murder, most of the news coverage came from reporter interviews with victims' families, employers, neighbors, teachers, or other outside sources.

Also, murder is one of the most sensitive crimes regarding police security. The wrong word, the wrong detail, a too exact identification of where a police probe was centered, could easily give the criminal an advantage in the "cat-and-mouse" aspects of the systematic inquiry into a murder case. Investigators knew a case could be blown wide open by the premature publication of too much detail. With this in mind, they usually told me nothing, or as little as possible to get me off their backs. In police jargon, they blew a little smoke at me.

On the other hand, I never wanted to be responsible for a murderer—or any other felon, for that matter—to escape detection and prosecution because of my inattention or insensitivity to police security. I would hardly be serving the public interest if I was guilty of either. Throughout the years I tread an extremely fine line: police security and the cause of justice versus the public's right to be informed.

the chiefs

DURING THE THIRTY YEARS THAT I WAS SHELTERED AT POLICE Headquarters, I worked with and acclimated myself to eight police chiefs and to their differing styles, talent, and especially to their widely divergent law enforcement philosophies. This was no small feat— more than most officers within the department would be called upon to do. A degree in psychology would have been helpful. Seven of the eight chiefs danced to the tune of the City Manager, their boss. A candid summation of those three decades would indicate that the influence of City Hall over the department was, in many instances, less than beneficial.

There was constant political posturing, demands for favors. I witnessed one city councilor physically thrown out of the chief's office for pompously making such a demand; city managers who thought they knew more about law enforcement than thirty-year professionals; and departments held hostage for much needed improvement appropriations, if the chief did not yield to political pressure. Year after year, when it came to requests for new apparatus or cruisers, uniforms, buildings, equipment, and for living wages, police and fire personnel were treated like second class citizens, or municipal after thoughts.

Only one police chief and one fire chief had the intestinal fortitude to stand up to City Hall, usually by using me to plead cases and causes in print. Both enjoyed only limited success, but, they felt, that to fight was better than settling for too little or nothing. Some were forced by the politically-motivated stinginess of the city manager and council to close entire divisions and to threaten the closing of fire stations. Both chiefs were very close to and very protective of their men.

Each chief had his own set of external constraints that often hampered his efforts to improve the image and performance of his troops. In addition to political pressure, from each succeeding generation there were greater public demands for "emergency" services—there were requests for police to cope with barking dogs, disobedient children, pesky neighborhood kids, property line disputes, late school buses, "boogie man appearances," sassy kids, loud radios, etc, etc. The cop was expected not only to serve and protect, but to be mediator, judge, jury, enforcer, and badge-carrying weapon against others. To accommodate to this situation, each chief, gradually, had to alter his professional beliefs and practices. The world continued to change. Some chiefs adapted, while others stubbornly held to former practices.

As the years unfolded, new, more liberal Supreme Court decisions hastened the process. New crops of more highly educated, more sophisticated recruits, many with college degrees, pressured the internal decisions or orders of each chief. In summary, some of the new breed were just smarter than their chiefs—not street smarter, to be sure, but academically sharper. During the early days, they served chiefs who never went beyond high school. From the time I started police reporting to the day I retired, rookie training went from a single day to twenty weeks. Chiefs and subordinate officers were also forced to come out into the open. During my early years on the police scene, officers might not see their precinct captains for the first year they were on the job and, quite often, they did not meet their chiefs for the first five years. Representatives of authority were totally isolated. The officer dealt strictly with his sergeant and that was it.

Gradually, the chiefs initiated improvements in communications. There were "wind boxes" on poles every mile or so; emergency equipment was summoned by telephones borrowed from residents; until eventually every officer carried a portable radio. In the early days, all cops—save a few sergeant street supervisors—were on foot. To alert downtown foot beat officers that a car had been stolen in the city, a red light flashed on a department store roof. This was the signal to call in for details at the call box. Every chief could take partial credit for each progressive improvement. The knee length, choker collar, twenty-eight-pound overcoat was replaced by waist-length leather or nylon jackets. Motorcycles were added to the Traffic Division. They were far more mobile than cruisers and response time was shortened.

In dozens of instances, my news stories motivated local politicians to acquiesce to the chiefs' requests. Soon, chiefs in both fire and police departments knew that perhaps they had the ultimate weapon in me—news exposure. Few politicians can stand up under the fire of newspaper headlines. To do so, would mean a flood of negative phone calls from constituents.

It must be kept in mind that police procedures in the late fifties were extremely primitive compared to what the public sees and expects today. Some of the chiefs were quite secretive and seldom seen, even by me. Others were overly quiet, not given to making public statements. Still others were coarse in demeanor, while others were outgoing, flamboyant, seeking the public spotlight and with great public appeal. And finally, there were the others, quietly studying for advanced college degrees to better themselves and to improve their ability to command. It took all kinds throughout the years, motivated mostly by a Civil Service exam and not necessarily by talent.

The first chief I encountered did not want me there in the first place. I was a threat—about to tell the world what he was, or was not, doing. He made his dislike for reporters quite clear. He refused to be a source of any information at all. He wanted everything swept under the rug, not exposed, or even talked about, in the press. It was during his reign that I learned the old police adage: "Screw the public. What they don't know won't hurt them." The best defense against the public was to tell them nothing.

I learned to work around him. From what I could determine from the troops, he made no attempts to upgrade departmental policies or improve working conditions. He was a sort of "show up and collect the pay check" leader. He was a status quo type chief—just tread water and make no waves. Very little news was reported during that period, mostly concerning fires and automobile accidents. The only improvement I remember him making was to enlist frog men (scuba divers) to recover drowning victims rather than dragging the bodies with hooks and handing them to grieving loved ones.

He made sure that his last day on the job I was not invited to his coffee party. I was told that he retired to the psychiatric ward of a local hospital, and when last heard of, he was walking in his underwear around the hospital parking lot.

His successor was the "Silent Chief," who smiled nicely and quickly and silently walked away before any questions could be asked. He was quieter and even more secretive that his predecessor. I was not allowed to tread on his turf. His men took their cue from their leader and acted accordingly. I do not remember ever writing a single story with his name in it. All my stories were developed from outside sources. He managed to obtain a polygraph machine for the department but apparently, as far as I could determine, it was too complicated and was never used. He also urged his upper echelon officers to return to the classroom in order to improve their management skills. A few did so, provided the classes were on company time. However, his tenure was short and little damage was done to the "public's right to know."

He retired to Cape Cod but, in his later years, returned to live in the city. Eventually, he committed suicide in his apartment, at the North End Housing for the Elderly. Though he had been gone for thirty years, police, most of whom never knew or heard of him, continued to protect his image and were loyal to the symbol he once represented. They refused to release details of his death.

THE NEXT CHIEF, A CAPTAIN, WAS ELEVATED TO THE POSITION upon the death of the candidate ahead of him. The first candidate died only weeks before the appointment was to be made. The sudden elevation of the captain from second to first touched off a flurry of back room political hustling in the remote corners of City Hall. The effort was to prevent this silver-haired maverick from sitting in the chief's chair. Cronyism and hack favoritism came crawling out of the woodwork. The fear that this man could not be controlled and not maneuvered politically, was well merited. He was his own man and already a legend in the department for his past performance.

The city manager knew that others on the eligibility list might be more manipulable but to by-pass the maverick would bring down on the manager's head a firestorm of criticism from the public, and more importantly, from the newspaper and its rib-rock Yankee editorial board. The chief applicant was eminently qualified for the job, had a thirty-year unblemished service record and was, to his credit, not one of the City Hall "good old boys."

The day after his swearing-in ceremony, he publicly announced that he and not the city's political element was running the police department. The gauntlet had been thrown down. And run the department he did as no chief before or after him was ever able to do. It became the golden era of police news reporting. The new chief, through the media, became a legend. And, to some extent, he took me right along with him.

A tiger had been released from its cage, and the influence peddlers in the city, those who previously had power at headquarters, discovered that they would never again be able to get the tiger back into the cage and slam the door shut. Henceforth, every departmental demand, every controversial issue, every departmental need or improvement, every change for the better in the working conditions of his officers, every building upgrade, every needed organizational modification was tried in the paper through my gradual takeover of Page One. His Irish eloquence won over his enemies—and he had many—while his biting, critical wit regularly tanned the hide of his boss in City Hall. He tagged me with the name "monsignor." He seldom requested, but, in his aggressive style, he invariable ordered.

Brick by brick he built the foundation of today's department. During his three-year tenure he brought about improvements, created more effective divisions, assigned more highly talented officers, and fine tuned training to a degree never thought of by previous chiefs. He brought about an imaginative metamorphosis not yet surpassed or even equaled. At headquarters, there was not a nook or cranny that he did not touch in one way or another.

The departmental table of organization was modernized, heavy discipline was meted out to slackers or deadbeats—one deputy chief had to punch a time clock—motor patrol routes were realigned to areas of heaviest crime incidence. Internal pipelines to City Hall were plugged. Political pull became a thing of the past. The chief knew where all the skeletons were buried and was ready to exhume them if the need arose.

His aggressiveness produced brickbats from City Hall. "Why don't you just once try being a cop half the time and a politician the other half, chief," I advised. "You just might get what you want a little sooner. Ask sometimes instead of demanding. It might grease the skids." He smiled, but made no promises.

A street cop at heart, uncomfortable behind a desk, he cruised the streets late at night keeping his thumb on the performance of his men, with many of them looking over their shoulder checking to see whether he was behind them.

As a youth, he had delivered milk by horse and wagon and never lost his humility. When someone asked him, now that he was chief, whether he would be moving out from his three-story tenement to the more affluent west side, he retorted, "Why should I? I was born and brought up here. It's my home."

Departmental morale soared. Footmen walked taller and more proudly. Many improved their appearance with creased uniform pants, ironed shirts, and general spick-and-span. The city began to notice and become proud of its police force. For a while the chief had to contend with two almost separate departments: the all brawn "old breed," and the more highly educated, more sophisticated "new breed," who expected more than the traditional outcome from their careers. The integration of both groups was awkward, but not for long. Their chief deftly brought both sides together into one cohesive, well-oiled unit.

It seemed as if there was nothing he could not accomplish once he made up his mind. He opened the doors for nearly 100 officers to take police science courses at five area colleges. A man of astute vision, the chief was looking twenty-five years into the future. Some officers tested his resolve and lived to regret it. His punishments were swift and severe. But, his compassion for others was also deep.

The chief even reached into the court system for information to improve the testifying procedures of officers. Every week, another long ignored and sorely needed innovation was implemented. The passage of time would demonstrate that none of his successors ever reached such heights of perfection within the department. He had a rather simple credo: "Give me eight hours of honest work for eight hours of pay and I will back you to the hilt, even if you screw up, but if you goldbrick on me, I'll hang you."

He became the modern knight in shining white armor. The power brokers of the establishment in the city treated the fiery chief like a messiah. Then one day, in an instant, it was over. On my day off, the paper informed me that the chief had died in a moment, at his desk, of a massive heart attack at the precise time when, on my working days, he and I chatted in the afternoon.

Higher-ups at the paper, feeling they could compose an appropriate eulogy, wrote of the chief the city had lost. I dictated a tribute over the telephone to a City Room reporter and it was chosen to be the one used. It was no contest for I knew the man better than any of them did. I described him as a man of vision who set goals knowing they might not always be met but still he never stopped trying. The eulogy was engraved in a golden metal plaque which I was asked to present to his widow. He was a maverick and so was I. I have always felt that was the reason we bonded so strongly, almost like a father and son.

THE NEXT CHIEF, NICKNAMED THE "GRAY GHOST," BECAUSE OF HIS mane of silvery hair, was largely unknown to his troops for he had spent thirteen years of his police career in the U.S. Navy. Suddenly, he was thrust into the limelight and expected to fill some very large shoes. When promotional exams were taken, he had become a thorn in the side of some of the department's top brass. His Civil Service veterans' two-point preference gave him an advantage that disgruntled applicants felt he did not deserve. He served as acting chief for a year before being appointed to the top slot.

He was a quiet, reserved man, and did not associate freely with others in the department. Although friendly enough, he was a loner by instinct. So was I. We clicked right away and I was given free run of the station and all police reports. When he learned I had a son who had a presidential appointment to the U. S. Naval Academy at Annapolis, he could not do enough for me.

He worked well with people, but only on the other side of an invisible barrier. He weighed his words well and seldom had to retract something he had previously said. In true military fashion, when assigned a task, he carried it out to the nth degree, overlooking no details. He was a strong administrator, but never acquired the loyalty of his troops, especially that of his superior officers. He had been away from the department too long and had not proven himself on the street, an accomplishment exacted by every cop when one from within their ranks was promoted.

He also had ideas for the department. Primarily, he wanted to resume planning for a new station. City Hall thwarted every effort in that direction. Station plans were gathering dust in some remote City Hall closet and would remain there, undisturbed. To meet the wave of the future, the chief strongly felt the need for a regional police radio network. To this end, he enlisted Ralph Thomson, executive superintendent of the Fire Alarm Division, to get the project off the ground. Thomson was a pioneer in such advanced technology, and today is still considered the leading authority in Massachusetts on emergency radio technology. To assist, he immediately recruited a savvy police chief from a nearby suburban town. Eventually, a slightly abbreviated network went on the air connecting Worcester with Massachusetts State Police, the Registry of Motor Vehicles, and nine towns on three sides of the city.

Lastly, the chief demanded that training courses be greatly expanded for all his troops. From sergeant to deputy chief, he urged his men to enroll in classes in leadership, report writing, command training, community relations, criminal investigation, conference leadership, and management. He assisted his superior officers in enrolling at Harvard University, Babson Institute, and the FBI Academy, all in the Boston area. Then he added classes in riot control, water safety, Civil Defense evacuation, and advanced firearms and first aid training. Because the city refused to provide classrooms for its "finest," in-house training was shunted from the antiquated station, to various military reserve centers, and finally to the Worcester County jail.

To provide more centralized coverage and protection, the chief dissected the city into east and west geographic sectors. Improved results were never realized and the strategy was dropped a few years later. Never one to give up, the chief then split the city into four quadrants to achieve the results he envisioned and to provide closer supervision of the troops by sectional lieutenants. Called saturation enforcement, this plan worked slightly better for a while, at least.

As others had done before him, the chief often sought my opinion and that of the newspaper. To his credit, he tried to keep his finger on the pulse of the community, feeling that by so doing he attained a better insight into how to respond to its problems and fears. He established a Community Service Office, staffed with multilingual personnel. Their job was to funnel rat and landlord complaints to the city Health Department, to remove abandoned cars, search for lost children, seek relief for battered wives and children, recruit minority police and fire candidates, expedite rubbish removal, assist minorities in finding employment, and befriending emotionally disturbed school children. It was thankless work and, in the end, the greatest stumbling block to its success was the people themselves, many of whom were beyond help, police said. Police Service Aides (PSAs) were added to the department to handle the less serious "garbage" calls, thereby freeing up police officers for the more pressing emergencies. This led to friction with the patrol officers' union, for the inefficiencies of many cops were often exposed by the effectiveness of the PSAs. The International Brotherhood of Police Officers (IBPO) used the opposition paper to air their views. Several feisty female PSAs used my pages to answer them, far more eloquently. A Robbery Strike Force and a Burglary Task Force were formed, both of which proved their worth repeatedly.

One day, without a word to anyone, he quietly walked out of the building, and retired, after nearly seven years as chief—no party, no goodbye, no nothing. Again, it was his way. Had he not been so strongly under the interfering influence of City Hall, I am sure he could have accomplished much more.

THE NEXT CHIEF WAS SO MUCH A GENTLE MAN, HIS MEN ALWAYS claimed he should have been a priest rather than a cop. As soon as he was sworn in, I did a profile on him—my usual first introductory story with the advent of each new chief. I described him as quiet, methodical, pleasant but almost shy, non-communicative, a solid family man, and the best golfing chief in the history of the department. I saw him as a good exam taker (police called them "good book men") with an unobtrusive manner, and a disciplinarian without fanfare. I was right on the mark. He turned out to be all of those, and more too.

When releasing news, the new chief, closely guarded police security and was extremely reluctant to discuss departmental matters with non-members of the force, notably the media. On a number of occasions, he carried this to the extreme. Instances developed when the IBPO, or the Civil Liberties Union, or some other faction produced a negative headline in the city's morning newspaper. The chief called in sick or found some unexpected committee meeting that required his attendance rather than face any follow-up questions I might have on the issue for the afternoon edition.

During his tenure as chief, he maintained an executive manner, one that paid close attention to administrative detail. Not much got by him. He possessed a broad knowledge of the law and placed great emphasis on self-improvement. Year after year, he returned to the classroom to attend police seminars. He set an example for his men by eventually obtaining a master's degree in criminal justice from Clark University. He was the first chief in the city's history to hold a college degree. Like his predecessor, he pushed hard for a better educated police force and for closer community relations programs between police and the public.

He was a master at blowing a smoke screen at interviewers and telling them nothing. Generally, he did not involve himself in departmental problems, delegating them instead to deputy chiefs or division commanders. No matter how many times I reminded him that I was not the enemy, I never penetrated his defense shield. It eventually got to a "I won't bother you if you don't bother me" attitude. During this period in my career I had to rely more heavily on outside sources than ever before. Getting information from him was like pulling hens' teeth.

An incident early in our relationship perhaps illustrates better his prim and proper attitude at times. A local bank was honoring one of his men for bravery during a supermarket holdup. The three of us were walking to the affair when the chief told me to take off a baseball cap I was wearing for it was not dignified and he did not want to be seen with me wearing it. "Then walk behind me." I responded, somewhat amused. He did.

The "reluctant dragon" side of the man came out when one of my sons, my wife, and I conducted a ten-week scuba course for members of the police SWAT team at a Girls' Club pool, and then took them for an open water orientation dive at a local lake. It would have been an extremely valuable addition to the department's emergency capability. When the Swat Underwater Rescue Force (SURF) was presented to the chief, he was aghast at the thought of his men "going that deep under water. Too dangerous." He refused to acknowledge the ten weekends his men had volunteered to improve the department's performance, and also the contributions my family had made. Never was SURF allowed to respond. Civilian divers were used instead.

The chief formed two units that proved quite successful: an Arson Squad, assigned to the Juvenile Division, and an Auto Theft Squad (ATS).

When he got wind of my upcoming 20th anniversary at the *Gazette*, he threw a surprise cake and coffee party for me, in the station's abandoned former District Court room. It was an extremely thoughtful gesture and I thanked him and the department quite eloquently.

Little by little, he fitted the pieces into the puzzle. The robbery and burglary, and arson and car theft units all bore fruit. Crime figures declined in the city, not drastically but steadily nonetheless. His next move was to streamline the Bureau of Records, to provide faster access for his men to information stored there. While this was being improved, a vigorous Crime Prevention Bureau out-reach program had its members pounding away for crime awareness in schools, churches, service clubs, civic organizations, businesses—anywhere, anyone would listen to them. Again, the chief was harking back to his primary interest—education.

When he retired, his sixty-three-month tenure at the helm was still being referred to by most as the "status quo era," not an accurate evaluation in my estimation. Perhaps, he was judged too harshly. Most of the criticism was not deserved. He was guilty of no serious flaws in enforcement judgment. However, the jury, his men, ruled that they had managed to keep the department going in spite of him. But, here I should add that in the thirty years I was in a police environment I never once heard a cop compliment a fellow officer.

OUT WITH THE OLD, IN WITH THE NEW. A LAST SUNSET, A NEW dawn. Soon, they all begin to look alike. The next chief was a transplanted Englishman who, during his five-year spotlight role as the city's highest law enforcement personality, became one of the most popular, flamboyant chiefs. He created a persona through widespread involvement in community projects, organizations, and affairs. He sat on the board of directors of the American Red Cross and local hospitals, was active with the Worcester Horticultural Society, the Mechanics Hall Restoration Committee, the American Automobile Association, the Worcester Center Boulevard Beautification Committee, and numerous other worthy causes. Tall and almost regal looking, he was dashing in a tuxedo.

"I'm not a cop. I'm an administrator," he announced, soon after being sworn in as chief. He worked hard at living up to that title. His popularity and wide respect within the department had been earned through the years as commander of all the department's uniformed and investigative units. He had paid his dues. He had proven himself to be a keen-minded thinker, a long-range planner, and an articulate commander who was guided by the strength of his convictions.

He made instant command decisions. "I'm never completely sure whether I am right or wrong but at least I will make a decision," he once boasted to me. An accomplished speaker, the chief was in constant demand and invariably enhanced the image of his department. With his flamboyant mannerisms, he met problems or matters of concern head-on. He handled disciplinary problems quietly and expeditiously. He dovetailed the operations of some divisions to strengthen interaction between each, thereby maintaining a more centralized effort.

Once, during this chief's term, friction developed between his men and the media, because the in-house reporter did his job correctly by printing both sides of an issue. To me, this was impartial reporting. But, to many officers this was anti-police bias. They reasoned that there was only one side to any issue: theirs. Their version of an incident, many of them felt, was absolute law. For the police reporter to take any other stand was to invite combat.

Officials became reclusive, often shunning me. Some took deeply defensive postures. If I dared to question their word, the turnoff became even more pronounced. The water in the puddle was muddied even more by a steady influx of new, younger officers who differed greatly from their older and more mature counterparts as far as police philosophy was concerned.

The chief, however, never turned his back on me as long as what I wrote was accurate. He never once tried to influence my reporting, nor placed any roadblocks in my path. I was given total freedom to question anyone I wanted in the building, and, more importantly, to read any and all police incident and crime reports.

Toward the end of his police career, he delegated a department spokesman, seen widely by other officers as one being groomed and showcased to the City Manager for the next chief's job. The so-called liaison officer dealt primarily with the media, during which time he attempted to be as suave and as cool as the chief. With his image in the community perhaps stronger than the City Manager's, the chief was able, on occasion, to stand up publicly to City Hall over budgetary constraints placed upon him. He once took ten cruisers off the road because, "City Hall doesn't give me enough gas money to keep them rolling."

My working relationship with this chief was always strong. When he heard I was being feted by the state Civil Defense Agency, he sprung for a "coffee and" party. Not long afterward, I received a call from an excited chief telling me to get to Communications Division fast, there was a major story breaking. When I zoomed into the room, notebook and pen in hand, there was the entire day relief with a huge cake commemorating my 25th year at the paper. I had forgotten the date. The chief had not.

During the years I had already been on the beat, the Police Department was reorganized repeatedly by six previous chiefs. Notwithstanding the many times those with the gold stars on their collars created organizational turmoil, the department always seemed to keep rolling along as if nothing was happening.

The resiliency of the troops was remarkable. As his thirty-nine-year police career ended, I wrote of a man who brought integrity, candor, humor, military-trim appearance and progress to the department. On his last day, the "Little Chief" slipped quietly out of the building and went home to the "Big Chief," his wife.

THE LIAISON OFFICER GOT THE JOB AS THE 33RD CHIEF IN THE department's long history, but he turned out to be an enigma: friendly, with a sly smirk on his face much of the time, but behind the mask, a withdrawn loner. His thoughts, emotions, and opinions remained concealed, for the most part, behind a smiling countenance. In all the years I wrote about him, rode with him, and associated socially with him, I never was able to penetrate his inner personality. I never fathomed whether it was Irish clannishness—much of it was, I am sure—or a latent air of superiority he kept well under wraps. All I know is that I gave him much more friendship than he ever returned.

When the chief was sworn in, a wave of optimism swept over the force. He was perceived as a "cops' cop," one who had worked up through the ranks the hard way, out on the street, and who, like everyone else, had earned his battle scars. He had a master's degree, a twenty-seven-year performance record serving in every division in the department, both uniformed branches and plain clothes investigation units, and had proven his bravery repeatedly in the Vice Squad. He was swept into office on a tide of popularity, hope, and optimism.

Previously, he had been an excellent news source, one who underplayed his own role in various incidents. But, somewhere along the line something happened and our once strong alliance began to erode. In-house analysts claimed the chief's debt to the City Manager for his support through the years was such that he was compelled, like numerous chiefs before him, to knuckle under, to become completely subservient to the manager. He became, in the minds of many, a follower rather than a leader—a puppet no longer sympathetic to the needs of the men on the street. Some accused him of living on past glories and using the system for personal gain.

I digested all the squad room stories, the street analysis, the patrol car harping, the locker room opinions but refused to allow them to sway my respect for the chief. I gave him the opportunity to prove himself in the new position. I tried throughout my police beat career—and it was not always easy—never to form opinions not based on fact. I gave the chief breathing room to prove himself. Soon, he too appointed a liaison officer, the so-called parrot for the department, so he could sequester himself further from the public and the media. It should be remembered that reporters too are only parrots repeating in print what someone has said or done. By journalistic dictum, reporters are not granted the luxury of an opinion. This eternal verity, in my day, was carved in granite. Opinions were granted only to sports writers, columnists, and editorial writers.

The chief's chair was not even warm when I interviewed him on his goals for the department. He envisioned stronger community involvement, one on one contact with the citizenry, linking with the

public through neighborhood meetings, and listening to public concerns. He promised total warfare against drugs, an area in which he
had been involved for many years in the Vice Squad. He made the top
brass more readily available to the cop on the street. One of his first
moves was to assign a captain as a civil rights officer to hear and investigate all complaints of possible civil rights violations, either by his
men or anyone else. The move, he said, was a firm commitment to the
protection of all citizens.

A fourteen-man Neighborhood Strike Force was created to drive
drug traffic and prostitution out of the beleaguered South End.
Residents there found cops all over the place. Fifty-three arrests were
made in three days. The chief kept the heat on as arrests reached into
the hundreds. Crime continued but went underground. But, as the
chief set loftier goals and strived to achieve them, his health started to
fail, eventually resulting in a heart attack. Gradually, the chief's work
load was lessened. A deputy was named as department spokesman and
served as acting chief for the ensuing two years. It was disturbing to
listen to the accusations that he was only a "figurehead chief," especially after so many, at the outset of his tenure, had expressed high
hopes for him. During his last months on the job, the disappointment
in him through the rank and file became stronger, more accepted, and
more outspoken. A quiet man had worked hard to be a strong chief,
but perhaps had just given off the wrong signals to his men, many of
whom felt they had not had the chief they anticipated.

THE LAST OF A LONG STRING OF CHIEFS WITH WHOM I HAD TO
work, was by far the most popular one with the troops. Never once
did I hear a disparaging word about the man. This type of loyalty is
almost unheard of in police ranks. Strangely missing were the misfit
malcontents with never a good word about anything and everything.
He knew every officer on the force by his or her first name and he
jogged with his men every noon to stay in top shape. You name it, the

chief had probably done it: a former Marine, street drummer, marathon runner, hunter, fisherman, artist, football guard and quarterback, and a strict parent. By reputation, he had excelled in every endeavor he had undertaken. Like several other chiefs before him, he had served in every division.

In all my years, I had never met anyone more personable. I have always regretted I had only eleven months of association with this most enlightened and captivating chief. During that time, he seemed to do everything right: making well thought out decisions, responding swiftly and honestly to citizen concerns, never displaying self glorification as had some other chiefs before him, and working diligently to please the public and his officers.

I was not around for his eventual retirement brought about by a disagreement, I was told, with a rather dictatorial new city manager. If true, his forced retirement was one of the greatest disservices to the city, in modern times. But, perhaps he had the last laugh. In what might be called poetic justice, the city manager's service to the city was terminated not long afterward.

the evolution of law enforcement: constitutional and civil rights

DURING THE FOUR DECADES BETWEEN 1950 AND 1990, LAW enforcement experienced a more striking metamorphosis than probably it had for any similar period in the twentieth century. Communications evolved from street call boxes or borrowed telephones to multi-band, secure channel, two-way radios. Cramped, rusted-out Cadillac ambulances were replaced by ultra-modern rolling hospitals. Armament went from six-shooters and shotguns to arsenals of automatic rifles, machine guns, stun grenades, chemical canisters, and life saving flak vests. But most importantly education, within police ranks, evolved through the years from grade school level to advanced college degrees including sophisticated legal methodology.

During the early sixties, the U.S. Supreme Court restrictions imposed on police across the land constituted more than anything else the biggest transition affecting and protecting the American citizen. Matters, such as how to handle a situation, or to effect an arrest, how to amass evidence or testimony, or how to prepare a criminal case for court, previously part of the individual officer's prerogative, were taken out of the hands of the street cop and standardized.

In June 1961, in a landmark case, *Mapp versus Ohio*, the Supreme Court interpreted seizure provisions strictly. The ruling brought all state rules of evidence in line with federal court standards; evidence obtained illegally could not be admitted in court. Prior to that decision, evidence presented in Massachusetts courts was generally admissible, regardless of how it was obtained by police during their investigations. As a result of the court decision, search warrants had to be minutely detailed before they were issued by the court.

Three years later, in June 1964, in the case of *Escobedo versus Illinois*, standards were set for all future methods of interrogation by police. In essence, the ruling insisted that the right to a lawyer was absolute when the investigation progressed from the investigatory stage to the accusatory stage, a very fine line that was often a matter of interpretation.

In June 1966, in the third major decision altering law enforcement, in the case of *Miranda versus Arizona*, the Supreme Court spelled out more clearly the rights of the accused before police interrogation could take place. In an extension of the *Escobedo* case, the court required first that police warn all persons accused of a crime, that:

1. They had the right to remain silent.
2. If they chose to speak, anything they said could be used against them in a court of law.
3. They had the absolute right to have an attorney present during questioning.
4. If they could not afford counsel, an attorney would be provided at public expense.

If the defendant was detained, he or she had to be allowed to use a telephone at his/her own expense, to contact friends, to engage a lawyer, or to arrange for release on bail.

The issue at stake was the matter of self-incrimination, a protection that extended back to seventeenth century English law. Henceforth, to satisfy liberal lower-court standards, police, forced to

"Mirandize" suspects at practically every turn in their investigations, felt the process would mark the end of confessions considered the foundation of any criminal case. Instead, the *Mapp*, *Escobedo*, and *Miranda* rulings forced police to develop new, more professional investigative procedures now that they could no longer rely on confessions. The net result was, over the years, the development of higher police standards and a more modern approach to police work in general. Without the ingredient of a confession (and there were very few once the criminal element learned it did not have to make them), police were forced to resort to other means to build their cases, mostly with the procurement of stronger evidence and broader witness testimony. Never again would there be the shortcut provided by a criminal admission.

Old and grizzled street cops found themselves back in the classroom redefining their trade. Another by-product of the court mandates was the unofficial abolition of "alley courts," in darkened back alleys, where crime prevention, retribution, and justice were beaten out of suspects. By the mid-sixties, the street court judicial system, a widespread adjudication practiced by many street cops, had all but disappeared.

All over, training seminars sprouted as police struggled to keep the playing field level. Officers took courses in report writing, conversational Spanish, neatness, courtesy, evidence procurement, Constitutional law, stress training, court procedures, community and human relations with special emphasis on sensitivity toward minorities.

The Supreme Court guaranteed that no longer would there be forced entry into a dwelling or business property without a properly documented and legitimate search warrant. Thereafter, the courts rejected testimony or confessions that were grilled out of a suspect without legal counsel. In three precedent-setting decisions in 1961, 1964, and 1966, the Supreme Court delineated precisely how evidence must be obtained and seized, and how police accusatory interrogations had to be conducted.

The guidelines imposed by the court were nothing more than strict interpretations of Constitutional law, but laws that were seldom read or adhered to by police, prosecutors, and lower courts across the land. The high court renderings forced police—kicking and screaming in many cases—to quickly alter their methods. Change is never easy. It is often easier to accept and bring about change if it is done gradually. That was not the case in the issue between the court and police. These decisions were abrupt, triggered by examples of poor or sloppy police work, in Ohio, Illinois, and Arizona. Many stunned police officials felt that the traditional and proven effective way of cracking a case was being abolished too abruptly and being replaced by radical, diametrically different, and unproven investigative techniques. There was no orientation or acclimation period. The old adage that an old dog cannot be taught new tricks is a truism. But for thousands of old dogs fighting crime on the nation's streets, the new tricks were being crammed down their throats repeatedly and with such force by the lower courts that many almost choked on them.

Police, in most cases, struggled to conform to the literal court interpretations of Constitutional law. Even when police managed to function strictly within these mandates, ultra-liberal judges in lower courts nit-picked the cases to death, releasing suspects in droves on minor technicalities. District, Superior, and Juvenile courts often made a mockery of reason and common sense, trying to ensure that criminal rights were fully protected. Thoroughly investigated and well-prepared criminal cases were thrown out of lower courts for no plausible reason on obscure technicalities and law interpretations that no police officer on the street could possibly be expected to know or understand. It appeared that each judge was fighting to be considered more liberal than the next bench warmer. It was a trying time of transition for police.

It seemed that the only one concerned about the rights of the crime victims was the police officer investigating the crime, and he was rapidly being rendered ineffective by the courts. Law enforcement, and society in general, were being pummeled by judges with judicial haymakers and uppercuts. To protect themselves, some judges resorted to seemingly outlandish decisions stacked so far on the side of the defendant that justice screamed for relief. Police openly criticized the courts, something that traditionally they were reluctant to do. After all, they had to work through the courts and to have judges ticked off at those testifying before them would be detrimental to the police cause.

Appeals clogged court dockets. The whole judicial system was in danger of bogging down, police said. "The public suffers at the hands of these judges for police or prosecutors have no right to appeal these odd decisions, but the defendant can, and does, appeal almost everything," one chief complained. "So you have two forces, law enforcement and the criminal element. You remove the dialogue between the two because of the Supreme Court, and it is often fatal to society. This is an excruciating experience for the public, one that creates apathy. Every day, all over the country, police departments are turning loose and without prosecution dangerous criminals, because they know that police, trying to protect the public, would not stand a chance in court," complained one police official.

In early 1962, when I first broke in full-time on the police beat, cops still joked about a captain detective who hanged suspects by their fingertips from third floor windows, and then threatened to mash their fingers with a billy club, if they did not confess to whatever he requested. Law enforcement back then was still pretty raw. Fists flew first, questions were asked later. With my sensitivities shocked, I watched a small, skinny teenager, his hands cuffed behind his back, take a shot to the back of his neck by a 200-pound cop, as he was being pushed roughly up a flight of stairs to the Youth Aid Division. The sucker punch sent the kid sprawling face down onto the marble steps. I learned later that the youth had beaten his mother and also mugged an elderly woman. The incident was the street cop's way of expressing an opinion: sucker punch retribution.

Search warrants were practically unheard of in the early days. I knew of a case where a man complained his watch had been stolen. He said he knew who the thief was. The cop broke down the suspect's door, searched his apartment, found a gold watch and waved it under the victim's nose. "Is this the watch?" Assured it was, the stolen timepiece was returned to the owner. Case closed successfully. Effective? Certainly. Legal? No way.

IN WORCESTER, POLICE AND THE DISTRICT ATTORNEY'S OFFICE moved swiftly to adjust to the new court interpretations. Seminars were scheduled and booklets explaining the new law procedures were distributed to all police officers. Prosecutors found themselves faced with more pretrial hearings on motions to suppress evidence. Trials dragged out longer and court dockets became even more hopelessly clogged. By 1967, district attorneys were admitting openly that the Supreme Court rulings were a major factor in crime increases nationwide. The pendulum swung so far to one side, the DAs were eventually proven correct in their prognostications. One local judge reminded people that their Constitutional rights had always been there but had become somewhat obscured by the passage of time. The rulings were merely a reaffirmation, not a change in the Constitution.

Police pointed out that the necessity for more thorough, time-consuming investigations slowed all other police efforts and prophesied that unless more police were hired, the number of investigations they could undertake would fall off sharply. Police, the courts, and the district attorney found some common ground: they all agreed the only way out of the court-imposed dilemma was through education. This was a new ball game and the players had better be ready to play.

The first step toward compliance with the court decisions was teaching more extensive police subject matter, delving deeper into interpretation, and reaching further in scope. In a hurry, department administrators were faced with the formidable task of turning their troops into street lawyers. Public defenders and district attorneys opened their doors to guide police through the intricacies of local, state, and federal laws. They showed police how to build their cases and then evaluated them when investigators felt they were ready to proceed into court. This alliance continues today on an almost daily basis, especially regarding felony cases or capital crimes.

The federal court decisions gave some police officials a new fad about which to grouse during the mid- to late sixties. They growled about how they, not the criminal, were being handcuffed by the court. I became their sounding board, sort of a pipe organ to public sympathy as police aired their frustrations and grievances in print. Their discontent made good copy, while serving to educate the public on the constrictions being placed on traditional police practices.

But lost in the legal tidal wave that washed over police everywhere was another development in the war against crime. The Supreme Court interpretations had a sharp effect on budding criminals, the juvenile delinquents who were hearing for the first time that they too, like adults, had Constitutional rights. One outspoken Juvenile Division commander claimed that court decisions put delinquents on a pedestal where they enjoyed a position of great self importance. He said the court rulings would not serve to correct delinquents, but instead would defend them and their criminal actions. The effective days of a stern warning, maybe even a mild threat to first time offenders was effectively taken away from police, he added. "The child who was once a juvenile delinquent has now been afforded the stature of adulthood. This suddenly important youth now appears on the witness stand, not at all afraid of impending punishment, but instead sees himself being defended staunchly for his wrong actions. Kids learn quickly. They flaunt the fact that they do not have to tell us anything. Suddenly, these kids know their rights. It is good-bye juvenile crime suppression." He also pointed out that the guidance that probation was meant to offer was becoming a thing of the past. Previous to the court decisions, Juvenile Court sessions were usually a closed hearing attended by a judge, the police officer complainant, the youth's parents, and the offender. Now delinquents were armed with batteries of lawyers. Police cited the case of the unprovoked racist fatal stabbing of a seventeen-year-old near his home as a classic example of police frustration and inability to bring criminals to justice, even for capital crimes. The case was never solved when the eventual prime suspect's mother repeatedly refused to allow police to interview her teenage son. In the absence of the ability to question a suspect, the only recourse police had was to prepare circumstantial evidence cases, which police abhorred because that was tantamount to sloppy workmanship.

Influenced by the constant griping of police officers empathizing with the victims of crime, I published a series on the subject. After interviewing dozens of men, women, children, and the elderly, I chronicled their comments and opinions. I then poured over police statistics, dissecting each crime into categories and figures that could be easily understood by readers. Afterward, police told me that it was the first time they had heard the voices of crime victims raised in protest. My findings clearly illustrated that victims of crime, on the whole, were receiving no redress from the courts or from any other facet of the judicial system. I also showed how the legal cards were stacked against the victim, and arranged almost solely in favor of the criminal and his or her Constitutional rights. The articles were hard-hitting, but, as the cops chided me afterward, nothing changed in the courts. "Probably not," I responded, "but I gave the city something to think about and that's how change is effected."

Confronted with the continued liberalism of the courts, police turned to specialized enforcement by creating burglary, robbery, arson, and car theft squads thus offering concentrated enforcement by special teams, solely concerned with specific crime categories. Police experimented with different strategies. The department was organized, reorganized, and then reorganized some more. The city, ostensibly to strengthen supervision and enforcement, was geographically bisected, trisected, and quartered. Many of the strategy adjustments were effective for a while, but just as often the moves eventually reverted to the original methods used. It was for the department a period of fine-tuning its offense. Repeated attempts were made to regionalize law enforcement, for the reason that there is strength in unity, especially where police intelligence can be exchanged. Every time, however, a reluctance to forgo autonomy defeated this innovative approach to police work. It was probably just as well, for the bickering I observed between cities and towns over autonomy negated any possibility of cooperative effectiveness.

While all this upgrading of police efficiency, and this profound challenge to police ingenuity were taking place, another much desired improvement in law enforcement was subtly transpiring. In my early days on the police beat, racism and bigotry were prevalent and perpetuated, it seemed, by some more than by other ethnic groups. But as the world changed with the times, so did this insensitivity practiced by many police officers. With the infusion of a new breed of cop, better educated, more tolerant, more attuned to society's social problems of the seventies and eighties, the racist epithets disappeared from police jargon. By the mid-eighties, racial slurs were no longer even remembered by the new generation of officers.

As devastating as the Supreme Court decisions had been between 1961 and 1966, the negative predictions that successful criminal prosecution would be impossible without confessions failed to materialize. Police adapted, the lower courts reverted to common sense decisions, and criminals were taken off the streets and incarcerated as they always had been. In 1987, I conducted a survey of police officials and chiefs throughout Massachusetts, asking them what effect the *Mapp*, *Escobedo*, and *Miranda* decisions had on their departments. Unanimously, they agreed the decisions had been beneficial, and had in fact, forced them to upgrade their performance, something that they all said was long overdue. One police chief called the Supreme Court decisions "the catalysts that promoted professionalism in policing."

The sometimes haphazard crime investigations of the fifties and early sixties, many of them based on hearsay testimony, sketchy evidence, and loosely gathered case components, were not that long ago. That period in law enforcement history may seem archaic to today's police officers, but to those who ground their way steadily through the generations, it was only yesterday.

I was fortunate to remain on the job long enough to observe monumental changes in police work: sidecar motorcycles replaced by high speed, sleek two-wheelers; rumbling old "radio cars" transformed into today's high powered cruisers; baggy woolen uniforms redesigned into spiffy nylon or leather jackets; manual files and finger picking typewriters replaced by computers and word processors; grade school education improved to master's degrees in criminal justice; one-hour training indoctrination expanded to twenty-week college mini courses.

Some of all the dire consequences that police predicted sometimes happened. Cases were lost. Guilty hardened criminals with expert lawyers walked away unpunished. In many cases, justice was never served. But overall, the Supreme Court interpretations of the sixties were the strongest factor in transforming police departments into what they are today. Indeed, there was an evolution, a wonderful transformation for which the entire country and our society as a whole should be thankful. It was just another cog in the wheel of keeping up with the times.

vehicular fatalities

IN AMERICA, THE PRIMARY CONCERNS OF POLICE ARE DEATH BY violence and the means to prevent it. In most cases, if violent death is caused by homicide, it cannot be forestalled. Murder, police say, is largely a private matter, often unpremeditated and committed away from public scrutiny. However, violent death on the highway is an entirely different matter. To some degree, police say it also is unenforceable but, in the same breath, they say they have a good shot at preventing it.

Annually, in the country, no single cause is responsible for killing more people violently than highway accidents. It is no wonder that police spend so much time, money, and effort in attempting to prevent it. Police radar cars and motorcycles slow drivers. Roads and intersections are rebuilt to higher safety standards. Traffic lights are updated. Warning signs are posted. Yearly, the media pours out tons of ink printing accident prevention warnings. Every year, more highway safety laws are passed in every state although most of them seem to have little preventive value.

The bottom line is that the elimination of highway bloodshed is almost solely in the hands of individual drivers or pedestrians. With this truth in mind, the prevention of highway fatalites by police or any other means takes a hit from the motoring public. By and large, drivers ignore traffic lights, speed limits, safety signs, and most vehicular laws already on the books. Drivers drink to excess and drive nonetheless; they speed recklessly ignoring safety warnings; they drag race; they show off; they drive defective, unsafe vehicles; they settle arguments from behind the wheel; they brazenly dare trailer trucks. In other words, too many drive aggressively, and seldom defensively.

During my career, the National Safety Council reported, nationwide, an average of 46,000 highway fatalities each year. Of the estimated 8,000 accidents I covered during my years as a police reporter, about 450 of them involved highway slaughter. No two were alike. Elderly pedestrians died, new drivers died, reckless teenagers died, drunks died, and babies died, some by fiery incineration when gas tanks ruptured, others by massive, decapitating trauma when two tons of metal slammed against unyielding trees, bridge abutments, behemoth trucks, or other vehicles.

Weather, highway conditions, and equipment failures also contribute to the annual loss of life, but only to a negligible degree. The overriding factor was summed up for me once by a thirty-year veteran Traffic Division investigator of fatal accidents. "There is absolutely no way we can protect drivers from themselves," he stated. "That's where the whole problem lies."

During the early days while I honed my skills on what the paper called the "county beat," my introduction to highway fatalities was emotionally harsh. It came suddenly and tragically when three teenagers showing off on a straightaway lost control and shredded their car against a huge boulder outcropping. My job, beside reporting the accident, was to visit three devastated families for pictures of their dead loved ones to accompany my story. That was the method used by newspapers back then: the personal touch. I shall never forget what a grieving mother said as I thumbed through a family album searching for a picture of her dead daughter. "Nothing you can do, sir, can hurt me any more than I am hurting already." Obituary pictures today, whenever possible, are obtained through undertakers. This much gentler, more sympathetic approach came too late to help me emotionally.

WHEN WORKING OUT OF POLICE HEADQUARTERS IN WORCESTER, my initiation to highway carnage was no less startling. During the last week of August 1964, three young people, possibly driving too fast, died in a fiery explosion near a local college. The crash woke up neighborhood residents, some of whom ran from their homes to assist the victims. Those first on the scene related horror stories of the screaming of the victims echoing through the night air. Within minutes, fire apparatus, illuminated by a twenty-foot ball of flames obliterating the vehicular coffin, came roaring around the curve where the accident took place. Within minutes, the broiling fire was extinguished. Mercifully, the voices inside had already been stilled by death. All that remained were charred corpses that forensic pathologists and police were charged with identifying.

Police, city traffic engineers, and an accident reconstruction team from the Registry of Motor Vehicles studied the road layout and lighting, trying to determine the contributing factors to the accident. Excess speed and alcohol were investigated but, in the end, no firm conclusions were drawn. There were only suppositions and no survivors, no witnesses to interview.

By this time, I had been on the beat long enough to be using police terminology when discussing highway accidents involving deaths. They were not called highway fatality accidents, they were just termed "fatals." To develop an insight into the problem, I often rode with radar enforcement cars and police accident reconstruction teams.

In the radar cars it was hilarious to record all the lame excuses used by those stopped for traveling fifty miles an hour in a twenty-mile-an-hour zone. The alibis made good copy and became just another segment of my own accident prevention programs. Speeders fell basically into two categories: males who glumly accepted their fate or per-haps, in a few instances, made sarcastic remarks; and females who often became verbally abusive, even swearing at or vilifying the offi-cer. Some males were name droppers. This worked only if the name was that of another police officer. A call to headquarters or some other police unit to confirm that the speeder was actually a member of the police family or a close friend or associate decided the fate of the errant motorist.

Women, on the other hand, when they were not howling in right-eous indignation, reacted differently. Some fluttered their eye lashes and tried to project sex appeal in subtle seduction attempts to distract the officer's attention. Some resorted to tears, others to pleading for mercy, while a few brought up the carefully veiled subject of bribery. At least, while I was in the back seat, none of these tactics worked. Courteously, citations were handed out, usually with pleasant reminders about safety.

"You have to learn to accept the insults," the radar cop explained. "You just let them roll off your back. It's part of the job. These peo-ple don't consider themselves law breakers. When you remind them that they are, their egos can't handle it."

It was not always so with the Registry of Motor Vehicles, whose inspectors tended to be a little more authoritative and stern toward wayward motorists. Riding with Inspector Fred Hughes one morning in the city's West Side outer perimeter, I eavesdropped unobtrusively while he patiently listened to an irate speeder. Finally, his patience at an end, Hughes matter-of-factly cautioned the fuming driver, "Keep right on talking, sir. I can keep writing (violations) as long as you want. I don't get writer's cramp for quite a while." The vitriolic outburst from the driver was reduced instantly to unintelligible grumbling.

ONE OF THE MORE BIZARRE "FATALS" INVOLVED A TWENTY-FIVE-year-old city man whose life was snuffed out, police said, after he was allegedly involved in a suburban town coffee shop fracas. When police arrived to quell the disturbance, one of the combatants jumped into a car and sped away east bound on Route 9 toward Boston. A police bulletin was broadcast describing a white Buick sedan wanted for questioning in regards to a possible armed assault. The radio bulletin also mentioned the driver might be armed. The wanted vehicle was spotted a short time later traveling at a high rate of speed on Route 495. The pursuit was on. As adrenaline starts pumping, high speed chases become contagious. The pursuit becomes one on one, a wild competition: the cop against the bad guy. A desperate, fleeing driver versus a police officer adventurously performing his duty at all costs.

The getaway car picked up speed trying to evade the pursuing police cars. Soon, cruisers from four other towns joined the chase. The pursued sedan, tires trailing clouds of smoke, lurched violently from one side of the highway to the other as its driver fought to maintain control. With his foot jammed to the floor, the wanted driver, now in full flight, desperately rammed the chase speed up to 120 miles an hour. Without slowing, the car blurred through a roadblock set up by police.

A few miles further, an empty trailer truck used by police as a roadblock suddenly loomed out of the darkness before him. One narrow lane had been left open. The high pitch screech of smoking tires resounded through the night as the driver slammed on his brakes. In one last violent, evasive maneuver, the car seemed to pirouette before it disintegrated in a blinding explosion against the truck. The trailer box was pushed twenty feet sideways by the impact. When the smoke dissipated, only fragments of the car and of its driver remained. He was alone in the car when his life came to a shattering, millisecond end. Police said they never determined why the suspect fled so desperately or what he was trying to hide. All they wanted was to question him about a coffee shop disturbance, a misdemeanor.

DURING THAT SAME PERIOD, A CITY MAN LOST HIS LIFE WHEN HE drowned during a high speed police chase. An auto theft detection investigator, on routine patrol on the boulevard marking the eastern approach into the city, observed a stealthy figure casing used cars in a lot in the middle of the night. Spotting the police cruiser, the man jumped into a nearby parked car and fishtailed away with tires squealing. With the cruiser riding his rear bumper, the getaway car careened onto one side street after another, trying to lose its tail. With lights out, the fleeing car roared toward the outskirts of the city, wildly skidding into more side streets. The chase continued to a municipal park where the suspect swerved onto a boulder strewn access road, the police car nose-to-tail behind him. Apparently unfamiliar with the area, the getaway car swung onto a 100-foot long dead end street where, without warning, it suddenly disappeared into the night. Illuminated momentarily by the cruiser headlights, the car was spotted again for a split second sailing through the air, whining wheels still spinning furiously. The police cruiser burned rubber sideways as the investigator fought to stop. He was familiar with the abbreviated street and remembered there was no barrier separating the roadway from an eighty-foot embankment to Lake Quinsigamond.

Police estimated that the getaway car flew more than 100 feet through the air before crashing nose first into the lake. Car theft officers jumped from the cruiser and scrambled down the steep banking to the water's edge. Shining their flashlights on the surface of the lake, all they saw were waves lapping at the shore line and a large gasoline slick forming on the surface. A hurried emergency call went out for volunteer SCUBA divers. Perhaps the driver was still alive. Using underwater lights, the divers located the car about sixty feet from shore, perched vertically underwater, its front bumper and grillwork dug into the muddy lake bottom. The body of the driver was found crammed beneath the dashboard where he had been unable to free himself before drowning.

REPEATEDLY, THROUGH THE YEARS, I WAS ASKED BY VARIOUS POLICE departments, bereaved families, and the Registry of Motor Vehicles to publish follow up stories on unsolved hit and run "fatals." It did not matter whether it was about a couple killed together crossing a city thoroughfare, an eighteen-year-old teenage girl bicyclist on an inter-state highway—where she was not supposed to be—an immigrant father only a short time in this country, a Halloween trick-or-treater, an elderly woman on her way to Easter Mass at a neighborhood church, or a small tot on a tricycle, the police appeal for information-al assistance was always written willingly. Police chiefs from several suburban towns knew they had a willing media outlet when their investigations "hit the blank wall."

Highway "fatals," especially those at night, are difficult to solve if there are no witnesses and if police are unable to recover physical evidence at the scene. The most formidable enemy that police inves-tigators confront in such accidents is public apathy, the instinctive desire not to become involved in anything relating to police. But, if hit and run victims were young, or the family loss occurred during a holiday season, public emotions were stimulated. Police accident investigators say they become so totally involved in each case that every minute detail becomes indelibly etched in their memories. These are the officers who are forced to view the crushed, battered bodies on highways or at morgues, and have to interview mourning loved ones afterwards. Fatality accidents take on a very personal aspect for police officers. Some told me that it was the ugliest crime with which they dealt.

IT WAS SNOWING HARD ON DECEMBER 29, 1969. CELEBRATIONS were already being planned for New Year's Eve. For one family, the holiday festivities were abruptly shattered by death—sudden, violent death on the highway.

Fate destined a tragic chain of events leading up to the death—an innocent victim being at the wrong place at the wrong moment. The victim, who dabbled in real estate to help support his family, had been repairing some property he owned in the city. His work done, the man started driving his pickup through a snow storm to his home where a party was planned. On the way, the truck bogged down in snow. With no help available anywhere and the truck hopelessly disabled, the man found a telephone and told his family he was going to walk home, a distance of more than five miles. The night was dark and cold but he was dressed warmly and he was strong and young, only 49. His family offered to intercept him on the way in another vehicle. Head bent against the storm, he trudged slowly toward home, walking on the wrong side of the highway. He never made it to his destination. On Interstate 20, an east bound car, weaving from side to side, changed the life of a whole family in one blinding, sickening split second. The victim was thrown cartwheeling over the roof of the car. The car stopped; a woman in a car behind it screamed. Startled, the driver, who witnesses told police appeared to be drunk, lurched back into his light blue Plymouth sedan and sped away into the night. Witnesses said the car was still operating erratically when it disappeared from sight into the darkness and they gave police a partial description of the driver and the death vehicle. Family members searching for the victim and seeing the police cruisers at the accident scene, instantly, knew the worst. Police worked feverishly against time on the man, but he succumbed a few minutes later at a local hospital from a fractured skull and massive body injuries.

Investigators from Worcester police and Registry of Motor Vehicles shoveled and sifted through snow drifts beside the roadway throughout the night. Pictures were taken. From physical evidence found at the scene, investigators were able to determine the year and make of the hit and run vehicle. Paint chips and broken parts were analyzed later by State Police. Officers from almost every town in Worcester County canvassed parts outlets and auto body shops.

Thousands of partial registration numbers were cross-referenced through Registry computers. More than 40,000 vehicles fitting the description of the hit and run vehicle were spit out. Eventually, the list was culled down to 200. Investigators created a profile noting the truck, the driving schedule of the driver, time and location of the accident, who, owning such a car, would be at that spot at that time. It was slow, tedious, painstaking digging. I composed several emotional appeals to the public for information. Generated leads were checked out—all dead end. The killer was never found.

THE POLICE DISPATCHER'S BASSO PROFUNDO VOICE BROKE THROUGH my morning routine with an announcement that a runaway dump truck had rolled down a steep hilly western approach to the city and had rammed several cars, one of which was buried under tons of gravel.

When I arrived, the scene resembled a war zone. The ten-wheeler had strewn wreckage across an entire four way intersection, a rear ended doctor's car had been catapulted almost 100 feet into the front display window of a florist shop and seven injured people were being attended by rescue workers. Twisted car parts were scattered everywhere. Fire Rescue Squad crews were furiously using air bags to lift the truck off the crushed car beneath it while others shoveled gravel to uncover the car. Most of the car's roof and rear fenders had been torn off by the impact.

Witnesses told me that the truck was rolling between sixty and seventy miles an hour as it entered the intersection with air horn blasting.

As police cordoned off the area and detoured traffic from the scene, fire fighters continued in their attempt to uncover the gravel smothered car. It was not known whether any of the occupants survived. Fire fighters started waving their arms, yelling "listen, listen," for silence. The faint, frightened voices of an elderly couple could be heard emanating from the crushed car. Over and over they cried for help. The diggers began shoveling faster, throwing gravel all over the square. After what must have seemed like an eternity for the couple trapped inside, rescuers using pry bars and brute strength, were able to yank and tug one door open. "We're OK. Just get us out," were the words that greeted the extrication crews. What had all the potential for multiple fatalities, had instead involved mostly minor injuries.

I raced to check out the victims at the Emergency Room of the city's municipal hospital. The supervisor who was the firmly established senior "pro" in the city's emergency medical circles, responded, "Just a few bumps and bruises, Rock. We put some band aids on them, gave 'em a pat on the rump and threw them all out." The supervisor, perhaps the warmest, most competent, and cooperative medical contact with whom I had to work daily, was the widow of a former police chief who, just before I arrived on the police scene, had committed suicide in his office. Many police officials said accusingly afterwards that his death had been brought on by constant departmental criticism by the newspaper. I never determined the true reason for if it was true I was not sure I wanted to know about it.

SOME FATAL ACCIDENTS ARE JUST THAT—ACCIDENTS. OTHERS ARE vehicular homicides. Late one night, on Interstate Route 20, in a suburban town, two young men died, one beheaded when he was impaled on a highway guard rail in what would today be classified as road rage. The deaths were an aftermath of a barroom brawl exploding into premeditated violence which then escalated into a high speed car chase that lasted more than a mile.

In an interview with two of the terrified survivors of the death car—I hesitate to call it an accident—they described a two A.M. drunken gang fight involving eighteen to twenty people in a watering hole parking lot, a few feet east of the city line. The fight spilled all over the lot, witnesses claimed. Some of the combatants, outnumbered by their assailants, ran away. One was found bleeding and walking beside the highway about 300 feet from the altercation.

When his friends picked him up, the group returned to the café and rammed a parked car repeatedly, shoving it against the café building. A group ran from the joint and started throwing bottles at the car inflicting the damage. Then the chase began as the first vehicle tried to flee. Two others joined the chase, one of them rear-ending the fleeing car before pulling along side it and repeatedly ramming it, trying to push it off the road. As the two vehicles careened all over the highway, tires screeching, occupants of the lead car leaned out windows, arms waving, crying for the chasing car assault to stop. Instead, the speeds increased, drunken rage boiling in both cars.

Finally, the chasing car rammed the other vehicle with such force that, in a blinding moment, the chase ended when the lead car was hurled against a highway guard rail. The force of impact curled a section of the rail like a giant pretzel and propelled it through the passenger front window. Two men died instantly, one of them decapitated with his mangled head thrown onto the car floor for police to retrieve later. The pursuing car sped away before police arrived.

Police found the demolished car still suspended off the ground by the guard rail. The score: two eventual arrests and two more needless violent highway deaths.

It is not often that a highway victim disappears before police arrive at the scene. When the police squawk box in my pressroom called for investigators of Traffic Division accidents, it was usually a sure sign that another fatal accident had occurred in the city. It was my signal to scrub out. This one turned out to be in the Swedish section of the city and had happened at the foot of one of the city's steepest streets, one on which I had sledded hundreds of times as a small boy. A huge rubbish compactor truck had lost its brakes on the hill and, despite futile attempts to down shift, had hurtled across a busy thoroughfare and rolled onto its side, throwing a passenger beneath it. The driver had been given no alternative but to ride it out and pray. On coming traffic had swerved onto sidewalks and veered into gutters to avoid the runaway truck. Witnesses told me that the truck's blasting air horn could be heard reverberating off neighborhood three-story dwellings all the way down the hill.

When I peered beneath the overturned truck, the helper had been reduced to a few shredded pieces of bloody flesh and a small puddle of blood. Nothing else remained. The helper had literally disappeared. I questioned what I was seeing. An accident investigator standing nearby said, "That's all that's left, Rock. There is no more."

A DRIVER FROM NORTHEASTERN MASSACHUSETTS WAS KILLED ONE winter night in a two car, head-on collision as a result of a nature created ice rink on the outer West Side. The story I filed of the accident rattled cages all the way from City Hall to the police chief's front office. It was the only time I remember that top police brass actively tried to hamper, even prevent, my news reporting. Following up on a rumor I had heard, I researched the accident more deeply than normally. I found that the ice rink had been formed when an underground water main burst, flooding large sections of the street. The bitter cold night turned the water to ice almost instantly.

Discovering the hazardous condition while on routine patrol, a route car called for sand. Five times, police Communications Division logged calls to the city Department of Public Works. Each time the calls went unanswered. DPW workers later told police the phones had been shut off at 6 P.M. due to budgetary cuts. I reported all this in my story.

Suddenly, everyone started crawling under the rug trying to avoid responsibility for the deadly foul up. For several days the controversy raged and blame for the accident was hurled back and forth between the two municipal departments. Finally, both decided to vent their rage on me for reporting the truth of the matter in the first place. A gag rule was placed on the whole station. No one was to speak to me or give me or any other reporter information relative to the accident.

They tried to make me believe that sometimes the public is better served if it is not told everything that goes on in the city. Personnel of the Communications Division were scolded for giving me, in the first place, the initial information about the multiple requests for city sand.

It was journalism under pressure, something that police reporters faced in different forms almost daily.

ONE OF THE WILDEST AND MOST TRAGIC HIGH SPEED CHASE DEATHS involved a sixteen-year-old car thief shot to death by a State Trooper. Before the chase was over, three police officers were injured, three cruisers demolished, and a teenager dead. The chase started on the east side of the city when a police cruiser swung in behind a speeding car. Spotting the cruiser in his rear view mirror, the youth started zig-zagging furiously at a high rate of speed trying to shake the officer off his tail, passing cars on the left and right, bouncing over median strips, across a bridge and into an adjoining town. One after another, the teenager crisscrossed several side streets, U-turning in parking lots, weaving a checkerboard pattern through several residential sections. Repeatedly, he slammed on his brakes trying to make pursuing cruisers rear end him. On a narrow, winding north south side street in the town, the youth navigated the street's seventeen curves at high speed like an experienced race car driver before violently skidding sideways onto west bound Interstate Route 20. By this time, the fleeing car's tires were gone and bare rims were showering pursuing police with wild showers of flames and sparks. For another mile the chase, now joined by State Police, continued into the city.

Without warning, the stolen car coasted to a stop beside the road. Cruisers cautiously boxed in the smoking car, not knowing what to expect next. As the officers stepped from their cars, guns drawn, the youth waited until all were on foot and then jammed his car forward violently, trying to hit as many as he could. Back and forth his car lurched, viciously damaging three cruisers as he tried to ram his way free. As the state troopers jumped out of the way, they fired three shots at the youth. Other officers scattered as the youth's car struck a retaining wall. He was slumped over the wheel, blood gushing from a head wound. He died the next day at a local hospital. He was well known to police. Several weeks before he had attempted to run down a police officer only a mile away from where he was shot.

The troopers were exonerated after an internal investigation into the circumstances surrounding the use of lethal force.

THE EXUBERANT FROLICKING OF A GROUP OF YOUNGSTERS RESULTED in the death of a thirteen-year-old student run over by a school bus; another, in a series of so many accidents that never should have happened. It was another of the hard to understand tragedies in life that seemingly could have been avoided. Playful children seldom give thought to death or the possible consequences of their actions. As children are wont to do, they push, and shove, and wrestle when a group gathers. It is nothing more than the release of energy. Such a group, while waiting for the school bus, gathered in front of one of the city's private academies. The bus was late and the group swelled to almost fifty youths milling around, police said. Finally, the bus arrived and as it slowed down, the pushing and shoving to get on first started in earnest. One boy lost his balance and was thrown against the moving bus. He fell to the ground and beneath the bus wheels, crushed instantly. The boy, only five weeks short of his fourteenth birthday, was DOA (dead on arrival) at a hospital only a block away. Police attempts to save him had been to no avail. The driver was found not at fault.

HIGHWAY DEATHS IN THE CITY ALWAYS SEEMED TO AFFECT THE station hard, especially when it was the demise of one of their own. A pall of sadness fell over headquarters when it was learned that the department's most popular female cost analyst had been killed during her lunch hour in a head-on collision, again on Interstate Route 20, scene of more than a dozen deaths during my years on the police scene. Route 20 as it wound through Worcester County was well known as a deadly highway. The analyst was on her way home to feed her dog, Sam. Many times she and Sam had visited my home by boat.

She was a bundle of energy, usually talking with such exuberance it was difficult to keep up with her. She was the consummate professional, designing federal criminal justice programs for the city. She had been the primary author of the $812,000 federal grant for the highly successful Impact Program operating in one of the city's major crime ridden neighborhoods. The driver of the other car, a hostess at a country club where I frequently performed as a musician, also died of injuries sustained in the accident.

The last words of the member of the police family, according to police, was for someone to take care of Sam.

THE FINAL ACCIDENT INVOLVING FATALITIES THAT I COVERED during my career was one to remember. The car in which a young man was killed and another critically injured, had been shattered into multiple pieces of wreckage one day after it had been registered. The rear seat and trunk compartment had been thrown thirty-five feet in one direction, while the front seat and engine remained wrapped around a utility pole. The impact literally molded the driver into the dashboard. District Fire Chief, John Horgan, my son's EMT instructor, and the Fire Rescue Squad crew labored for thirty minutes to extricate the two victims. A reconstruction team stated that the car had been driven down a steep hill at eighty miles an hour and had bottomed out, catapulting it airborne nearly half a city block. When it slammed back to earth, it skidded out of control another 100 feet, scattering parts over a wide area before slamming against the pole. The determination: reckless operation.

In practically every highway death, investigators say that the blame rests squarely on the shoulders of drivers. Driver error, either in judgment or in operation, is the major cause of most serious accidents, police say. A little less booze, a little less speed, keener awareness behind the wheel, and a defensive driving posture would not necessarily eliminate highway carnage, but these measures would go a long way in that direction. Just ask the cop who week in and week out picks up bodies splattered all over the highways. He is an authority on the subject.

gun play

MANY AMERICANS HAVE AN AFFECTION FOR, AND AN ATTRACTION to guns. The founding fathers guaranteed the Constitutional right to bear arms, but it is highly doubtful they meant for the arms to be used so often as they are today. Bearing arms was to protect ourselves from foreign invaders. Within strict limitations, we still have that right. So does a police officer to use a gun to protect himself or anyone else by the use of lethal force. Too often, however, the right to use a weapon is abused. Readily available in many homes and on the streets, guns are used for revenge, for drug rip-off pay backs, to settle arguments, as punishment for infidelity, as a reaction to lost tempers, for kicks, as statements of importance, or to rob. Only rarely are they used in self-defense.

Police are ambivalent about guns. On the one hand, they are the last to want to deprive anyone of the right to own a gun. On the other hand, they wish there were not so many available and easily accessible to the wrong people: those emotionally or mentally unstable, those with criminal intent, or heavy drinkers. In the hands of such people, law enforcement authorities say that guns carry a potentially deadly threat to police officers on the street and to the public in general.

To be sure, in every state, there are gun laws on the books to protect the public and police officers. But all too often these protective laws fail to shield from injury. There is little legal protection against mental instability or a drunken rage, especially when readily accessible weapons are also involved. As well intentioned as gun laws are, people seldom stop to read them before they indulge in gunplay.

EARLY APRIL 1965 WAS LOVELY AND WARM, ALREADY SHIRT SLEEVE weather. I was enjoying a second cup of coffee and a doughnut in the Cell Room, sipping and munching my way through the sports page. Deadline was out of the way and it was time for a little self-indulgence. The radio calls droned on in the background but hardly anyone paid attention to them. Suddenly, shortly before noon, squawk boxes all over headquarters blared out the news that a disgruntled former employee of a North End manufacturing company was running amok with a pistol—shooting people at the plant.

Sirens reverberated off downtown office buildings joined in the distance by a chorus of others coming from, it seemed, every direction like a chorus of banshees. More sirens wailed throughout the recesses of headquarters as ambulances, the patrol wagon, detective cars, and traffic cruisers screamed away, all heading for the Worcester Expressway at breakneck speeds.

The newspaper and coffee went flying as I swept notepads and pens into my jacket pocket and raced for my car parked in a lot across the street. The puzzled lot attendant threw up his arms in defense as I gunned the car out the gate without even slowing down. What would usually be a seven-minute drive to the north end of the city was completed in three. Even at that, cruisers were passing me all along the way.

When I swerved into the company parking lot, officers stopping traffic recognized my car and flagged me through the cordoned-off police lines. Confusion at the company was such that, without being challenged, I was able to sprint with detectives up the stairs to the corporate suite.

Company workers had overpowered the gunman, a distraught former service engineer, and disarmed him, but not before he had shot three top executives. I stood in the background scribbling down everything I saw or heard at the outset, and then started interviewing anyone who was emotionally able to talk to me. As this went on, the gunman sat sullenly glowering at me, his hands handcuffed in his lap. Company employees, still in shock, talked openly, perhaps not fully understanding that they were talking to a reporter. During the initial confusion, I had not taken the time to identify myself. If the misconception existed that I was a cop taking investigative notes, I could tell them otherwise later. One company manager described the gunshots he heard in an adjoining office as sounding like hammer blows. Moments later, women began screaming, he said. When he ran into the office, the gunman was calmly standing in the middle of the floor reloading a .32 caliber, nickel-plated revolver. The manager said he asked the gunman to give up his weapon. "Get away or you'll get it too," the shooter screamed in response.

As the manager tried to inch his way behind the gunman without being noticed, the attacker left the office and headed down a flight of stairs to the company's main lobby and the parking lot. At the front door, the gunman was confronted by a company sales manager blocking his way. The gunman whirled and shot the man in the arm. Defying the pistol that was being waved menacingly in their faces, the wounded man and another employee jumped the gunman, grabbed the pistol, and wrestled the man to the floor. After a violent struggle, they subdued him until police arrived.

I grabbed the nearest phone I could find, called the City Desk and hurriedly dictated a story, informing them that staff photographers had pictures and were already on their way back to the paper.

When I returned to the shooting scene, detectives were digging slugs from a window and a wall. One of the executives was on the office floor, shot in the abdomen, while the other, the company president, was slumped in a chair bleeding from a neck wound. Ambulance attendants were stabilizing them before taking them to two area hospitals.

While all this was going on, I glanced out a second floor window and spotted one of the *Evening Gazette's* most competent reporters, being restrained by police officers guarding the crime scene perimeter. I bolted to the parking lot, shoved the names of the shooting victims at him and breathlessly dispatched him to two local hospitals to update the conditions of the wounded executives. I remained at the scene to cover the main story. I knew that I could accomplish more there when minutes were so crucial, because police were more apt to extend privileges to me than they were to an unknown reporter. Generally, I was reluctant to work with other reporters when covering major police incidents or fires, but this was one time, already past deadline, when I was relieved to see someone with whom I could team up.

A company receptionist told me the gunman came to the company earlier in the day to inquire about being rehired. At the time, he was told there were no openings. He left the building but returned later with a gun and, slightly staggering, walked through the lobby and up the stairs to the executive suite. Moments later, shots rang out, she said, trembling as she recalled the events.

As was so often frustratingly true, the breaking story occurred at noon, a full hour past normal deadline. Fortunately, on a newspaper, Page One is put together last, affording a one-hour deadline extension. Because at the crime scene all the pieces fell into place quickly, and police placed no insurmountable barriers in our way, our effort was rewarded, in the final edition, with twenty-three inches of copy and five pictures.

IN 1966, ON MEMORIAL DAY, EVERYONE AT HEADQUARTERS WAS looking forward to a quiet holiday; just about everything was closed;

a parade was scheduled to honor the country's war dead; and we all welcomed a respite from the daily activities of the city. In fact, I planned to sneak up to Main Street, for a few minutes, to catch the parade when it came by.

"Attention, all rolling stock. Attention, all units," a police dispatcher intoned matter-of-factly over the air. "We have a hostage situation on Pleasant Street, corner of Newbury. Shots have been fired. All units, approach with extreme caution. Are there any DB (Detective Bureau) cars on the road? All DB cars to Pleasant and Newbury Streets. Are there any officials on the air? Who's responding?"

As station monitors spit out more details, distant sirens could be heard in the pressroom, converging downtown from the north and west sections of the city. Knowing that the City Desk also monitored police calls, I yelled into the phone, "I'll handle it! Keep the kids away! Too dangerous! Whadda ya mean—what number Pleasant? Tell the photographer to look for all the police cars and listen for the shooting," I bellowed, slamming down the phone and bolting out the door.

As I came wheeling onto the scene, police were already rerouting traffic away from the area. Puffing out of breath, I ran the last two blocks and worked my way to the back of the building, where I climbed porch stairways to the top floor to join a cluster of detectives bunched up there. I inched my way into a back hallway to the apartment where the gunman was barricaded. Muffled gunshots popped away inside. Suddenly, there was a different sound, an almost indistinct snap, inside the apartment. Moments later, lung-constricting tear gas seeped out from under the kitchen door, forcing us to scramble quickly down the back stairs, trying to find breathable air. As soon as the tear gas canister was thrown into the apartment, gas-masked officers rushed the apartment and rescued the gunman's terrified wife and their infant daughter, both of whom were being held at gunpoint. The gunman, a well-known cop fighter and general troublemaker, pulled back under the tear gas attack and barricaded himself in a bedroom on the west side of the building. There, he smashed out a window and started shooting indiscriminately at the ground. All the while, he repeatedly pounded his face against the shattered window sill. His face was soon masked with blood as shards of broken glass slashed his cheeks and forehead.

Unable to breathe because of the tear gas, I retreated to a car parked beside the building, upwind from the gas. From that vantage point, I could see the gunman with his pistol hanging from the jagged window. Crouching with me behind the car was the berserk gunman's wife, a priest, and a detective. For twenty minutes, the wife and clergyman tried fruitlessly to convince the gunman to give up his weapon. More shots peppered the parking lot as we ducked for cover. Ignoring pleas to surrender, the gunman continued to scream incoherently and fire off rounds in our general direction from the top floor bedroom window. "Why don't you cops get a rifle and pick me off like they do in the movies?" he screamed at those on the ground. "I can't breathe. Please, Father, take care of my wife."

The man's head disappeared momentarily and another gunshot was heard. He had shot himself in the leg, we found out later. When he did this, police knew the end was near, that he was probably on the verge of committing suicide. There was no more time for negotiations. The bedroom door was battered in and a team of gas-masked officers overpowered the crazed gunman as he put a .32-caliber pistol to his head. A large kitchen knife with which he had stabbed himself in both arms during the half-hour siege was also wrestled from his other hand. One last live round was found in the man's gun when he was overpowered. More than fifty rounds of ammunition were found beside him.

After he was released from City Hospital, he was committed by the court to a state mental facility for psychiatric evaluation.

ONE MORNING, LATE IN JULY 1970, THE POLICE SWITCHBOARD lighted up frantically, when a fusillade of gun shots was fired in the

Greendale section of the city. City cruisers scrambled, but by the time they arrived, other police agencies already had in custody two fifteen-year-old escapees from the Shirley Industrial School, one of them wounded in the left knee. The escapees had led a siren-screeching, eight-cruiser caravan on a 75-mile-an-hour chase along Route 12 through three North County cities and towns and into north Worcester, where their fleeing stolen car eventually went out of control after striking a traffic island and blowing a tire. Skidding sideways, it slammed against a building with such force that the youths were trapped inside. When pursuing police officers thought they heard gunshots coming from the wrecked car, they returned the fire. Both teenagers squeezed through car windows and fled on foot, one of them limping badly. The wounded boy was captured a few minutes later as he staggered along, dragging an injured leg behind him. The other youth was apprehended about two hours later in woods about three-quarters of a mile from where the chase ended. Both juveniles denied having a gun and searchers never found one.

When I arrived at the scene, troopers and cops from four cities and towns were vying for position to be interviewed, each claiming to have played the dominant role in the caper.

ONE OF THE MOST HIGHLY PUBLICIZED CRIMES COMMITTED IN THE city, through the years, was the theft, by two masked gunmen, of two million dollars worth of valuable paintings from the Worcester Art Museum, in May 1972. During the robbery, a fifty-seven-year-old security guard was shot in the hip when he attempted to block the bandits' escape. He told police that he was standing at the main entrance talking to a female visitor when the masked robbers came running from an upper gallery and carrying the paintings in plastic bags. As they approached the guard, one yelled, "Get out of the way. We're coming through." The security guard said he grappled with one man and, as he did, the other thief turned and shot him. As he lay bleeding on the mosaic floor of the museum, the guard managed to crawl to the doorway and get a description of the getaway station wagon as it sped away toward the downtown business district. The guard told police that, a block south of the museum, the escaping vehicle sped through a crowded intersection and headed west out of sight.

Within minutes, the entire city was emptied of police patrol cars and unmarked detective cars as all converged on the museum. A description of the station wagon was broadcast by the first officers to arrive there. State Police were alerted as an all points bulletin was broadcast to suburban towns on the regional police network. Roadblocks were thrown up on all major arteries leading away from the museum, but to no avail. The station wagon used in the robbery was found abandoned on the Worcester Polytechnic Institute campus, two blocks from the art museum. It had been reported stolen earlier. The gunmen had been able to transfer casually the valuable art works into a stashed car, undetected all the while by dozens of students walking to class nearby. The robbery had been planned down to the last detail. No masks, guns, gloves, or other identifiable items were left behind when the robbers switched cars. Police interviewed two high school girls who saw the men remove the paintings from a gallery wall and had been ordered, at gunpoint, to sit down and be quiet. They were unharmed.

Investigators, questioned the next day, speculated on what recourse the thieves had in order to dispose of the paintings. Police were concerned they would be damaged by rough handling or improper storage, especially if subjected to moisture. The museum curator told police that if attempts were made to cut the paintings out of their frames, irreparable damage would be done. Police pondered on the thieves' options if they tried to obtain ransom for the paintings or disposed of them on the black market. One thing was sure: the robbers had on their hands some very hot and difficult paintings to dispose of.

When a detailed inventory was taken, the paintings were identified as "Portrait of St. Bartholomew," a 1632 oil painting by Rembrandt;

"The Brooding Woman" and "The Head of a Woman," both by Paul Gaugin; and "Mother and Child," by Pablo Picasso. I included reproductions of the paintings with my robbery story so that everyone who read the paper could view reproductions of the missing paintings.

Acting on an anonymous tip, a suburban detective and I staked out a house, guarded by a Doberman Pinscher and believed to be the hideout of the robbery mastermind. After eight hours of mutual staring by the dogs and us, the surveillance was called off.

Eighty-two hours later, a break in the case came when a woman, picked up for questioning and trying to make a deal with police, squealed on her accomplices. She gave investigators very little, but enough to get them moving again. A special fourteen-man squad surrounded a three decker in the southern extremity of the city and scooped up a laborer known to be interested in any kind of shady deal offering a fast buck. Both the woman and the man were charged with complicity in the art theft.

Although all sorts of state and federal agencies were involved in the investigation, city officials were my main contacts from the first hour. They held numerous closed door strategy conferences with FBI agents throughout the day and into the night. Twenty investigators were assigned to the case full time. As the investigation became more sensitive, detectives started clamming up. Soon, I was frozen out completely. Interviews stopped and a lid of secrecy was clamped over the entire probe. Even my most faithful contacts dried up. When major cases were reaching a climax, police often became antsy about the prospect of premature information leaks that could undermine their case. I understood this and begrudgingly accepted the news blackout.

As the police network across the state tightened, the heat on fences was intensified. Street informants were called in and offered deals. One investigator told me quietly in a lavatory that the paintings were getting hotter to handle by the hour. "The thieves know it, we know it. The breaking point is coming soon," he said. I hung loose in anticipation of an imminent break in the case.

Without fanfare, police recovered the stolen art, mostly undamaged, from an undisclosed location. Primarily, I assumed, to protect the street informants who had given police the crucial tips, the site was not even disclosed during the trial of the four culprits. As a result of the recovery of the paintings, two more arrests were made. When yet another tip was received, an arrest warrant was issued for a South County man, known in the underworld as, "Junie." As the heat of the investigation became too much for the art thieves, one by one they "rolled over" and incriminated others involved, either during or after the robbery. Each tried to cut his or her own deal with police. Investigators, working under tremendous community pressure to solve the case, took advantage of a strong bargaining position and promised very little. All were eventually convicted and imprisoned.

ON A VERY COLD NIGHT WHEN THE MERCURY HOVERED AROUND zero and a punishing wind made outside activities difficult, a fellow musician and I were returning home about midnight from a band engagement in the Greater Boston area. When we approached the city the night sky in front of us lighted up with flashing blue strobe lights at a Route 9 motel. The highway was clogged with police cruisers.

I pulled over, knowing that, although I was not responsible for news from that town, this one had to be big to attract so much police attention. Cops were running fast to and fro. As I pulled in, an ambulance with sirens wailing was leaving the scene and heading toward the city. Known to most of the officers, I was allowed into the motel lobby. There, a detective, not wanting to be overheard, said in hushed tones, "One of our guys, 'Pudge' [James] Lonchiadis has been shot. It doesn't look as if he's going to make it. He's at Memorial [Hospital]."

Disturbed, I continued home, knowing the next morning would be difficult for me. Although I was on vacation, I knew the City Desk would enlist my help because of the magnitude of the story and because suburban police were normally reluctant to talk to most reporters. Without ever regaining consciousness, Lonchiadis died before dawn of a single gunshot wound of the chest. As anticipated, I received a call from the managing editor of the *Evening Gazette* who had offered the suburban police chief a full news page devoted to the murder of Lonchiadis. "The cop killing is yours all the way, Rock. Get on it," I was ordered. Vacation be damned, I got on it.

In a smoke-filled back room, I grilled detectives for almost eight hours as they poured out details of the investigation. Every time one of them hedged on a fact I wanted, I threatened to terminate the interview. Never before had I conducted such an intense skull session. All during the interview, police and federal agents from all over the state dropped by to volunteer their help in the case or to exchange information. State Police composite sketches were drawn, based on descriptions given by witnesses. The FBI entered the case almost immediately.

Finally, totally wrung out from the non-stop, head-to-head questioning in a cramped interrogation room, I headed for the City Room to write the story. Four hours later, it was finished and edited.

After the officer was shot, one of the killers ran to a local doughnut shop four blocks away and, at gunpoint, stole a gold colored Cadillac from a customer. He sped away heading west across White City Bridge and into Worcester, where he disappeared into the night.

Police were already moving in when the shooting took place. Minutes before, a call had been received that a police officer was being held at gunpoint outside the motel. One minute later, another call was received by police saying that one of their own had just been shot.

Investigators swarming over the crime scene determined that the young officer was shot behind his cruiser but was able to drag himself to his car in an apparent attempt to radio for help. His service revolver had been taken from him but had not been used on him. Instead, he was shot at close range through the heart with a .32-caliber pistol already carried by one of the killers. The cruiser trunk was open and investigators theorized that the killers had planned to stuff the officer inside. No weapon was ever found, despite an intensive search for days of woods, swamps, alleys, brooks, gutters, fields, and rooftops throughout the area.

Emotions were running high. Lonchiadis, who had been on the job for only ten months, was popular in the department. Two months before he was killed, he had purchased a new home for his wife and two small children. Police wanted his killers badly. Tightly, they turned the screws on the underworld, rousting every hot-car man, junkie, drug pusher, bookie, burglar, and armed robber. Someone had to know who the cop killers were and police wanted them "turned." To loosen tongues, a $5,000 reward was offered. For a time, the investigation hit a blank wall, the dreaded fear of every homicide investigator. But when a cop's murder is involved, emotions run deep within the police brotherhood.

The first break came when the getaway car was recovered in Warwick, Rhode Island. This could mean the killers were from that area. The investigation immediately shifted some of its emphasis to Rhode Island. A massive task force of police and volunteers from all over began checking out hundreds of other leads in Framingham, Virginia, and all along the eastern seaboard to Florida. Tediously and frustratingly slow, the investigation dragged on for months. More than 900 people were questioned. More than 41,000 man-hours were expended on the case. Inquiries were made to more than twenty major cities as far west as California and into Canada. Information was funneled in from several cities and towns in Connecticut, Massachusetts, Rhode Island and from New Mexico, California, Maine, and New York.

When police became cagy, subtly avoiding me, I took it as a good sign: they were getting close. Nineteen months after the officer was murdered outside the Worcester City Motel, three Providence, Rhode Island suspects—two men and a woman—were arrested. Before dawn, I was on the phone for details but was informed that the district attorney, wanting the headline for himself, had placed a gag order on the case. Livid with rage, I exploded, complained, and fumed, but to no avail. I reminded the chief I had given up twelve hours of vacation time to help his investigation. He shrugged, a victim of a direct order from the DA. But, I was urged to be patient. He had a plan, and it turned out to be a good one. When the three accused killers were scheduled for arraignment in Kent County Superior Court in Warwick, I was passed off as a police lieutenant so I could penetrate the heavy courthouse security. I got my Page One banner headline, and I can only imagine that the DA has not figured out yet how I did it. I also extracted the sweetest revenge of all by not once mentioning his name anywhere in my story. The accused triggerman told police he sold the officer's service revolver to a Providence underworld figure. It has never been recovered. Today, a picture of Lonchiadis hangs at headquarters. Not long after the suburban police officer was gunned down, Worcester police started wearing bullet-proof vests while on duty on the street, but for one officer, it was not soon enough.

A CALL WAS RECEIVED THAT A NORTH END MAN, DURING A DOMESTIC dispute, was killing his wife in the family kitchen. From all over the city, officers converged on the house. All knew that domestic disputes are the most volatile, the most potentially dangerous calls for police officers to handle. An eight-year veteran of the department was the first to arrive at the modest Cape Cod style house where he knocked on a rear screen door. Without responding to the knock, the enraged home owner fired a pistol shot through the door. As the officer jumped back defensively, the door flew open and the home owner fired another round at him, this time striking him in the stomach. The officer lurched backwards away from the house, bleeding profusely.

Backup units, sprinted around the house and prepared a four-sided assault. Other officers dragged the wounded officer out of the line of fire and placed him in a cruiser until an ambulance could be summoned. Several officers jockeyed into combat position, some ready to barge through front and rear doors, others to dive through windows. As the officers positioned themselves closer to the house, a muffled shot was heard, then silence. Bullhorns called for the gunman to surrender. Phone calls were made to the house. No one answered them. The tension heightened. Officers crouched outside could hear the telephone ringing inside until it stopped when frustrated police supervisors hung up.

On a pre-arranged signal, the flak-vested officers stormed the house. The gunman lay dead in a hallway between the kitchen and a bedroom, his finger still clamped inside the handgun's trigger housing. He had placed the pistol under his chin and committed suicide. A single bullet was lodged in his brain. Police found his wife's body on the kitchen floor. She had been shot several times in front of two terrified children and a mother-in-law. Eventually, the wounded officer recovered but he resigned from the Police Department six months later.

IN THE REALM OF LAW ENFORCEMENT, VIOLENCE IS SELDOM EVER preceded by a warning. During a local package store robbery in early November 1976, a customer was shot by a masked gunman. Within seconds after the store clerk called 911, a police radio bulletin was issued describing the bandit and his getaway automobile.

A route car patrolling nearby was the first to respond. Suddenly, out of the night, a car matching the description of the vehicle used in the robbery sped past him. The officer wheeled around and gave chase with one hand, calling for backup units with the other. Despite the fact that the bandit's car was weaving from side to side, the cruiser was able to pull in close behind it. As he did, three shots rang out from the robber's car. One of the bullets shattered the cruiser's windshield and grazed the side of the officer's head. Bleeding, he radioed the robber's location to other police units and then broke off the chase. Almost immediately, other officers spotted the car and boxed it in. The package store thief was apprehended as the wounded officer was being transported to a nearby hospital for treatment of his head wound.

For several days, incensed cops grumbled over a rumor that the chief, when told that one of his men had been shot, replied that the officer used poor judgment in following the bandit's car so closely during the pursuit and that it was some of the lousiest police work he had ever seen. I was never able to confirm that such a remark was made by the chief, but the rumor persisted.

IN EARLY JANUARY 1985, A ROUTINE TRAFFIC STOP ON THE CITY'S West Side illustrated how precarious a police officer's job is at all times, especially when risk is least expected.

A Traffic Division accident investigator pulled over a car for having expired registration plates. While he checked out the operator on his police radio, the driver of the car appeared alongside the cruiser window with a .45-caliber semi-automatic pistol in his hand. He held it inches from the officer's face while he reached inside and removed the officer's service revolver from its holster. Now unarmed and believing he was about to be shot, the officer instinctively grabbed for the muzzle of the automatic in the gunman's hand. With a pounding roar, the gun exploded in his face. He was hit in the left hand. The shooter then sprinted back to his Volkswagen sedan and fled north out of the city. A civilian, witness to the shooting, jumped out of his car and fired two shots at the fleeing car as it passed through an intersection at Pleasant Street. He missed both times. Another witness ran to the bleeding officer's cruiser, where he ripped his own shirt off and bound the officer's wound.

The gunman sped north onto Route I-190. Within minutes after the alarm went out that an officer had been shot, a wild ninety-mile-an-hour police chase ensued, involving Worcester, State, and North County police. During the chase, the gunman commandeered two other cars and kidnapped two people. Shots, police said, were fired during the chase. When the gunman rammed a pursuing State Police officer off the highway, he lost control of his own car and slammed into a concrete highway barrier. According to police reports, the gunman jumped out of his demolished car and tried to command passing motor vehicles. The first car, driven by a woman, refused to stop for a huge black man standing in the road waving a gun at her. In anger, the gunman fired a shot through the woman's windshield. She was not hurt and still refused to stop. Another approaching motorist, seeing a pistol aimed at him, stopped and was taken hostage when he was roughly shoved aside as the gunman jumped behind the wheel.

Swerving repeatedly up and down on and off ramps, the gunman tried to dodge police as the terrified hostage hung on desperately beside him in the front seat. Roadblocks were established, but somehow the gunman managed to evade them. After several miles, the car commandeered by the gunman became disabled. At this, he jumped out and ran to another car stopped nearby at a stop sign. The driver did not move as the gunman approached his car, the gun leveled in a two-hand grip at his head. The driver was taken hostage as the gunman slid behind the wheel.

The state trooper who was forced off the highway by now had his car back on the road and resumed the pursuit. The gunman's desperate dash for freedom ended in a North County city, where, now on his own familiar turf, he abandoned the getaway car and managed to escape underground. Despite an intensive police search with ground troops and helicopters, the gunman melted into the city. Police identified the gunman as a former Norfolk State Prison guard who had been given a suspended sentence to Walpole State Prison in September 1984 for kidnaping and assaulting his estranged wife. A Northeast District (New England, New York, New Jersey and Pennsylvania) all points bulletin was issued for the gunman.

I interviewed the wounded officer in his home the next day. For me, he relived every moment of his harrowing experience. He considered the shooting a learning experience, saying that he would make traffic stops quite differently in the future.

Some weeks later, the gunman was apprehended and convicted of the attempted murder of a police officer.

IN LATE OCTOBER 1988, AN OFF-DUTY WORCESTER POLICE OFFICER, while giving chase, was shot in the knee by a motorcyclist who had struck his car and then taken off. The officer, a well-known Central Massachusetts marathon runner, had just gone off duty and was heading home in his car when a motorcycle carrying two men came out at high speed from the wrong way out of a side street and sideswiped the officer's car. The "bikies," police said, raced away with the officer in pursuit. About two miles away, he tried to pull along side the motorcycle to flash his badge and identify himself. He never had the chance. The bike abruptly veered to the left and again struck the officer's car. This time, the impact caused the motorcycle to tip over, spilling both riders onto the highway. Although stunned, they split up and fled, weaving and stumbling into the darkness, one of them disappearing behind a nearby junior high school. Gun in hand, the officer inched his way around a corner of the school. The back yard was illuminated with outside floodlights, but these cast some shadows which the officer's vision could not penetrate. Instinctively, he felt that someone was behind him. Two shots rang out, one knocking the officer to the ground shattering his left knee. From the ground, the bleeding officer returned the fire. The gunman broke out of the shadows and ran through the illuminated area and, in seconds, was again swallowed up by the night.

Painfully, the officer pulled himself to his feet and with his left leg dragging behind him, limped after his assailant. The gunman whirled and fired more shots at the now partially disabled police officer. Finally, the officer, his strength ebbing from loss of blood, could go no further. He collapsed. When he looked up, neighbors who had heard the gunfire were running to assist him. None of those who responded to help knew he was a police officer. All they could see in the darkness was a black man on the ground with a gun in his hand. But still they came and gave first aid and comfort until other police units arrived. At headquarters, the switchboard was clogged with calls from West Side residents reporting gunshots outside their homes. Cruisers converged on the area and were directed to the officer by those performing first aid on him as he lay bleeding on the ground. State Police tracking dogs were called in and a widespread search was conducted behind Worcester State College.

About an hour later, one of the motorcyclists was apprehended while walking a quarter mile away with one shoe missing. The next day, a .357 Magnum revolver was recovered behind the college by a man walking his dog.

Several days later, the second biker was arrested in Miami and returned to Worcester to face charges of attempted murder of a police officer. When the recovering officer was released from the hospital, I interviewed him. He shared with me that moments before he was shot he had a premonition that someone in the shadows had a clear shot at him.

GUNPLAY IN MAJOR CITIES IS ALMOST A DAILY OCCURRENCE. TOO often it results in death or crippling injury. To compensate, many police officers now carry 15-round semi-automatic pistols to combat criminals armed with Uzi machine guns or TEC-9 machine pistols. No matter how heavily armed the police officer may be, those they face on the street are packing even heavier armament. Not many officers advocate taking all guns out of the hands of law-abiding citizens. Their wish is that a certificate of law-abiding maturity, responsibility, and common sense would supplement gun permits when they are issued.

a look inside headquarters

LAW ENFORCEMENT IS NOT A WORLD OF BRAVE SUPER-HEROES charging on white horses to vanquish the evils of the world. Instead, it is a world of real people who, just like everyone else, feel pain and sorrow, practice self-indulgence, and sometimes weaken under the stresses of the job. The cop's world is one of violence and tragedy, a filthy environment of cruelty, indecent behavior, and emotional punishment. Sometimes it can be a cesspool of greed, sexual weakness, alcoholism, drug abuse, dishonesty, freeloading, and malingering to beat the system; the same weaknesses in moral character that infect many in the civilian world.

A cop is no smarter than anyone else; he just tries to be. He or she is no braver than anyone else. Cops just rise to the occasion when they have to, and hope their response is enough. Police officers are no bigger or stronger than anyone else. They are average people trained to perform, to the best of their ability, one of the most difficult, trying jobs in society.

When once asked about the proficiency of the average police officer, I drew on experience and personal observation, while living at their elbow, and offered the following opinions. Fifty percent of the police officers were doing the best job they could with the brains, appearance, and strength given them; another twenty-five percent, I felt, performed with dedication and a strong desire to serve the public with distinction. These are the mentally, morally, and physically strong who daily meet the public with compassion head-on; they are the ones who measure up fully to the public's expectations. The remaining twenty-five percent of the force—many of them social misfits with deep attitudinal problems—should never have been allowed to don the uniform and wear the badge. Today, I still hold pretty much to this belief, although, in all fairness, I should add that increased training and mandatory psychological evaluation, during rookie training, are weeding out most of the misfits before they are sworn in. The percentage of top cops is increasing every year.

From the inside, over the years, I watched cops duking it out in the privacy of the station, bouncing one another off the walls to settle disagreements.

On a few occasions, I stood by helplessly while prisoners, some handcuffed, were assaulted in retaliation or to "smarten them up." I knew of, but did not personally observe, the beating of a prisoner by several cops who had him on the Cell Room floor. To their credit, when officials heard of the incident, the offending officers were given lengthy suspensions without pay.

I watched a cop, bombed drunk at seven A.M., crawl on his hands and knees across a street near headquarters to respond to morning roll call, and then, after officials chose to ignore his obvious inebriation, saw him driving the patrol wagon at five miles an hour picking up drunks off the streets in the city.

I once babysat a cruiser while a patrol officer disappeared into a run-down tenement for a morning "quickie" while I manned his cruiser and nicked the siren when he had a call.

There are certain groups of police officers who, apparently, seem intent on screwing up their careers, always thinking, that they can get away with all sorts of stupid antics: the on duty cop sleeping in a patrol car on a darkened street or secluded area; the officer with tom cat morals demanding "sloppy seconds" when he came across two night-time lovers in a tryst. Then there was the suburban town police ambulance attendant who was summarily fired from the job after he propositioned a bleeding female accident victim as she was being loaded onto an ambulance Gurney. Jail time was served by an alcoholic officer who propositioned a grieving woman as she knelt praying at her husband's cemetery grave. And the officer who without any warning signs went over the edge suffering a nervous breakdown, babbling incoherently at roll call formation, as his fellow officers mimicked him. His weapon was taken from him and he was referred for evaluation before being terminated. He was a veteran of the force but finally the job caught up with him.

I followed with some degree of disdain the devious antics of a uniformed freeloader hustling freebies at the newspaper loading dock and then suing the paper with the false claim that he tripped over a length of bundle wrapping wire, suffering "mortal" injuries. When he was bought off with a small nuisance claim payment, he immediately started strong-arming newspaper employees again for free copies.

I was witness to a gaggle of high ranking police officials consuming a corn beef and cabbage lunch and then stiffing the restaurant and even the waitress of her tip. Disturbed by this obvious parsimonious treatment, I threw three dollars on the table for the overworked server. A grateful smile was my repayment.

I wrote of an officer who filled the trunk of his cruiser with automobile batteries while investigating a nighttime burglary at a gas station; and another who loaded up with meat and liquor from a burglarized Chinese restaurant before backup units arrived.

Invariably, serious in-house offenses were reported in the paper. The less serious—the so-called in-house misdemeanors—were not. It was a method I used to balance a police officer's right to some privacy and, at the same time, fortify police confidence that I could be trusted not to report every miscreant action I uncovered or observed. With some sadness, I watched a good cop turn murderer when the city failed to diagnose properly his demented depression.

The alleged thieves in the department, I avoided. The freeloaders, I tolerated, rationalizing that they were just part of the overall scheme of law enforcement. The mentality of "everything-for-nothing" and "the world-owes-me-a-living" had been a police tradition for generations. It was not about to disappear just because I came on the scene. A free coffee soon snowballs into a free doughnut and then into a free meal or a bottle of liquor. One restaurant owner told me that free meals to one officer often escalated into "Here's my partner. Take care of him too." When I questioned some cops on what right they had to do this, I was told these were "gratuities for services rendered."

During the early days on the beat, I witnessed "alley court" sessions in back alleys where budding juvenile delinquents, abusive husbands, and combative petty criminals were tried, convicted, and sentenced. Effective deterrents to crime, but highly illegal.

Throughout the sixties and early seventies, I cringed as disgusting racial slurs were passed off as normal in-house conversation. Fortunately, the next generation of police officer displayed more sensitivity toward minorities.

I had to tolerate screamed invectives and manhandling from jealous cops when I wrote puff stories about more deserving officers. These intense rivalries between officers were part of the police beat; they went with the territory.

I was physically pummeled one morning by a police lieutenant who swarmed all over me as I sat quietly drinking coffee in the Cell Room. I asked the lieutenant a question, obviously the wrong one, about how many criminal cases his Bureau of Criminal Identification had solved by fingerprints. It would, I thought, make a good feature. After three officers subdued him, wrestled him to a nearby passenger elevator, pulled the wire cable sending him skyward to his office, and then slamming the wire cage door shut so he could not escape again, I was told he was emotionally disturbed. After the dust settled, one of my rescuers shared with me that no crimes had ever been solved that way. "He thought you were ridiculing him," I was told.

I sat amused in the Detective Bureau one morning as a popular black, female radio dispatcher sneaked up quietly behind a white, outspoken racist detective and kissed him on top of his bald head. As a room full of other detectives fell off their chairs laughing, the racist ran to a men's room to wash his head. The dispatcher, with a wide grin and a fist-in-the-air black power salute, sauntered out of the room amidst applause from everyone.

Fascinated, I watched when, one morning, a brawl broke out in the same Cell Room. An enraged cop, a favorite of mine, was being forcibly dragged from the driver's seat of the battered old patrol wagon, a descendant of the old Black Maria. Several officers were struggling with my friend, having a hard time subduing him. All I could hear above the din was my friend screaming, "I know where he parks. I'll get him. I'll ram the bastard's car." The struggling officer, normally one of the department's more happy-go-lucky characters, had just been told that his car had been ticketed for illegal parking by a cop who was infamous for constantly bragging that he did his duty without fear or favor.

Many police officers had a reputation for having a short fuse. I witnessed the explosions many times and once asked an official about the situation. "Violence begets violence," was his curt answer. One such time I rescued an over-zealous television reporter from being decked by a police sergeant when the reporter insisted on pushing a little too hard for information at an East Side tenement fire.

With collaboration from Bernie Stalilonis, I posed as a deputy chief to get an obnoxious, hot-shot Boston TV personality thrown out of a crime scene so I could corral the exclusive story to myself. The bewildered reporter was reduced to interviewing small children fascinated by his nearby helicopter. Bernie was without a doubt my favorite street sergeant, one who made my job easier every time he could, especially when under extreme pressure at fire scenes. He was a true friend in the department.

On occasion, perhaps out of a sense of sympathy for the job conditions that made them that way, I failed to report when alcoholics were subjected to forced retirement. For some of them, I had been a sympathetic confidant when they poured out their frustrations and marital problems. I protected what was left of their dignity and reputation when they needed it most. The fact that everything that transpired was not necessarily reported in the newspaper served to cement the bond of trust between myself and most on the force. Some of them considered me a cop without a badge.

It was not until after his retirement that I learned of a scam perpetrated by a certain lieutenant of Precinct 2. His gambit was putting the squeeze on a tavern owner. The victim of the scam was told to soak a pair of men's long underwear in water and hang them outside, in the winter, to freeze stiff as a board. Then the bar owner was instructed to put a bottle of hooch in each leg every week. When the underwear was hung, that was the signal for the pickup. As the shakedown continued, the cop's greed grew. Soon it was a bottle in each leg and each arm. Eventually, the extortion stopped when the bar owner, bled dry for months, threatened to complain to the chief. From that point on, the bar owner was compelled to protect his own property without the help of the greedy lieutenant.

Thinking it was an in-house problem, I closed my eyes when a captain and a sergeant went at each other. During the altercation, one of the combatants was knocked through an office glass partition. Upon hearing about the incident, the chief's comment was, "It's too bad they didn't both beat each other's brains out." Case closed.

BUT, IN DEFENSE OF THE DEDICATED, HONEST COPS INSTEAD OF the condemnation of the weak, I was witness, through the years, to many faith lifting events by the men and women of the department.

Most police officers have sympathetic, compassionate hearts, a fact generally unknown to the public. When police learned that monitoring police calls from a wheelchair in his home was the main diversion of Marty, a twenty-one-year-old cerebral palsy victim, they did something about it. Marty was transported by cruiser to headquarters and given a cook's tour, where he met a dispatcher, his radio voice hero. The young man's joy knew no bounds when the dispatcher, a polio victim himself, stepped aside and Marty was given the radio seat for a couple of calls. At that point, officials appeared and presented him with a regulation police jacket, complete with all the emblems. Then he was sworn in as a "special officer." Marty, the police buff, was overwhelmed. Worcester's finest often rose to the occasion when necessary. Truly, this was one of those times. I was very proud of them.

In mid-May 1979, a seventy-four-year-old woman was mugged by a gang of thugs, on the street, near her home,. During the attack, she sustained a painful head injury. While she lay bleeding on the sidewalk, another gang happened by and taunted her for nearly thirty minutes before anyone called police. She was operated on for a blood clot of the brain, at a local hospital. It was discovered, during the police investigation, that she had no family. Spontaneously, members of the police Impact Program adopted her as their "official mother." During her recuperation in the hospital, she was showered on Mother's Day, with flowers, candy, and gifts. Later, after she returned home and until other assistance could be arranged, Police Service Aides were assigned to check periodically on her welfare. A maiden lady, the grateful woman said she had never before received Mother's Day presents.

One of the longer lasting acts of police compassion was exemplified by one of the department's veteran ambulance drivers. At Halloween, an eleven-year-old girl trick-or-treating near her home, was struck by a hit-and-run driver. The impact left her with part of her skull pushed into her brain, her back broken, both hips dislocated, three ribs, and a collarbone fractured, compound fractures in both legs, and a hole in her head, the size of a golf ball. As her hysterical mother screamed at the officer to bring her daughter to a hospital a mile away, the officer, instead, headed for City Hospital and its top-rated emergency room. The officer's decision probably saved the nearly lifeless small girl. Unable to erase from his mind the sight of the battered girl lying on the road, the ambulance driver kept a vigil at the girl's hospital bedside. He brought her gifts daily. Through the years he sent her flowers on her birthday, and kept in touch with her even after she married, years later. A tough cop, who had seen it all during his career, offered his own special brand of love to a frail, battered teenager fighting for her life in a hospital intensive care unit.

Countless times, police officers approached me asking that I squelch some details of a story to spare the victim's family from further anguish. It was standard practice to prevent me, if possible, from publishing gory details of a case. They seldom gave me credit for having enough self-discipline and a personal moral conscience when deciding what to include in a tragedy story.

Worcester police have a long history of involvement in worthwhile projects involving children. Every year, "camper-ships" are granted to bus loads of underprivileged children from slum families, bringing them to a nature day camp, in southeastern Massachusetts. Each year, athletic teams are sponsored and charity softball games played for the Jimmy Fund. Money is donated by the police union to keep open a minority neighborhood municipal swimming pool closed by the city due to budgetary cuts. Every year, college scholarships are awarded to deserving students by the Worcester Chapter of the International Brotherhood of Police Officers.

Much goes on inside police bastions. In one respect, it is unfortunate that the public cannot peek within the walls. An inside view might offer the citizenry a keener insight into the men and women who serve and protect them. They would find that police officers are not infallible but on the whole are good human beings.

the curtain falls

DURING THE MID- TO LATE EIGHTIES, I BEGAN TO FEEL A LITTLE like a dinosaur. It was getting progressively harder to "get up for the game." My enthusiasm for the beat never wavered. It was still a ball: exciting, humorous, sometimes dangerous, vital, challenging, fascinating, pressure-filled, and important right up to the end. It afforded me the privilege to enter places that were off limits to others, and to meet and interview celebrities and criminals alike, both of whom were usually sequestered from the general public. But, above all, the overriding factor that sustained me throughout the years was the total journalistic freedom the police beat afforded me, especially from direct supervision and interference by management.

There were times when the newspaper tried to infringe upon my territory, to bring me back into the fold, but living in a police world had taught me how to deal with such distractions. An out-of-order phone, an inoperative beeper, or a "He was just here a minute ago" cover-up by some of my uniformed accomplices preserved my independence.

Toward the end of my tenure, there were days when I wondered whether I had lingered too long on the job, and whether youth and its inexperienced, immature approach to journalism was now governing my destiny. To myself, I admitted that the snowstorms were getting fiercer, the nights longer, the stairs and hills steeper, the winters more punishing, the screams of the dying more deafening, the rains more soaking, and the deadlines earlier and harder to meet. I watched myself becoming grumpier, more demanding, impossibly impatient, and neurotically more isolated. Like someone fighting off encroachment from the outside world, I zealously guarded my small fiefdom from all comers.

When I joined the paper, old-timers did not speak to me for ten years. Now, on the rare occasions that I visited the News Room, I was impatient with fledgling reporters who flocked around me to ask questions about police. I had lost sight of myself thirty years earlier, when the old-timers on the staff were frustratingly slow in acknowledging me. At that time, I vowed I would never treat others that way. But as time and job pressures took their toll, I just did not seem to have the patience I should have had toward the cubs. I rationalized that we lived in vastly different worlds. Theirs was protected and singularly focused, mine was one of stark realism, violence, foul language, squalor, and death. I had no desire to live in their cloistered environment and surely they were not prepared to live in mine. In retrospect, there were times when I did not like what I was becoming.

To compound further the changes I observed in myself, the limited, tightly controlled companionship that nurtured me at police headquarters was slipping away. Many of my favorite cops, with whom I had shared so many gratifying experiences, were retiring. I realized fully that I was someone who worked in two worlds and did not really belong to either. I had spent most of my adult life in a police environment but I was still only a partially accepted civilian there. I had been employed by the newspaper all those years but was still largely ignored and seldom accepted socially in that world. With perhaps just a tinge of bitterness, I began distancing myself from both worlds.

The Fourth Estate, the world of journalism, was a closed shop when I first tried to enter it. Desirous since childhood to be a writer, I applied for a position as a reporter at least a half dozen times between 1946 and 1957, and each time was abruptly thrown out by a coarse-mannered managing editor. Eventually, an opportunity presented itself, when as a file clerk in the "morgue" I sneaked in the back door. Assigned to the Marlborough Bureau, I endured a week when no one spoke to me, and then I was transferred to the Clinton Bureau to replace a reporter that the paper could not pour out of a whiskey bottle. After a week there, I was shunted off for another week to the Spencer Bureau where I was accused of screwing up the resident reporter's overtime. Back at Marlborough, a bureau chief with an elementary-grade education, informed the newspaper hierarchy that I had no talent and would never make it as a reporter. Disregarding this unsolicited evaluation, the paper sent me back to Clinton to replace the drunken reporter who just disappeared without a trace. In one month, I had been relegated from Worcester to Marlborough, to Clinton, to Spencer, back to Marlborough and back to Clinton: and I still had not learned how to turn on the damn Teletype machine.

It was an era without electronics, and with only antiquated, often balky, manual Royal typewriters. Pencils were still in use and folded sheets of manila copy paper were the forerunner of reporter notebooks or tape recorders. Stories were written long hand and then typed. To transport the stories to the City Desk (in my case, fourteen miles away) the reporter ran to meet the seven P.M. bus to the city. The bus was then met at the other end by a copy boy who retrieved the news envelope from the driver whose tip was one dollar. With experience honed by time came the skill to dictate major stories from a telephone booth to a rewrite man, all with correct paragraphing, proper punctuation, sentence structure, and accurate, detailed content, exactly as it would appear on the printed page.

Old habits die hard. Thirty years later, on occasion, I still recorded news stories on scrap paper or discarded envelopes stuffed into back pockets. The bus delivery system was eventually abandoned in favor of Teletype transmissions. This time-tested method of moving news copy was used at Police Headquarters until August of 1978, when the wonderfully reliable old machines were scrapped in favor of simplified versions of word processor terminals equipped with modems.

At fires, police reporters accompanied fire officials in still burning buildings, wading through several inches of hose water while rivulets of charred wood and brackish water cascaded onto them from upper floors. Information was gathered wherever it was available. Another major change in news gathering crept into journalistic work some-where along the way and I am not sure exactly when it was. Feet were replaced by telephones. Reporters today would not be caught dead pounding the pavement to retrieve a news story. Instead, the tele-phone on the desk is the new method of journalism. If a news source does not answer a telephone call, the story is not reported fully or properly. The fact that a source could not be reached by telephone is dropped into the release with a remark such as "so-and-so was unavailable by telephone today" or "so-and-so did not answer calls from this reporter." In either case, the basic premise of all newspaper reporting which is the reader's right to know is seriously and irrevo-cably compromised.

Especially when fighting deadlines and allowing time required by editors to scan stories submitted by reporters, expediency is often nec-essary at newspaper headquarters. But, a by-product of this expedien-cy can be lackadaisical performance by reporters, especially if rebuked on an initial attempt to question a news source. On newspapers, there should be no room for reporters who subscribe to the thesis that "if-at-first-you-don't-succeed-QUIT."

As time went by, the City Desk fell into the habit of calling upon me to bail out reporters confronted by uncooperative news sources, often, area police departments. The requests were flattering at first, but irksome later on, especially when I was struggling through a daily hectic work schedule myself. If police chiefs refused to talk over the telephone to unproven reporters and jolted these reporters and then demanded to talk to me instead, that was fine with me, because what was paramount was getting the story in the *Gazette* first. Some staff members and editors started referring to me as the fastest gun in the west, but I was getting really tired of being required so often to prove it. Perseverance, the foundation of all news journalism, was not even in the vocabulary of some reporters.

Soon, my impatience spilled over and I demanded that the desk not assign other reporters to assist me on major breaking news stories, no matter how big the stories were. This worked out well, for a while. When, on occasion, I found someone else from the staff wandering around in my protected territory—inside police or fire lines—I became impatient. What must first be understood is the overwhelming pressure on a police reporter to quickly, fully, and accurately report a major, sometimes catastrophic, event on deadline—or to try by sheer effort to bend that deadline. I carried this self-protective attitude too far at times. At an armed home invasion when the occupants were bound and robbed, I prevailed on a police sergeant to "get rid of that guy over there, he's a reporter," pointing to a *Gazette* staffer edging closer to the crime scene from across the street. The sergeant did, very abruptly. Another time, the same sergeant eliminated what I considered an infringement on my rights, by declaring a crime scene off limits to a pushy, pompous Boston TV personality.

POLICE REPORTERS WERE NOT WITHOUT PROBLEMS ON THEIR BEAT. There were always enough problems every day to go around for everyone. What difficulties did not emanate from police came instead from someone in authority at the newspaper. One morning, a case in point was one of the district attorney's collaborative police efforts. Fifty-three suspects were scooped up in massive, simultaneous police raids for car theft, firearms, and narcotics offenses, gaming, and other related charges. Tipped off by my sources that the raids were sched-

uled for the next day, I was able, beforehand, to infiltrate a news photographer into a remote wooded area where a massive parking lot of
recovered stolen cars had been established by police. A female editor
who never in her career had written a news story and who was thus
relying on her keenly honed instinct for news story value, parlayed the
story into a single-column spread buried inside the paper. "This was
just a staged media event, not news," she sniffed when I howled. It was
true, to some extent, but the paper had nonetheless blown a major
story of broad reader interest.

I began to notice a strange, subtle de-emphasis on police news.
Events that had previously warranted a full spread above the fold (of
the newspaper when printed) were being reduced to a few paragraphs
at the bottom of the page. Replacing the hard news of the day were
society's social problems emblazoned across the top of the pages, the
sole interest, it seemed, of the new generation of editors. They reasoned incorrectly that their interests were shared by all age groups.
The importance of my coverage was waning at the paper, but by that
time it did not matter much any more.

IN LIFE, ONE NEVER KNOWS WHEN THE GUILLOTINE BLADE WILL
fall until it is already on its way down. On Monday, October 26, 1987,
I walked through the City Room at the paper to pick up my mail,
waved casually to a friend on the Copy Desk, and then went home for
the day. Later, the friend remarked that I appeared to him tired and
drawn. An hour later, on a gorgeous Autumn afternoon while raking
leaves in my yard, I suffered a massive heart attack that brought me to
the brink of death. Cardiologists told my family that I had only a slim
chance of survival. When I first opened my eyes, in the Cardiac
Intensive Care Unit (CICU), after twenty-one days in a drug induced
coma, the first thing I requested was a pen and some paper. I had a
story to write: the agonies of being felled by cardiac infarction. It was
important, I felt at the time, that readers be brought into the shatter-

ing, frightening world of a severe heart attack victim. Flat on my back, I interviewed everyone in sight about what had transpired while I was unconscious in CICU.

The day I was released from the hospital, I wrote the story in my cellar, on a borrowed manual typewriter, and then called for an office boy from the newspaper to pick it up. After it was published, I received stacks of inspirational mail.

Recuperation was slow. But, in one respect, the down time proved beneficial for it offered me an opportunity to rearrange my priorities, and to reflect back on what had been a totally rewarding and fulfilling career. There were so many poignant memories, like the day I arrived at work, in the old station, and found a badly chipped bud vase holding a bouquet of crude, hand-made plastic flowers on my desk. Propped up against the vase, which I knew had been reclaimed from a rubbish bin, was a poem. It read: "It is my joy of life to find at every turning of the road the strong arm of a comrade to help me onward with my load. And since I have no gold to give and love alone must make amends, my daily prayer is while I live God make me worthy of my friends. Good Luck, Rocky, Chester Cannon." Cannon was a deformed, former mental patient who worked as a janitor at headquarters. I was deeply touched by the gift. Afterwards, Cannon explained that I was the only one at the station who did not tease or make fun of him. The poem is one of my most cherished memories of the police beat.

Twice, during my recuperation period, I sneaked back to Police Headquarters, dug up stories and filed them over the word processor lines. Both times I was berated by a newly appointed managing editor for coming back to work without medical authorization. After several months' recuperation, I was not sure what to expect. I was told by doctors that the heart attack was brought on by the repeated, year-in, year-out, on and off adrenaline surges. After three decades, working under pressure in punishing weather, the loss of sleep, and the constant stress of fighting deadlines had all caught up with me.

Like a punch in the nose from which the pain never subsides, I admitted to myself that my life hinged on a drastic alteration in my work habits. Somewhat begrudgingly, I gave in to the suggestion of City Desk that younger reporters be assigned to the more physically taxing stories. The very close call sobered my personality and softened my combativeness.

For a year, I existed on a steady diet of features while others on the staff coveted the news. I walked instead of galloped. I was no longer driven to give 110 percent effort every work day. With some difficulty, I learned to ignore deadlines and, instead, afforded myself time to research each feature more deeply, giving each one a depth of perspective that had been impossible in the past. I exuded a confidence that disguised the aging process. Above all, I continued to convince management that their man in the cop shop was still on top of all situations. The police beat was still a madly whirling carousel on which the music never stopped, and I did not want to get off.

The darkest day in my journalistic career came in a letter, dated late December 1988, suggesting that I consider taking an early retirement. It was a devastating blow. I was the recipient of three keys to the city; had been chosen in 1984 as the man of the year by the Registry of Motor Vehicles; had won three National Safety Council awards; and had a mayor's proclamation designating July 18, 1987 as Roscoe C. Blunt, Jr. Day, in Worcester. I also had been given two awards by the International Association of Fire Fighters; a Governor's Council citation; numerous contest prizes by Associated Press and United Press International; a commendation from the Bureau of Alcohol, Tobacco, and Firearms Division of the U.S. Treasury; a state Civil Defense citation; a meritorious award from the International Brotherhood of Police Officers; and many, many more honors from service clubs and private concerns. In addition to this, I had lectured on police media relations at three colleges, and for numerous police departments. For some years, the State Police Public Relations Office in Boston deferred to me as the dean of police reporters in Massachusetts, and possibly in all New England. I found myself trying to live up to the title. And now I was being asked to surrender it all. If I opted to stay on the job, I would become a reporter for the recently merged *Telegram & Gazette*. I had been a *Gazette* reporter for more than thirty years. I was not about to abdicate that honor for any reason. I agreed to retire.

As my retirement party approached, my wife, Bea enjoined me to "Be a nice boy for once. Don't burn your bridges," during my swan song address. She knew me well.

Slowly and silently, the curtain was being lowered. I had written approximately 25,000 stories, and by-lined more than 2,300. I had reported nearly 4,800 fires, 480 or so highway fatalities, and nearly 400 murders. My presence had been established throughout the region and now it was time to give my two typing fingers a rest.

The flame of youth had been extinguished. The long hours, the roller-coaster life of a double murder in the morning, a five-alarm fire in the afternoon, followed by hours of boredom until the next crisis erupted had taken its toll on me. I was tired, more emotionally drained, and physically worn out than I had ever been before. Even though I could not understand it at the time, and probably would not have admitted it even if I had known, it was time to step down. I had my day in the sun and now the sun had set and I was living in the shadow.

On the last day at headquarters, unsuspectingly, I joined my coffee drinking buddies in the office of the License Board Investigative Unit, where I was greeted by a decorated cake large enough to feed the entire department. Pictures were taken of me in my Balinese swimming jacket and floppy sun hat, normal attire for me at that time of the year. Then I was ushered into the Fire Alarm Division, my favorite dugout, for a full buffet and gold badge presentation by the "Mighty Servants Who Never Sleep." My last official duty on the job was presenting my Salvation Army easy chair, in the press room, to Superintendent Ralph Thomson's high professional fire dispatchers.

Finally, it was off to the Operations Division squad room where practically the whole department responded to say good-bye and to watch me receive another gold badge, the first that the department had ever presented to a civilian. I graciously gave all credit for any successes I enjoyed on the police beat to those in the department—cops and civilians alike—who had made it all possible by helping me shape my life and destiny. It was a liturgy of all the sincere emotions I had ever felt for them. The reception line afterwards resembled those at a wake. I had dreaded the thought of all the emotional farewells. Both mentally and physically, I was ready to go. But, the honors did not cease when I walked out of headquarters for the last time. Later, I was voted into the Worcester County Chiefs of Police Association, an honor rarely afforded a civilian. When leaving the newspaper on June 26, 1989, I knew I would never again feel the vibrant pulse of world events. The next day at the *Evening Gazette* "coffee and" retirement party, a simple affair for those looking for a free coffee, I forced myself to be a "good boy" as my adoring wife had enjoined. But, it would not be me if I did not get in a few pointed, but good natured barbs, as long as I did not watch my wife's reaction.

Before the final curtain rang down or the last alarm bell sounded, I requested of the City Desk that I be allowed to write a final by-lined story to open up the wondrous world of police reporting to my readers. I wrote of the evolution of the newspaper industry and of local law enforcement. I wrote of tears and laughter, of the deep responsibility involved in news reporting. I pontificated on the goodness of mankind and the temptations of those evil-bent. I said good-by to my readers and thanked them for their loyalty. As mentioned before, I was once called by the mayor of the city "delightfully and refreshingly disrespectful." That, I was, I guess. But, it was the only way I knew to do the job correctly and professionally. If, to achieve this it meant, under certain circumstances, telling off a few self-important people then, so be it. A police reporter's job is to tell his or her readers just how wonderful the world is and, at the same time, inform them how terribly bad it also can be. Police reporting was reporting at its deepest, basic core; it was an opportunity of which others on the news staff were deprived: telling of the naked realities of life.

Police reporters, often the envy of other scribes, usually own Page One on a newspaper. The page goes with the territory. The police beat means being an amateur psychologist, knowing when to push, when to lay back and listen, when to play shy, or when to be an aggressive fighter. If a police reporter goes a little over the line and pushes too hard, cops invariably clam up. The secret is to keep the mouth shut at times and the eyes and ears open; and above all, not to ask silly questions, a common failing of TV alleged reporters. A police beat is truly seat-of-the-pants reporting, often with unorthodox methods needed to gather news accurately.

Perhaps more than on any other news beat, police reporters, when conducting interviews, have to acquire an instinct as to how to strip away the fat, and cut to the bone instantly, without time-consuming wasted effort. This can be perceived sometimes as abrasiveness. Often, it meant interviewing a cop in the middle of the night when and where his supervisors were not within earshot to inhibit him. During the dark, lonely hours, a certain camaraderie often exists between police officers and police reporters.

A police reporter must, under all circumstances, go to great lengths to retain objectivity, and always, whenever possible, present both sides of an issue. Often, that is not easy. A police (or court) reporter is constantly aware of the sword of Damocles hanging over his or her head: the sword of libel and social responsibility. There is an awesome power attached to a police reporter's typing fingers: the ability to create a hero, or, just as quickly, to destroy someone or something.

When the last siren was heard and the last alarm answered, I knew I had never cut corners for the sake of expediency and had always strived for excellence and perfection in my reporting. An editor once described me as an "exhaustive" reporter, that I left no question unanswered, that I covered every aspect of my stories before writing them.

I hope that was true. FBI Special Agent, Jim Ring, upon hearing of my impending retirement, dropped me a letter in which he said that he always respected me for, at all times, writing with concern for others. I saved the letter for it was the nicest accolade I received from anyone as I walked out the door for the last time. Despite all the hardships, the insulting indignities, the often smothering daily diet of horror, I knew when I retired that, all in all, there had been no higher calling in life, no more noble cause, no more important service to the community than having been a police reporter. I felt, with great satisfaction, that my life had not been wasted. I thought that, at least on some occasions, I had made the world a little better place in which to live. For nearly a third of a century, I had been one of the privileged few to have a ringside seat watching history being made—the greatest sideshow on earth. It was great while it lasted and I would not have missed it for anything. It was truly one helluva great ride.